Y0-BKB-450

A UNITED NATIONS PEACE FORCE

by

WILLIAM R. FRYE

Prepared under the auspices of
THE CARNEGIE ENDOWMENT FOR INTERNATIONAL PEACE

OCEANA PUBLICATIONS, INC.
New York City
1957

Copyright, 1957, by OCEANA PUBLICATIONS, INC.

Text may be quoted or reprinted with due acknowledgment of the source.

Library of Congress Catalog Card Number 57-12990

Printed in the U. S. A.

Contents

AUTHOR'S PREFACE v

FOREWORD ix

CHAPTER I: NEW HORIZONS 1
    UNEF is born in crisis . . . Behind-the-scenes story of midnight diplomacy against backdrop of war in Egypt . . . Pearson persuades Hammarskjold

CHAPTER II: AN IDEA TAKES SHAPE 6
    The General Assembly endorses Pearson's ideas and wins a cease-fire . . . Hammarskjold outlines the role and functions of UNEF . . . Vital precedents set

CHAPTER III: THE FORCE EMERGES 21
    From drawing board to operating force in eight days: how troops were obtained, others tactfully refused . . . Capodichino and the American air lift . . . Race against Soviet "volunteers" . . . Hammarskjold's troubles with Egypt; the case of the Queen's Own Rifles

CHAPTER IV: THE NEXT CRISIS 32
    What might have happened in the Egyptian case if a force had been available . . . in Hungary . . . What might happen in Kashmir . . . in Algeria . . . and elsewhere

CHAPTER V: THE LONG ROAD 46
    Efforts in the past to set up international police forces . . . for a fighting role . . . for lesser duties. Pre-World War I . . . Between wars . . . Article 43 of the UN Charter . . . the Military Staff Committee . . . Korea and the Uniting for Peace Resolution . . . The Collective Measures Committee . . . Trygve Lie's Proposals

CHAPTER VI: CAN THE UN ENFORCE PEACE? . . 66
    Is public opinion ready now for a step forward? Some indications of public sentiment . . . A plan for a force "in being" of 6000-7000 men: what it would cost, how to obtain it, what problems it would provoke . . . Conclusion: probably impracticable at this time

Chapter VII: What Can Be Done — Now? . . 81
A UN force pledged by member states and in readiness for quick assembly . . . Advantages and disadvantages . . . What preparations would make it most useful? Availability of troops . . . Logistics . . . Headquarters and commander . . . Morale . . . Political control . . . Relations with "host" state

Chapter VIII: Conclusions 90
How the General Assembly could create such a force . . . How it would fit into UN peaceful-settlement activity . . . Exclusion of Big Five . . . Role for a study committee . . . Should it be the Peace Observation Commission? . . . Would the plan work?

Chapter IX: Looking Ahead 103
Need for a way to prevent or halt small wars before they touch off atomic holocaust . . . a UN police force capable of meeting aggression will be needed some day . . . How practical first steps today could evolve into a safer, more peaceful world

Appendices

Where and Under What Circumstances Might a United Nations Police Force be Useful in the Future? 111
—by Paul H. Nitze

A United Nations Force: Its Usefulness in the Resolution of Various Crises 122
—by Richard L. Plunkett

The Problem of "Consent" in Relation to a UN Force 148
—by Charles P. Noyes

Military Aspects of a Permanent UN Force . . 161
—by Lt. Col. Charles A. Cannon, Jr., USA and Lt. Col. Amos A. Jordan, USA

Efforts to Establish International Police Force Down to 1950 172
—by Leland Goodrich

A United Nations "Guard" and a United Nations "Legion" 195
—by Stephen M. Schwebel

Index 217

Author's Preface

Professors, soldiers, government officials, and lawyers may write books freely without danger of losing their professional standing. So may dentists, third-basemen, ex-Communists, and drug addicts. Not so newspapermen. No matter how many hundred of thousands — yes, millions — of words they may have written, for them to put their thoughts between hard covers is, in the eyes of their colleagues, to become "authors," and this is inexcusable. It is almost as bad as becoming public relations men. They have deserted the atmosphere of the city news room, with its hourly deadlines, its editors' inanities, and its sense of the frantic, and have instead retired into chambers; they have sacrificed the sharp tang of fresh ink on newsprint for the musty fragrance of the ivory tower. So the legend goes.

In my case, however — if I may be permitted this defense — it was precisely because I felt I was *not* climbing into an ivory tower that I undertook the task of designing a United Nations peace force. The Carnegie Endowment for International Peace persuaded me there was a real opportunity to perform a useful service. UNEF, the United Nations Emergency Force, had given the UN a valuable new tool for peacemaking. Why not make some such machinery permanent? It was an obvious question; many were asking it; but few seemed to be doing anything specific about it. Perhaps a thorough study of the problems and prospects — an effort to plow the ground — would be useful if and when the UN General Assembly came face to face with the question on its agenda. It might, indeed, help to encourage the subject being placed on the agenda, by stirring informed public discussion of the issues involved. At least, so it seemed to me.

Such an undertaking requires many things. It requires a sponsor; the Carnegie Endowment was prepared to play that role. It requires an indulgent editor, ready to humor a correspondent's temporary aberration; and in Erwin D. Canham of *The Christian Science Monitor*, I had that. It requires a wife willing to eat supper alone night after night while her husband wrestles with documents and copy paper; and I had that too. Most of all, however, it requires expert advice and assistance. For this purpose, the Endowment helped gather together an advisory committee made up of some of the best-informed men in the United States. This committee was an anvil on which my ideas were hammered out; but it was far more than this, and although I would not wish to saddle its members — individually or collectively — with responsibility for the conclusions in this book, their suggestions, comments, and discussions shaped my thinking to a very considerable extent. No newspaperman, if he must become an author, could possibly have a more helpful team of consultants.

Nor is this by any means all. Attached to this book as a series of annexes are several special studies from which, as will be seen, I have drawn heavily in the text. That by Lieutenant Colonels Amos A. Jordan and Charles A. Cannon, Jr., of the United States Military Academy at West Point, is perhaps worthy of special mention. It kept me from falling into many pits which a civilian, dealing with military subjects, is certain to encounter. John N. Irwin, II, Deputy Assistant Secretary of Defense, arranged for briefings by a team of Army, Navy, and Air Force officers in the Pentagon whose practical advice also was indispensable. I am particularly obliged to Colonel Philip H. Greasley of the Office of Plans, who coordinated my requests for information. The same gratitude should be expressed, with even greater force, to the State Department, where Francis O. Wilcox, Assistant Secretary for International Organization Affairs, and many members of his staff, including John E. Fobes, Ware Adams, Joseph J. Sisco, Ronald I. Spiers, and Vincent Baker, helped steer me away from political and diplomatic reefs. So too, in New York, did Henry Cabot Lodge, chief United States delegate to the United Nations.

Nor was this solely an American undertaking by any means. I spent many extremely useful hours in Ottawa, where the Rt. Hon. Lester B. Pearson, then Secretary of State for External Affairs, John W. Holmes, Deputy Under Secretary, Brigadier G. C. Leech, and many others in the East Block, in Defense, and in Parliament shared with me their rich experience with UNEF and their thoughts for the future. Miss Dorothy Osborne of the United Nations Division steered me into many of the right offices at great sacrifice of her time and energy. In New York, UN delegates of a score or more countries offered advice and suggestions. Secretary-General Dag Hammarskjold; Andrew W. Cordier, his Executive Assistant; Dr. Ralph J. Bunche; David B. Vaughan; Oscar Schachter; and Alfred G. Katzin were among the members of the UN Secretariat who offered invaluable assistance.

The list could be extended at length. I had the privilege of consulting with Professor Julius Stone, the Australian international law authority, with Professor Louis B. Sohn of the Harvard Law School, whose works on similar subjects are so widely known and respected. Members of Congress helped. Many men and women, hearing about the study, sent suggestions by mail. There is an extraordinary reservoir of interest in the subject of a UN police force, and if this book does no more than help bring that interest to focus, it will have served a useful purpose.

Finally, by way of acknowledgments in the family, as it were, I must certainly put on record my unusual debt to Joseph E. Johnson, President of the Carnegie Endowment, who gathered together the advisory committee, acted as its chairman, and read the manuscript with great care; to Lawrence S. Finkelstein, Director of Studies, who shepherded the project from the beginning and also made scores of helpful suggestions on the text; and to many others on the staff, including Roger Lyons, a prime mover in the undertaking, Lee Ash, whose Library was indispensable, and Leslie Paffrath, another whose suggestions on the manuscript were of great value. The work could not possibly have been done in time for the deadline — and deadlines in terms of months, I found, can also be pressing — had it not been for my indefatigable research assistant, Miss Susanne Davis, and her unique capacity to win cooperation from others. Miss Ruth Jett, Miss Anita E. Sedler, and their fellow workers did incredible stints with the typewriter, days, nights, and weekends alike.

The end product is offered as an aid to thinking and action in the field of peacemaking. It looks to the future, not the past. It is not an attempt to write a history of UNEF, although the highlights of the UNEF story were directly relevant and therefore have been sketched in the first three chapters. To historians must be left the task of writing a complete and definitive account of the events of October and November, 1956. This book starts where those events left off and attempts to answer the question: "Where can and should the UN go from there?"

WILLIAM R. FRYE

August 1957

Foreword

In October and November 1956 two simultaneous crises presented the United Nations with a test as severe as any it has confronted. Most people would probably agree that the events in Hungary and the Middle East brought the world as close to disaster as it has been at any time in recent years. Probably few are completely satisfied with the course of UN action in these crises. Nevertheless, almost all would agree that, in the Middle East, the United Nations Emergency Force (UNEF), created in the frantic hours when the peace of the world may have hung in the balance, has performed a highly useful service. UNEF encouraged an end to the fighting and offered a means for bringing stability to the area. It demonstrated anew the great potential of the United Nations, attributable in part to its capacity to adapt to changing needs and circumstances.

This book attempts to appraise whether some such instrument as UNEF might be made available to the United Nations on a permanent basis, for similar peace-keeping functions. It discusses frankly the obstacles that lie in the way, and the reasons why no such force has ever been available on a permanent basis. It also points out that such a force may now be possible and outlines a modest but useful plan that would encounter the least resistance and thus have greatest short-run feasibility. The report, it seems to me, has the great virtue that it does not minimize or try to wish away the real difficulties to be faced. But there is a bias in this report, a bias that was implicit in the motives of the Carnegie Endowment when it launched this study project. That bias is that the peace-keeping potential of the UN should be strengthened in every possible way and, for that reason, the idea of a permanent force deserves full exploration and wide and thoughtful consideration. It is my earnest hope that this volume will be a contribution to those ends.

The reasons for this motivating assumption are apparent to all who have been disturbed by the growing destructive potential of modern weaponry, existing in a world rent by tension and controversy. To be sure, there is reason to believe that the awful knowledge of the atom may serve to inhibit deliberate unleashing of its full destructiveness. Both the United States and the Soviet Union have tacitly acknowledged new restrictions on their freedom to act because of the danger of atomic involvement.

But Suez and Hungary proved again, if indeed further evidence was needed, that the world still runs a real risk of conflagration by accident. One may perhaps be hopeful that the great powers will not deliberately unleash massive atomic destruction on each other and thus on themselves. There is no special reason, however, for confidence that another Suez, anywhere in the world, might not involve the great powers, even against their will.

The Suez experience was evidence that, in such a situation, a small patrolling and observation force, equipped mainly with the prestige and authority of the United Nations, can play a useful role in smothering a raging fire. The embers are still smouldering in the Middle East but the roof now seems in less danger of going up in smoke. A significant aspect of this experience was that all the great powers, the Soviet Union implicitly among them, were willing to have such a force employed. Significant also is the fact that it was possible to create a force of small nation contingents, thus avoiding the risk of dangerously involving the great powers through their military units in the field.

The appearance of this volume in time for the twelfth session of the UN General Assembly demanded extraordinary effort and teamwork. First of all, the credit should go to William R. Frye, who directed the enterprise and has written this volume, on leave of absence from his post as UN correspondent of *The Christian Science Monitor*. The skills and insights Mr. Frye has brought to bear will be apparent to all who read the work that follows. What may not be equally apparent are his energy and devotion to the task. He has virtually had to work around the clock in order to complete the manuscript before the printer's deadline. The volume owes much to *The Christian Science Monitor,* and particularly to its editor, Mr. Erwin D. Canham, for having permitted Mr. Frye to take on this assignment.

Although Mr. Frye alone is responsible for the form and contents of the book, he has had the benefit of close consultation with a small advisory committee whose discussions and ideas have contributed a great deal to the final product. The members of that committee included:

Harding F. Bancroft, Secretary of *The New York Times,* former Deputy U. S. Representative, UN Collective Measures Committee;

Philip C. Jessup, Hamilton Fish Professor of International Law and Diplomacy, Columbia University, former Ambassador at Large;

Lt. Col. Amos A. Jordan, Deputy Head, Department of Social Sciences, U. S. Military Academy;

Frank C. Nash, lawyer, former Assistant Secretary of Defense, former U. S. Alternate Representative to the UN Commission on Conventional Armaments;

Charles P. Noyes, Rockefeller Brothers Fund, former U. S. Deputy Representative on Interim Committee of the General Assembly;

Joseph E. Johnson, President, Carnegie Endowment for International Peace, (Chairman).

In addition, Mr. Frye was able to consult with many other officials and private individuals of many nationalities, to whom the Endowment owes much for the information and good advice they gave.

In the course of his work, Mr. Frye was able to mobilize considerable assistance in the form of staff papers on various aspects of the overall problem that seemed to need special treatment and expert knowledge or judgment. Some of these staff papers have been incorporated as appendices in the present volume. They were prepared as the work progressed, as various hypotheses were being considered, tested, and in some cases discarded. Therefore, the appendices do not all, as they could not in the circumstances, reflect Mr. Frye's final conclusions. The authors of these papers are alone responsible for their form and contents. To those who prepared staff papers, often laying aside other concerns, to conform to the demands of the rigid timetable, much gratitude is owed.

Finally, a word should be said about those members of the staff of the Carnegie Endowment for International Peace whose energetic assistance was essential to the completion of this work according to the rigorous schedule that was established for it; they will know who they are without having their names mentioned here.

JOSEPH E. JOHNSON
President, Carnegie Endowment for International Peace

August 1957

CHAPTER I

New Horizons

The United Nations Emergency Force is an accident of history. It was created in such haste that even its parents scarcely recognized it. It was sent out to do a man's work while still an infant, with few tools and fewer instructions. At home, the parents have quarreled over who should feed it and clothe it and over how long they should permit it to live.

Yet, somehow, UNEF is a success. It has won the hearts of nearly everyone, from Lt. Col. Gamal Abdel Nasser of Egypt to Senator William F. Knowland of California and from Foreign Minister Malik Firoz Khan Noon of Pakistan to Marshal Josip Broz Tito of Yugoslavia. In part, this is because it has managed, despite all handicaps, to do its job; in part, it is because so many people have felt for so long that its parents—the United Nations—really should have had children. UNEF has succeeded so well that many hours of careful thought are being devoted to keeping it alive, even after its present task in the Middle East has been completed. Many students of world affairs want the UN to obtain, as a regular part of its peacemaking machinery, a permanent police force. This book outlines one practical method of accomplishing that goal.

If any one man could be said to be the author of UNEF, it would be Lester B. Pearson of Canada. Even Mr. Pearson, however, did not originally conceive of it in its present form. He and his key advisers in the East Block, Ottawa, home of the Canadian Department of External Affairs were profoundly concerned over developments during the critical days of October 30, 31, and November 1, 1956 when war broke out in Egypt. Their first idea was to run up the blue and white flag of the United Nations over a police force consisting primarily of British and French, with soldiers from other countries to come later as window dressing—not to give UN respectability to the Anglo-French intervention, but to change its character and make it serve different ends. The ostensible purpose of British-French action in Egypt was to separate the belligerents (Israel and Egypt) and protect the Suez Canal; very well, the Canadians said, why not take this policy at face value and deputize London and Paris to perform those tasks on behalf of the UN General Assembly? Mr. Pearson abandoned this idea very soon after he arrived at UN headquarters and sampled the atmosphere. The Afro-Asian nations, frightened and infuriated by the Anglo-French action, regarded it as a case of naked aggression and were in no mood to let London and Paris act on behalf of the UN. On the contrary, they were determined to condemn the British and French with all the force they could muster. The United States and the Soviet Union, broadly speaking, had adopted the same approach, so there was no future for the original Pearson plan.

The question that was really at stake, at the core, was whether the Anglo-French-Israeli use of force in violation of the Charter was to succeed in improving the bargaining position of London, Paris, and Jerusalem in negotiations with Egypt over Suez and Palestine, two overriding political issues troubling the Middle East. Once the British and French were to seize the canal and hold it, they would be able to dictate the terms of a Suez settlement. At least, they could try to "sell" the withdrawal of their troops to President Nasser or his successor for a useful price; the presence of the troops would represent bargaining power. Similarly, Israel might be able to extract a political price for the withdrawal of its forces. This stratagem might work almost as well if the occupation force consisted of Canadians or Pakistanis or New Zealanders or Colombians under UN control. At some point, Egypt might pay a price to secure their withdrawal if it could not get rid of them without doing so. Mr. Pearson, believing that some increment to the bargaining power of London, Paris, and Jerusalem was vital to break the dangerous deadlock and bring lasting peace to the area, began to explore the idea of a UN force, made up of small countries, to separate the belligerents, provide a cooling-off period, readjust the political balance, and rescue Britain and France from the worst consequences of their desperate act.

All during the first critical night of November 1-2, while the (then) 80-nation General Assembly was exploding with indignation and demanding a cease-fire, Mr. Pearson, in his private contacts, argued for delay. Make haste cautiously, he counseled; divide the Assembly's pressure, exerting some on Egypt as well as on Britain, France and Israel; make use of the "incentive of fear" to pry from Egypt and her friends the first step toward a peace settlement. Pearson held an impromptu conference with United States Secretary of State John Foster Dulles on the floor of the Assembly while the debate was in process. Dulles was sympathetic to the idea of a UN force, but did not think it wise to delay the pending cease-fire resolution, which he had put forward. The best way to control the Assembly was to lead it, he felt. If the United States did not lead, the Soviet Union would—and the Russians would gain a political and psychological foothold in the Middle East from which they might not be dislodged for generations. Moreover, he said, President Eisenhower was no less indignant than the Afro-Asians, agreed that the British-French-Israeli action was aggression, and was determined that aggression should not be allowed to pay. There was even the possibility of atomic world war if things got out of hand. So the United States pressed ahead. Debate was shut off, and in the small hours of Friday morning, November 2, an American resolution—calling for a cease-fire, a withdrawal behind the Armistice lines, strict observance of the Armistice Agreements, a ban on "introducing military goods in the area of hostilities," and a free and open Suez Canal—was passed, 64-5, with 6 abstentions.

Mr. Pearson got a turn at the podium after the roll had been called. "Peace," he said, "is far more than ceasing to fire, although it certainly must include that essential factor . . . I regret the use of military force in the circumstances which we have been discussing, but I regret also that there was not more time, before a vote had to be taken, for consideration of the best way to bring about that kind of cease-fire which would have enduring and beneficial results. I think that we were entitled to that time, for this is not only a tragic moment for the countries and peoples immediately affected, but it is an equally difficult time for the United Nations itself. . . .

"The armed forces of Israel and of Egypt are to withdraw or, if you like, to return to the armistice lines, where, presumably, if this is done, they will once again face each other in fear and hatred. What then? What then, six months from now? Are we to go through all this again? Are we to return to the *status quo ante?* Such a return would not be to a position of security, or even a tolerable position, but would be a return to terror, bloodshed, strife, incidents, charges and counter-charges, and ultimately another explosion which the United Nations Armistice Commission would be powerless to prevent and possibly even to investigate.

"I therefore would have liked to see a provision in this resolution . . . authorizing the Secretary-General to begin to make arrangements with Member Governments for a United Nations force large enough to keep these borders at peace while a political settlement is being worked out. I regret exceedingly that time has not been given to follow up this idea, which was mentioned also by the representative of the United Kingdom in his first speech, and I hope that even now, when action on the resolution has been completed, it may not be too late to give consideration to this matter. My own Government would be glad to recommend Canadian participation in such a United Nations force, a truly international peace and police force. . . ."

This was the Pearson trial balloon. The Assembly adjourned at 4:20 a.m., too exhausted to go any further at that time, though Dulles endorsed Pearson's idea in principle and added: "The United States delegation would be very happy indeed if the Canadian delegation would formulate and introduce as part of these proceedings a concrete suggestion along the lines that Mr. Pearson outlined."

During the debate, Pearson had informed Secretary-General Dag Hammarskjold of what he had in mind, and at 4:30 a.m.— as dawn slowly battled with the blackness over New York—the two men held a preliminary discussion of the plan, Hammarskjold wary, Pearson convinced it was the only way out of an impossible dilemma.

There was little sleep for anyone at the UN that night. Men cat-napped in chairs, waking periodically to read cables and dictate replies. The British and French were bombing Port Said; Israel was decimating such Egyptian forces as it had caught in the Sinai desert. By mid-morning on Friday, November 2, it was abundantly clear that the cease-fire resolution would be ignored.

Mr. Pearson sat down with Mr. Hammarskjold and Andrew W. Cordier, Executive Assistant to the Secretary-General, for lunch. The Canadian explained his plan in greater detail. It was urgent for many obvious reasons, he said, including the fact that a police force was one of the British-French preconditions to a cease-fire. By way of a footnote to history, it was urgent, also, he said, because Canadian Prime Minister Louis St. Laurent was making a speech Sunday in Toronto, and wanted to deal with the subject at that time.

Hammarskjold looked out the window and studied the skyline of midtown Manhattan. The Swedish diplomat's youthful face was lined with fatigue and reflected the bitter dismay he had felt when his close friends, the British and French, had torn up the UN Charter and invaded Egypt at just the moment when he thought a Suez settlement by negotiation was within reach. He was still doubtful about the practicality of the Pearson idea. From which countries would the troops come? he wanted to know. Would there be a response? The idea must not start out with fanfare and then flop; it could backfire badly. The risk of acting must be weighed against the risk of not acting. Early in the fish course, however, Pearson was able to convince Hammarskjold that the obstacles could be overcome; and the rest of the meal was spent planning an approach to the General Assembly and deciding immediate next steps. By demi-tasse time, the Secretary-General had been fully persuaded, St. Laurent had his speech, and the UN had new horizons.

CHAPTER II

An Idea Takes Shape

Saturday night, November 3, the Assembly reconvened. In the interim, the Canadians had contacted London, the United States and Norway had been brought in on the planning, and strategy had been mapped out in detail. Pearson had put a proposed first step into writing in the form of a draft resolution endorsing the idea of a police force and asking an Assembly committee to work out the details. This draft, in a form revised by the United States to give Hammarskjold the executive responsibility, had been shown to as many influential delegates as Pearson and his aides could collar in UN corridors and lounges.

This process of lobbying continued during the debate that night, Pearson masterminding the process from his seat in the Assembly hall. A key move was a contact made with Arthur S. Lall, the permanent representative of India, head of the Indian delegation pending the arrival from New Delhi of Minister Without Portfolio V. K. Krishna Menon. Lall, on behalf of India, accepted the Pearson draft and promised to support it. Pearson in turn indicated support for a new and strengthened cease-fire resolution which India and a group of other Afro-Asian nations were offering. (Nearly everyone at the UN calls this process vote-swapping, though diplomats do it with subtlety and tact, avoiding the appearance of a deal.) Pearson accepted the arrangement, even though the Indian resolution represented considerable pressure on Britain, France and Israel, and such pressure was not entirely popular at home. Canada could go along if the Indians—and consequently, the 26-nation Afro-Asian bloc—would accept the UN force. Attaching the police force as a rider to the pressure was precisely the strategy Pearson himself had been urging.

It was happy for UNEF that it was Mr. Lall and not Mr. Krishna Menon who was in New York at the time. On Monday, two days after the Pearson resolution had been adopted overwhelmingly, Mr. Krishna Menon strode into a private meeting of the Afro-Asian bloc and started resisting the whole idea of a police force. There was a shocked silence; then someone pointed out to him that virtually everyone in the room, including the representative of India, had already voted in favor of the idea, and that it was being implemented. Krishna Menon subsided; and his government later sent troops.

The Canadian resolution, marking an endorsement in principle and hence the first step toward a UN police force, read as follows:

> The General Assembly,
> Bearing in mind the urgent necessity of facilitating compliance with the [original cease-fire] resolution adopted by the Assembly on 2 November 1956 (A/3256),
> Requests, as a matter of priority, the Secretary-General to submit to it within forty-eight hours a plan for the setting up, with the consent of the nations concerned, of an emergency international United Nations force to secure and supervise the cessation of hostilities in accordance with all the terms of the aforementioned resolution.

This Canadian resolution was passed 57–0 in the morning hours of Sunday, November 4. There were 19 miscellaneous abstentions, including all nine members of the Soviet bloc and Egypt. Egypt's aloofness cast temporary doubt on the consent of one of the "nations concerned."

It remained for Hammarskjold to produce the plan which the Assembly had requested. It was little short of a political miracle he was being asked to bring off. History records many futile efforts to set up international police forces, and very few successes indeed. Late Sunday morning an informal planning group consisting of Canada, Norway, Colombia, and India met with Hammarskjold at his invitation to discuss it. Ambassador Hans Engen of Norway proved to be a key member of this group. It was he who acted as liaison with the Scandinavian countries—and the Scandinavians were highly important participants in UNEF.

The plan which emerged from this Sunday morning meeting was first, to establish a "United Nations Command," headed by Major General E. L. M. Burns, chief of staff of the UN's

Truce Supervision Organization in Palestine, and give him a staff of officers; then, when the General Assembly had provided that nucleus, to send the foot soldiers. The first step would be relatively non-controversial, and could be taken quickly, preserving the diplomatic momentum; once it was on the books, the Assembly would have put its hand to the plow, and could scarcely turn back.

The Assembly had given Hammarskjold 48 hours to prepare his blueprint. The first installment was ready in scarcely more than 12. By the time the Assembly next met, on Sunday night, November 4, it was ready for formal Assembly approval. This was forthcoming. Shortly after midnight, in the small hours of Monday morning, a resolution sponsored by Canada, Colombia, and Norway was passed 57–0 with 19 abstentions, Egypt again among them. (Later Monday, in a cable from Cairo, Egypt "accepted" the resolution.) By its terms, the Assembly noted "with satisfaction" Hammarskjold's first report; established "a United Nations Command for an emergency international force to secure and supervise the cessation of hostilities in accordance with all the terms of" the first cease-fire resolution; named Burns to head that Command; and authorized the recruitment of a staff of officers from countries other than the great powers.

A cable went out to Burns notifying him of his new job. A few hours later, just having gotten to bed, sleepy UN officials were awakened by a long-distance phone call from Jerusalem. A puzzled, astonished, and none-too-enthusiastic Burns wanted to know what in the world it was he was commander of. Headquarters chuckled sympathetically. They didn't yet know, for sure, either.

The primary diplomatic objective at this stage was to stop the fighting. This—not the establishment of a police force as such—was what most delegates had in mind. The Israeli action in the Sinai peninsula was, to all intents and purposes, over; but the British and French were bombing targets in Egypt around the clock, and (beginning the night of November 4-5) making assault landings. London and Paris, in a joint statement read to the House of Commons November 3 by Prime Minister Sir Anthony Eden, had said they would "most willingly stop military action" as soon as three things had happened: Egypt and

Israel had accepted a UN "peace force"; the UN had set up such a force and decided to maintain it until Suez and Palestine settlements had been achieved; and finally, Israel and Egypt (in effect, Egypt) had agreed to let British and French troops occupy the canal area temporarily, "until the United Nations force is constituted." In private, the British and French seemed highly skeptical that a UN force, without their participation, could be put together and brought to the scene in time to be of any significance. Thus their public position must have been little more than an attempt to fend off pressure for a cease-fire.

Pearson, Hammarskjold, United States delegate Henry Cabot Lodge, and others believed the force could be put together in a hurry, and they set out to prove it. There were, however, several highly important questions that had not been answered. They had been postponed deliberately, in order to obtain quick Assembly approval of General Burns' appointment. But now, when governments were being asked to contribute manpower, these questions would have to be faced. What functions would the force perform? Where would it be stationed? How long would it expect to be there? Under what conditions would it withdraw? How would it affect the political and military balance in the area? Was Egypt amenable? Who would pay the expenses? Who would be in control?

There were pressures on Hammarskjold from many sides as he sought to answer these questions. His suggestions would have to be approved by the General Assembly and would therefore have to anticipate the Assembly's views. But which faction of the Assembly? Britain, France, Israel, Australia, and New Zealand conceived of the force as a means of exerting political pressure on Egypt. They wanted it to occupy the canal zone and the Sinai desert, and remain until satisfactory settlements of the two main political problems—Suez and Palestine—had been negotiated. Egypt and her friends took precisely the opposite line: to them, the purpose of the force was simply to obtain a cease-fire and usher foreign troops off Egyptian soil. It would cease to function, Egypt felt, as soon as the *status quo ante* had been restored.

Since the Assembly had decided that Egyptian consent would be required for the entry of UNEF into Egyptian territory, Cairo was in a strong position to influence the preconditions.

And there was no convenient way around this Egyptian roadblock. Bombs raining on Port Said and Cairo airports, and then British-French invasion troops, might normally have extracted consent from Egypt to a force on almost any terms. But this British-French pressure was counterbalanced by support from the Soviet Union. It took various forms: vocal backing in the UN; a proposal that Russian and American troops go to Egypt's rescue to "crush the aggressors and restore peace"; and letters from Premier Nikolai Bulganin to Britain and France with an ominous reference to "countries" which "could have used" rocket weapons, i.e., presumably atomic missiles, against London and Paris. (Talk of mobilizing Soviet "volunteers" to force troop withdrawals came later.) With such support from Moscow, Egypt dared to stand firm.

The United States—and only the United States—could have countered these Soviet moves, but Washington disapproved of the British-French action so strongly that although it did speak up when the Soviet threats became too blatant, its voice was muted. Indeed, Washington joined in exerting pressure on Britain and France, thus helping to strengthen Egypt. The Soviet Union, Washington felt, could not be allowed to appear to the Arabs to be their only great-power friend, lest the whole Middle East be lost to communism; nor did anyone in Washington want to do anything which could increase in the slightest the already great risk of World War III. For what it may be worth, Soviet leaders are known to have told Indian Prime Minister Jawaharlal Nehru, when they visited New Delhi in November and December, that at the time the Egyptian fighting broke out they believed world war was being set in motion.

Hammarskjold, threading his way through the many conflicting pressures, assessing the temper of the Assembly with consummate skill, drew up a statement of the principles, functions, legal status, and proposed financing of the force. It was embodied in what he called his "second and final report" to the Assembly on the establishment of UNEF.

A major state paper, the second report was produced by the Secretary-General and his indefatigable staff between Monday, November 5 and the early hours of Tuesday, November 6. Its principal conclusion was, in effect, that UNEF could not and should not be used as a means of exerting political pressure on Egypt; that Britain, France, and Israel could not expect it to enhance their bargaining position. At least, it could not be set up on such an assumption or with such an appearance. "It follows from its [UNEF's] terms of reference," the report said at one key juncture, "that there is no intent in the establishment of the force to influence the military balance in the present conflict and, thereby, the political balance affecting efforts to settle the conflict." Britain, France, Israel, and their friends protested vigorously, in private, against this judgment and long tried to reverse it in practice. But Hammarskjold's decision accurately reflected the views of a large majority of the Assembly, and of the United States, by far its most influential member. Had he decided otherwise, there is no assurance at all that Egypt would have admitted UNEF onto her soil, and every reasonable probability that she would not. Indeed, there is no assurance that troops would have been forthcoming from any but a very few countries.

American pressure applied directly on Eden, plus world opinion, and perhaps the Soviet Union's threats, extracted from Britain and France an agreement to cease firing on the basis of the second Hammarskjold report. London and Paris really should not have expected much more. It did afford them a certain amount of face-saving, inasmuch as it provided for, and foreshadowed the dispatch of, a "peace force" similar to the one they had been asking. And by this time, Britain, at least, was eager for a convenient way out of a very difficult predicament. A few hours after the report had been made public, the Secretary-General was able to announce to the world that the shooting would stop at midnight, November 6th, GMT.

Hammarskjold's two reports—like virtually everything else that was done—set vital precedents for any future peace force. He was constantly aware that this would be the case, and careful to make the precedents as constructive as he could, within the limits of his authority. The key points made in these two reports were as follows:

1. The great powers were not to participate in the force. Hammarskjold even politely rebuffed a British-French effort to take part in deciding the "composition of the staff and contingents."

The primary reason for excluding the great powers was to make clear that Britain and France were not to be deputized as UN policemen; a secondary, but scarcely less important, reason, was to keep Soviet troops out of the Middle East. London and Paris still wanted a role, but it was clear to virtually everyone else that the idea was wholly impractical. Even if a two-thirds majority of the General Assembly could have been obtained for it—which it could not—Egypt would never have agreed. Exclusion of the Big Five meant, of course, that no American GIs could take part directly; but had GIs been included, the Russians almost certainly would have demanded a role, and few diplomats—even from the Arab states—wanted Soviet foot soldiers in the Middle East.

2. Political control of UNEF was placed almost entirely in the Secretary-General's hands. "If the force is to come into being with all the speed indispensable to its success," his second report said, "a margin of confidence must be left to those who will carry the responsibility for putting the decisions of the General Assembly into effect." In practice, this "margin of confidence" was very wide indeed—and except for those who have criticized his handling of Egypt, there have been few who have regretted it. On the contrary, history may well record that this decision was the principal key to the success of UNEF.

At the Secretary-General's suggestion, he was given an Advisory Committee. Its members were Brazil, Canada, Colombia, India, Ceylon, Norway, and Pakistan. Committee members have differed with Hammarskjold from time to time, and he often has modified his policies in the direction of their advice. But the function of the Advisory Committee has been just what the name implies; it has not sought to make decisions or take responsibility. No votes have been taken; issues have not been forced to a showdown. Thus when fast action has been necessary, there has been no need to wait while seven UN delegates contacted their home governments by cable and awaited formal "instructions"— a process which normally takes days. Whether in another crisis the world community would be satisfied to trust a different Secretary-General with so much authority is an open question.

3. UNEF was to be a buffer force, with certain police duties, not a fighting army. "Although paramilitary in nature," Hammarskjold said, UNEF was "not [to be] a force with military ob-

jectives .... It would be more than an observers' corps, but in no way a military force temporarily controlling the territory in which it is stationed." Any thought of its fighting its way into Egypt was dismissed; it would not enter until after a cease-fire. It would not attempt to force Israel out of Sinai, or Britain and France out of the canal zone. In short, it would not seek to impose its will, or the will of the world community, on Egypt, Israel, Britain or France; it would simply assist in bringing about results jointly desired by the governments involved. Cooperation by those governments was assumed.

This was a limited definition of the force's objectives, but in many ways a realistic one. Much the same thing could be said of all the UN's activity in the realm of peaceful settlement of disputes. Settlements are not imposed; they are simply facilitated. UNEF was, in point of fact, to be an extension of the UN's peaceful settlement function. It was not to be an enforcement organ. Few countries, if any, other than Britain and France, would have contributed troops to a UN army which was to fight its way into Egypt, and none except the Soviet Union was ready to drive the British and French out.

4. The force would be as nearly neutral, politically, as possible. No force can be entirely neutral; it is bound to have some effect on the balance of political forces, and hence on bargaining positions of adversaries. But Hammarskjold, taking his cue from the Assembly — where a majority felt Britain, France, and Israel should not be "rewarded" for aggression — defined the functions of the force in such a way as to restore the political balance which had existed before the fighting. In doing this, he found himself in broad agreement with Egypt, and thus incurred sharp criticism from those who wanted to use the force to enhance the bargaining positions of Britain, France, and Israel. But use of the Force on behalf of Britain and France would have been nearly if not completely impossible politically. At a later stage, Israel was able to mobilize enough support in the Assembly and in Washington to obtain the help of UNEF in pursuit of two of her principal political objectives: free passage into the Gulf of Aqaba, and protection from fedayeen raids based on Gaza. Britain and France did not have that kind of backing.

Historians probably will debate for years the wisdom and necessity of Hammarskjold's decisions at this time. In theory, at any rate, it would have been possible to have given the force a broader, more ambitious task. He himself helped make this possible. Defining UNEF's functions, he said it would "help maintain quiet during and after the withdrawal of non-Egyptian troops, and . . . secure compliance with the other terms established in the [cease-fire] resolution of 2 November, 1956." Those "other terms" were broad. One paragraph urged

> . . . that upon the cease-fire being effective, steps be taken to reopen the Suez Canal and restore secure freedom of navigation.

The British and French argued that if UNEF was to "secure compliance" with the objective of "freedom of navigation," UNEF should be stationed in the canal zone until a political agreement had been reached guaranteeing free transit of the waterway. But this was not what the Assembly majority had intended, nor was Egypt prepared to consent to admission of the force on these terms. So Hammarskjold assured Egypt privately that, except for a possible "staging area" in the region of the canal, UNEF would have "no functions" there once the area ceased to be a battle zone. In point of fact, though the UN did an extraordinary job of salvage, clearing the waterway in 14 weeks, UNEF played no direct part in this operation or in political negotiations on canal management.

Other functions which might have been given to UNEF, in theory, and which still could be undertaken — if agreement could be reached among the governments concerned — may also be inferred from the November 2 resolution. A paragraph urged "the parties to the Armistice Agreements" (not merely the Israeli-Egyptian armistice, but all of them)

> . . . to desist from raids across the Armistice lines into neighboring territory, and to observe scrupulously the provisions of the Armistice Agreements.

In order to "secure compliance" with this provision, UNEF at the very least would have to patrol all the borders which separate Israel from the neighboring Arab states. Still another paragraph recommended

> . . . that all [UN] members refrain from introducing military goods in the area of hostilities . . .

To make certain this was done, UNEF would have to be given

the task of policing an arms embargo. But there has been little or no public talk about giving UNEF either of these functions.

It has been difficult enough for the force to carry out its principal task, that is, insulating Egypt and Israel. To be genuinely effective against border crossings, it would have to be able to shoot at marauders. But although General Burns requested this right, the most he could obtain from Hammarskjold and the Advisory Committee was authority to shoot in self defense, with "self defense" being interpreted very broadly. Some countries contributing troops did not want their men shooting at Egyptians (or Israelis) without the consent of the Egyptian and Israeli Governments, and Hammarskjold did not press them to do so. Instead, he sought the necessary permission from Cairo and Jerusalem. These capitals haggled interminably, through him, over the terms and conditions and places where UNEF would shoot. The negotiations finally broke down because Israel would not let Burns' men operate on its side of the armistice line, and Egypt would not let them operate effectively on the Egyptian side alone.

UNEF's success in quieting the Egyptian-Israeli armistice line therefore was something of a miracle, no doubt reflecting in large part the fact that — at least for the first few months — both Cairo and Jerusalem considered it to be in their national interest to have a quiet border.

5. The "very basis and starting point" of all that was done, as Hammarskjold told the Advisory Committee, was "recognition by the General Assembly of the unlimited sovereign rights of Egypt." At the same time, as he also pointed out, the world community had certain rights; and the effort to balance the two was perhaps the most difficult of all the tasks Hammarskjold undertook.

He attempted to lay down a guiding rule in his second report. The General Assembly, he said, "has wished to reserve for itself the full determination of the tasks of this emergency force, and of the legal basis on which it must function. . . ." On the other hand, UNEF "would be limited in its operations to the extent that consent of the parties concerned is required under generally recognized international law." The second of these statements obviously qualified the first very heavily, especially in the light of this further observation: "While the General Assembly is enabled to *establish* the force with the consent of those parties which contribute units to the force, it could not request the force to be *stationed* or *operate* on the territory of a given country without the consent of the government of that country." (Italics in the original.)

What this meant, in practice, was that while Hammarskjold and his aides — under authority delegated by the Assembly — would make decisions on the force's composition, movement, duties, etc., they would act in the full knowledge that those decisions could not be carried out unless Egypt were willing to accept them. Egypt's consent would be required at every step, and in order to avoid controversy and delay, it would be wise not to attempt any move, at least at first, which Egypt would be likely to resist.

This concept of a world organization recognizing the "unlimited sovereign rights" of a member state is abhorrent to public opinion in some countries. Many Britons and Frenchmen, for example, and not a few Americans failed to understand why Hammarskjold, when necessary, could not simply tell Nasser to go jump in the Suez Canal. Nasser had had a large share in the blame for the outbreak, hadn't he? He was being rescued from military defeat, wasn't he? Well, then, why should Hammarskjold "take orders" from a "petty dictator" in Cairo? they wanted to know.

The difficulty was that the UN is not a world government. It is a voluntary association of states which cling desperately to their sovereignty, and there is no clear evidence that world public opinion wants it to be anything more. The same Britons and Frenchmen and Americans who objected to Hammarskjold (as they saw it) "taking orders" from Nasser would cry out in rage if the UN were to try to station troops on *their* territory without their consent, or indeed, do anything else that affected their country's sovereign rights without its full agreement. How many Parisians, for example, would want a UN police force sent to Algeria against France's will to check the activities of the French army there?

So when it came to choosing countries to make up UNEF, Egypt had what amounted to veto power. As Hammarskjold told the Advisory Committee, while he could not "accept any conditions" as to the establishment of the force, he "agreed [with

Egypt] that a special unit could not be placed in a country without the consent of the country." On November 14, when Egypt agreed to let the force enter, she cabled consent to "the arrival of UN forces which have been the subject of mutual understanding between us."

There is nothing in this fact that need make UN officials as sensitive as they sometimes seem to be when the issue is discussed. Perhaps their feelings have been rubbed raw by criticism that they "knuckled under" to Nasser. But one of the principal prerogatives of a sovereign state under international law is the right to say whether or not foreign troops may be stationed on its soil. The fact that in the case of UNEF the foreign troops were to be acting on behalf of the UN should, perhaps, have made a difference to Egypt, and may in the future come to do so with other host states. But no such concept of a special status for representatives of the world organization had evolved in November, 1956.

Elaborate "status of forces" agreements have been negotiated to permit the stationing of American troops in NATO countries, for example, and in Japan. Hammarskjold and his chief legal aide, Constantin A. Stavropoulos, negotiated a status of forces agreement with Egypt which gives UNEF more freedom than American GIs have in Britain and France — more even, it is said, than Russians have in Poland. Among other things, UNEF personnel are totally exempt from criminal prosecution in Egyptian courts. A case like that of Specialist 3/c William S. Girard (the American soldier tried for murder in Japanese courts in the summer of 1957) could not arise with UNEF in Egypt. Hammarskjold succeeded in modifying Egypt's absolute sovereignty with the full voluntary agreement of Egypt.

Much the same thing might be said of another key problem with respect to UNEF in Egypt, namely, the length of its stay and the circumstances of its withdrawal. Hammarskjold told the Advisory Committee November 14 that in answer to a question from Egypt, he had said the force would stay until "liquidation" of the "immediate crisis," and that "in case of a difference of views as to when the crisis does not any longer warrant the presence" of UN troops, the matter would have to be "negotiated with the parties."

Later, on a trip to Cairo, Hammarskjold was able to obtain from Nasser a better understanding, from the UN's point of view.

> The Government of Egypt and the Secretary-General of the United Nations [its critical paragraphs read] have stated their understanding on the basic points for the presence and functioning of UNEF as follows:
> 1. The Government of Egypt declares that, when exercising its sovereign rights on any matter concerning the presence and functioning of UNEF, it will be guided, in good faith, by its acceptance of the General Assembly Resolution 394 of 5 November 1956 [establishing the UN Command].
> 2. The United Nations takes note of this declaration of the Government of Egypt and declares that the activities of UNEF will be guided, in good faith, by the task established for the Force in the aforementioned resolutions [all the resolutions establishing UNEF]; in particular, the United Nations, understanding this to correspond to the wishes of the Government of Egypt, reaffirms its willingness to maintain the UNEF until its task is completed.

This agreement did not say explicitly who would decide when UNEF's task *was* completed; but there was a subtle implication that the UN, that is, the UN General Assembly, would decide. It is in this sense that Hammarskjold and Nasser are said to have understood their agreement. No doubt in practice, Nasser would merely have to ask UNEF to leave, and so many contributing countries would withdraw as to destroy the force; but in such a case, Nasser could be charged with not having acted "in good faith," and the charge might carry enough weight with countries previously friendly to him to help deter the act.

Planners for a future force would do well to start from the premise that full consent of the host state would be required on virtually every key point. Circumstances and skillful diplomacy might be able to modify this requirement of consent, or obtain it from an otherwise reluctant host state, when that state stood to gain much from the presence of the force and to lose much by its departure.

6. On financing, the "basic rule" laid down in Hammarskjold's second report was that "a nation providing a unit would be responsible for the cost of equipment and salaries, while all other costs should be financed outside the normal budget of the United Nations" (i.e., paid by the UN but as the result of a spe-

cial levy on member states). In practice, this "basic rule" has been supplanted by a provision that the contributing state pays all expenses (except food) that it would have incurred in any event, as the result of maintaining under arms the troops comprising its contribution — basic equipment, clothing, salary, etc; while the UN pays such expenses as are directly attributable to the fact that the troops are serving overseas, rather than at home — transportation, special equipment, extra pay for overseas duty, etc. Even this formula, however simple on the surface, has been susceptible of differences of interpretation.

There has been a running dispute inside the UN General Assembly over apportionment of the UN's share among member states. There has been much eagerness among many countries to let someone else — anyone else — pay it. Hammarskjold has felt the full amount should be borne by member states in the same proportion as their annual contributions to the regular budget, which in turn are based on ability to pay. Since the whole world community benefits from peaceful conditions in any single troubled area—the world being an interdependent whole in this age of jet propulsion and atomic energy — his formula is clearly the most logical. But it could not command the necessary majority in the 1956-57 General Assembly, since many countries felt remote from the hostilities and/or were hard put for money, and an American compromise was substituted. Under it, the first $10,000,000 was levied according to the regular scale of assessments, and the rest — then estimated (much too optimistically) at $6,500,000 for the period to December 31, 1957 — was left to be met by voluntary contributions.

The United States offered to contribute half the $6,500,000 if other states would pay the remaining half. Their reluctance to do so is a strong hint that ambitious schemes for large permanent UN police forces, costing as much or more, are likely to get a very cold reception unless and until world opinion demands that funds be diverted to that purpose from armaments and other traditional sources of national security. Even in a country like the United States, with an annual national budget of more than $70,000,000,000 and a gross national product in the hundreds of billions, there was sharp and hostile questioning from at least one member of the House Appropriations Committee when the Administration asked for $6,583,000 to pay its share of the costs of

UNEF. Some countries which have contributed troops, finding the contribution is a considerable financial burden and feeling — with some justice — that they are carrying more than their share of the load, have threatened privately to pull out unless the UN shoulders a larger part of the cost.

Hammarskjold's blueprint for UNEF, embodied in his "second and final report," was endorsed by the General Assembly 64-0, with 12 abstentions, on November 7, the day after the cease-fire became effective. The nine members of the Cominform bloc comprised most of the abstainers; they did not want the Middle East pacified until after the Soviet Union had gained a political and military foothold there. Egypt, Israel, and South Africa were the other three who abstained from voting.

The force now existed — on paper. It remained only to get it onto the scene.

CHAPTER III

The Force Emerges

The United Nations Emergency Force was born, in a legal sense, at 7 p. m. on Wednesday November 7, 1956, when Rudecindo Ortega of Chile, President of the UN General Assembly, announced: "Sixty-four in favor, none opposed, twelve abstentions. The resolution [endorsing Hammarskjold's report] is adopted." Eight days later, on Thursday November 15, at 9:35 a.m., local time, the first UN troops, 45 Danes, landed at Abu Suweir airfield ten miles west of Ismailia, Egypt. It was one of the fastest diplomatic-military "crash" operations in history. And perhaps the most astonishing part of it is that the first of the men could have been there in three days — on November 10 — if Egypt had been willing to let them in.

UN Secretary-General Dag Hammarskjold began rounding up troops even before the Assembly had formally approved the force — indeed, before General Burns' Command had been set up. On Sunday morning, November 4, when he met with the delegates of Canada, Colombia, India, and Norway in his office on the 38th floor of the UN Secretariat building, he emphasized the importance of having men ready to go to Egypt immediately after a cease-fire, or as soon thereafter as physically possible. All four delegates — Pearson of Canada, Urrutia of Colombia, Lall of India, and Engen of Norway — indicated a willingness to cooperate, and thought their governments would agree; all got on the long-distance telephone to their home capitals urging that agreement. Later the same day, three of them — Canada, Colombia, and Norway — put their offers into writing. New Zealand orally confirmed an earlier offer. Already, in less than 12 hours, the nucleus of a UN police force was available.

Other countries came forward. Sweden, Denmark, and Pakistan offered troops the following day; Finland, Ceylon, India, Czechoslovakia, and Romania stepped up on Tuesday, November 6. Dr. Ralph J. Bunche, who coordinated the offers, soon had an *embarras de richesse.* Before the crisis was over, Burma, Yugoslavia, Brazil, Iran, Ethiopia, Indonesia, Ecuador, the Philippines, Peru, Afghanistan, and even tiny Laos — in roughly that order — said they "wanted in," too. Chile said, somewhat wistfully, that she knew she wasn't needed, but that if more troops ever were wanted, to let her know, and she would be ready. Twenty-four countries, in all, offered to participate, and others would have done so but were persuaded to hold off.

Immediately after passage of the November 7 resolution, Hammarskjold therefore could and did notify Egypt that the force was ready. Egypt, staggering from her military defeat, might have been expected to welcome the news; but she did not. The firing had stopped, and Cairo's political problem now was to secure the withdrawal of foreign troops without paying a diplomatic price for it. Tens of thousands of Russians were "volunteering," according to Moscow, to go to Egypt to drive out the "aggressors"; in Peking, the Egyptian ambassador to Red China was quoted as having notified President Nasser that no fewer than 280,000 Chinese had also "volunteered." So Egypt had a choice of methods. It is entirely possible that Nasser, Wing Commander Aly Sabry, his highly influential aide, and others in the inner Cairo circle seriously considered using Soviet manpower — or the threat thereof — instead of UNEF, to get the British, French, and Israelis out of Egypt. They may also have been suspicious of the aims and purposes of the UN force, having heard it described by Britain, France, New Zealand, and others as a weapon of political pressure on Egypt. Soviet propaganda worked night and day to heighten that suspicion.

Whatever the reason, Egypt withheld permission for the force to enter her territory and sent Hammarskjold a list of detailed questions about it. Where would it be stationed? How long would it stay? Would it leave when Egypt wished? What troops would it consist of? What would be its duties? Hammarskjold was able to satisfy Egypt on many of these points, as we have seen. He sent Burns hurrying to Cairo to discuss others. But on the composition of the force the Secretary-General was in a very difficult position. He was under great pressure to accept certain countries to which Egypt would object; but if Egypt were not satisfied, consent to entry of the force would not be forthcoming —and Soviet diplomacy was drastically limiting the pressure that could be brought to bear on Cairo. Hammarskjold decided the vital thing was to get a UN force on the scene. He and Bunche made up a tentative list of countries they felt would be non-controversial, accepted these offers, and deferred the rest. (No offers were ever "rejected"; some were simply "not activated." It is a distinction which only a diplomat, and a subtle one at that, would fully appreciate.)

Some countries whose offers were deferred were highly indignant. Bunche had his hands full explaining why they were not immediately accepted with enthusiasm. The force had to be "balanced" geographically and politically; Burns had not had "time to study the type of military organization" he needed. This was not persuasive. Delegates who had telephoned their home governments in frantic excitement begging for troops to save the peace now had to tell their prime ministers and foreign ministers that maybe the men wouldn't be needed after all — and they didn't like it. The New Zealanders were particularly outraged. Why, they wanted to know, should Nasser, the man who seized the Suez Canal company, and had a sad record of trouble-making over a period of years, be allowed to dictate to the United Nations General Assembly? But New Zealand had been voting in the Assembly with Britain and France, it was pointed out, and it was not reasonable to expect New Zealand troops to have a warm welcome in Cairo. Pakistan wanted to serve, too, and Bunche would have been glad to have had them. Among other things, their unit included an excellent military band. But the Pakistani prime minister had attacked Nasser publicly; Pakistan was a member of the Baghdad Pact; and India was not eager to have Pakistani troops in UNEF. So Pakistan was not considered suitable.

As time went by, the problem got worse. Canada had put a battalion of the Queen's Own Rifles aboard the aircraft carrier *Magnificent* in Halifax, all steamed up and ready to set sail. There was a first class row in the newspapers — and later in Parliament — when word leaked out that Egypt was objecting to Canadian infantry. In Brazil, the contingent had gone on dress parade in the streets of Rio, and the government had made considerable political capital out of its gesture of international mindedness. What an anticlimax if the troops were never to go! In the Philippines, the government didn't even wait for its men to be accepted — it simply telephoned Washington to ask the United

States (which by then was supplying an air lift) to come and get them. Fortunately, the misunderstanding was straightened out in time.

Delegate after delegate filed into Bunche's office, some of them repeatedly, day after day, wanting to know when their men were going to Egypt. Czechoslovakia — whose offer, it is safe to assume, was never seriously considered — put pressure on Cairo to demand of the UN that its troops be included. Some Egyptian officials did try to link Czechoslovakia with Brazil, saying they would accept both or neither. After a trip to Cairo by Cordier, and a face-to-face interview with Nasser, Brazil finally was accepted without any conditions.

All this trouble was embarrassing at UN headquarters, especially after the original eagerness for troops. Something had to be done. Moreover, there was the danger that Soviet "volunteers" were more than a bluff — and hence, there was a danger of world atomic war.

So it was highly important to demonstrate that UNEF was really coming into being, and quickly. Hammarskjold, Bunche, and Cordier were discussing the problem before dinner on November 8, the day after they first ran into Egyptian resistance. "We don't know when we'll get consent to go into Egypt," Bunche said in effect (though no one recorded his exact words). "But since we've got a number of offers, some of them with troops standing by, why don't we move them as near to Egypt as possible — perhaps somewhere in southern Italy? That way, we could use an American air lift all the way." It was not possible, under the terms of the resolution, to send American personnel directly into Egypt.

"A good idea," said Hammarskjold. "Call Vitetti [Dr. Leonardo Vitetti, the Italian delegate] and find out if he'll come in to see me after dinner."

Bunche made an appointment for 10 p. m., and the idea was broached. Vitetti promised to look into it immediately. Knowing how slowly the wheels of government normally turn, Hammarskjold and Bunche expected a reply in three to four days. It came the following morning. "You can have Capodichino," Vitetti called to say. "It's ready for occupancy now." Capodichino was the airport of Naples.

It remained only to get the troops moving. Countries whose offers had been accepted — Canada, Colombia and the four Scandinavians: Norway, Denmark, Sweden, and Finland — had been asked to rush military attachés to UN headquarters for consultation with Burns, who was due back at headquarters soon. Some of them flew in from Washington, where they were stationed, on the very day they were requested. They now pitched in, in earnest, to get the men to Capodichino. Brigadier G. C. Leech of Canada, Eduardo Carrizosa of Colombia, Lt. Col. C. G. A. H. Bernhoft of Denmark, Capt. Aimo I. Saukkonen of Finland, Lt. Col. Einar W. R. Sieger of Norway, and Lt. Col. Stig A. Lofgren of Sweden, together with Col. R. F. C. Vance, Col. John Gormley, and C. H. Owsley of the United States, worked virtually around the clock in Bunche's conference room solving the thousand and one problems involved in transporting, feeding, supplying, equipping, and servicing infantrymen away from their home base. Lt. Gen. John B. Coulter, Agent-General of the UN's Korean Reconstruction Agency, happened to be at headquarters and was drafted to sit in. David B. Vaughan, another high-ranking UN official — like Bunche, Cordier, and Coulter, an American — coordinated the logistics and did trouble-shooting. The UN Field Service, which is under Vaughan's regular jurisdiction, was invaluable in untangling knots, providing experience and know-how, and supplying communications for the troops. Other departments of the UN Secretariat — legal, financial, and administrative, men from dozens of countries — played important parts. Secretaries, clerks, messengers, document men, telephone operators, and many others put in hundreds of hours of overtime.

It was an extraordinary operation. At one point, Bernhoft had Copenhagen, Sieger had Oslo, and Vance had Wiesbaden, Germany, on the telephone simultaneously. Wiesbaden was headquarters of the United States Air Forces, Europe, and its Flying Boxcars and Skymasters were to be used to get the Scandinavians to Capodichino. The man on the phone on the other end in Norway did not know what airport would be best for the Skymasters to land and pick up the Norwegian contingent. "Get them going and decide later where they'll land," Vance said. Wiesbaden telephoned Oslo and said the planes were on their way to the Norwegian capital. "If that's wrong, let us know, and we'll radio them new instructions in flight," USAF, Europe, said. Norway got the men to Oslo.

Life was just that hectic the first eight days of UNEF. Night after night, men would knock off at 4 or 5 a. m., go home for a warm bath and a cat-nap, and be back at 9:30 or 10 a. m. to work another 19 or 20-hour day. Hammarskjold, Bunche, and Cordier found an all-night hamburger joint on Lexington Avenue where they went for pre-dawn snacks. The three of them, familiar with the elegant fare of prime ministers and queens, would sit perched on stools munching hamburgers and onions while taxi drivers, night-shift workers, and others who are awake on Manhattan's East Side at four o'clock in the morning looked on in astonishment. The Secretary-General was always willing to push aside the mustard and ketchup and write his totally illegible "Dag Hammarskjold" on the napkins and train schedules which autograph-hunters put on the counter in front of him. The UN has many sharp critics in New York, but at least a few of them may have gotten a new idea in November, 1956 of what is involved in peacemaking.

Back in the glass skyscraper, Vaughan, Bunche, and the military men concentrated on the American air lift. It was a remarkable operation. Air Force and MATS (Military Air Transport Service) Super-Constellations lifted Colombian jungle fighters from Bogota, and Indian paratroops from Agra, converging on Naples from opposite sides of the globe. The plane which lifted the Indians came from Hickam Field in Hawaii. It made the 8,500-mile flight across the Pacific to India in 20 hours, getting through on time because KLM (Royal Dutch Airlines) lent it a new magnetic generator to replace one that burned out in Bangkok, Thailand.

The air lift was an American contribution to UNEF; the United States absorbed its entire cost, estimated at $2,250,000. Canada, Switzerland, and Italy also provided air transport at their own expense in the early days. The United States made available, "subject to reimbursement" — that is, sold — the UN millions of dollars worth of C-rations and other material from Army stores in Leghorn and supply dumps in Metz and Dreux, France, airlifting it to Capodichino. The Italian Army and Air Force serviced planes and lodged and helped feed troops. Scandinavians and Indians were quickly educated to a taste for spaghetti. It took just three days — November 8, 9, and 10 — to get the first advance party into Capodichino; had Egyptian consent been available, they could have been in Egypt almost as quickly.

Another time, if such an operation were necessary, it would be greatly facilitated if problems of transportation and logistics could be worked out in advance, so that they would not have to be improvised. UNEF was in many ways a major miracle, because so many important details had to be handled on the spur of the moment. Bunche and Vaughan found, for example, that soldiers all over the world are reluctant to be separated from their vehicles. They will leave their wives, but never their jeeps. ("They might not get another," one officer cracked.) It was one thing for an air lift to transport personnel and light equipment, and quite another thing to fly jeeps and half-ton trucks. Hence the Flying Boxcars. Then when UNEF finally moved to Egypt, there was the problem of getting the vehicles across the Mediterranean. Swissair, which handled the leg from Italy to Egypt in the early stages, did not have Flying Boxcars available. The UN solved the problem by buying some British jeeps on the spot in Egypt, painting them white, and letting UNEF troops use them until their own vehicles could be brought later.

All troops were asked to carry with them from home a ten-day supply of rations, their personal sidearms, and tents. Thereafter, the UN — depending heavily on purchases from American supply dumps in Europe — took over. Because the deserts of North Africa are cold at night in November, tent stoves were one essential item. One of the detachments planned to take wood-burning stoves. It was pointed out that there would not be much wood in the Sinai desert, so oil stoves were substituted. Political troubles notwithstanding, UNEF was able to get oil.

Uniforms provided a special problem. One of the reasons why Egypt objected to Canadian troops was that their uniform was so similar to that of the British. Other uniforms, too, were patterned either on basic British or American styles. Since the British lacked a certain amount of popularity in Egypt, it was felt wise to provide UN troops with some item of uniform which was distinctive and eye-catching enough to deter snipers. Arm bands and shoulder patches were all right at close range, but what about snipers using telescopic sights? Bunche, Vaughan, and Cordier wrestled with that problem right up to the day before the first troops were to go into Egypt. They first thought of blue berets —

blue because blue and white are the colors in the UN flag. Vaughan ran up a formidable telephone bill calling around the world to find military berets which could be quickly dyed light blue. It was no use. Light blue would not cover American khaki; the Canadians had British Navy blue, which would not do; and no one else came close. Finally they decided to use American-style helmet liners, 1,000 of which could be had at a United States supply depot in Leghorn. They were sprayed the right color, and in less than 24 hours were issued to the troops just before they boarded the plane. There is a story that helmet badges were provided at first by painting the UN's insignia over some "I Like Ike" buttons left over from the 1956 presidential campaign, but UN officials say it is apocryphal.

"I am amazed" said General Burns on November 16, the day after the first troops landed in Egypt, "at the speed with which this plan has developed from the idea stage to its endorsement by the General Assembly and to its implementation in the field." He was not the only one amazed. Many of the men who directed the job at headquarters could scarcely believe it themselves.

Meanwhile, as the physical job of getting men to Capodichino was being licked, Hammarskjold had the at least equally difficult job of persuading Egypt to let them come the rest of the way. No one ever said so out loud, but the very tactic of sending the men to Italy—of having them knocking at the door, as it were—put great pressure on Egypt to accept the force. In many countries, there was a considerable reservoir of sympathy for Egypt, and she stood to lose much of this if she kept UNEF troops cooling their heels in an Italian anteroom, so to speak, or barred them entirely. Negotiations to obtain Egyptian consent went hand in hand with the build-up of the force, and as the force built up, the mounting expectations of world opinion strengthened Hammarskjold's bargaining position. He made no effort to exploit this source of strength; on the contrary, he and his aides, in their contacts with the press, sought to protect Egypt from criticism and to hide the difficulties Cairo was raising. But the pressure nonetheless existed. It was vital to have such pressure, for the stakes involved in the operation were immense. Hammarskjold was racing against time and the dispatch of Soviet "volunteers." UNEF was a means of averting Soviet incursion in the Middle East.

The case of Canada was illustrative of Hammarskjold's difficulties. One of the prime movers of UNEF — indeed, its original sponsor — Canada had offered a battalion of infantry; the offer had been accepted; and preparations had been made to send it immediately. Then on November 10, Hammarskjold phoned Pearson in Ottawa to say the Egyptians were concerned about the possibility that Canadian troops would be mistaken for British. Pearson flew to New York and saw Omar Loutfi, the Egyptian delegate, who confirmed that Egypt would have "certain difficulties" about accepting Canadian troops as part of UNEF.

The Canadians felt this was wholly unacceptable. Not only was it extremely embarrassing for the Government domestically, it would be, they felt, wrong in principle and a bad precedent for a "host" state not merely to decide whether a UN force could enter its territory but what its membership should be. Pearson saw Hammarskjold November 13, emphasizing how important it was, in his opinion, that Hammarskjold remain firm in the light of Egypt's attempt to impose conditions on admission of the force. The Secretary-General said he "hoped Canada would go right ahead" with its plans for a contribution, apparently believing Egyptian consent could be obtained. Canada did; an advance party of 34 men, in fact, had already been flown to Naples. Arrangements had been made with Italy for the Royal Canadian Air Force to bring some 300 more the following week, and for the *Magnificent* to land in Naples on November 28.

On November 12, Hammarskjold announced — prematurely, as it proved — that Egypt had agreed to the entry of the force. Two days later, on November 14, he finally got a cable from Cairo which enabled him to order UNEF into Egypt. Assuming the conditions were as Hammarskjold had outlined, it said, and assuming that the sovereignty of Egypt would be fully respected, Egypt agreed to the arrival of UN forces which had been the "subject of mutual understanding between us" — that is, the noncontroversial elements of the force. Hammarskjold cabled Burns a go-ahead, and then himself climbed into a plane for Cairo to try to iron out the remaining difficulties.

Meanwhile Canada found a valuable friend and advocate in India. On November 15, Krishna Menon told Pearson he personally and his government had intervened in Cairo more than once to try to remove doubts about Canadian participation. Later the same day, Krishna Menon again sought out Pearson in the delegates lounge and reported that the Egyptian Government would agree to have Canada provide air transport and a field ambulance. Hammarskjold reported similarly from Cairo.

To Pearson, this was not acceptable. The Egyptians could not be permitted to determine the size, composition, and nature of the Canadian contingent. Burns, himself a Canadian, arrived in New York November 16. At lunch with Pearson, he said he had told the Egyptians he would resign if they raised serious opposition to Canadian personnel and were sustained in that objection.

That night, things looked blackest. Hammarskjold reported from Cairo that the Egyptians were arguing they *had* accepted Canada by accepting Canadian air transport; this, they were saying, meant addition of Canada to UNEF. Hammarskjold reported this was as much as he felt he could achieve in Cairo at the moment. The following morning, however, things began to brighten. In Cairo, Hammarskjold and Fawzi drew up a statement which mentioned administrative personnel for the first time. "Canada is welcome as a country from which elements of the UNEF may be drawn," it read. "It is felt that the most important contribution that could be given at the present stage from that country would be air support in the transport of troops from Italy *and for the current functioning of the UNEF in Egypt.*" (Italics added.)

"The question of ground troops could best be considered when UNEF can assess its needs at the armistice line. The present situation seems to be one where it is not a lack of troops for the immediate task but of possibilities to bring them over and maintain their lines of communication. That is a cause of worry."

According to Hammarskjold, the Egyptians were not opposed in principle to Canadian ground forces, nor were they attempting to dictate conditions, but they were faced with very real practical problems, notably the problem of explaining to the Egyptian people the replacement of British troops by Canadians. The Canadians very easily could be mistaken for Britons; not only the uniforms, but the language, and even the name of the unit — the "Queen's Own Rifles" — contributed to possibilities of mistaken identity.

Pearson talked it over with Burns. After careful consideration, Burns decided that — national pride aside — it would in fact be more useful to have air transport and administrative personnel, 300 of whom were due to fly to Italy that same weekend, than it would to have 1,000 more infantrymen. Indeed, administrative personnel would be essential. There were plenty of infantry available from other countries, but no engineers, signalmen, maintenance men for vehicles, ordnance specialists, and personnel to distribute food, gas, and oil. Without these men, an army cannot operate. It would be useful to have all this administrative support from the same country, to eliminate language and organizational problems. Canada was the only country, outside the Big Five, which was in a good position to supply it. Burns therefore recommended that the Hammarskjold-Fawzi formula be accepted, with minor revisions, and Pearson agreed. So did Prime Minister Louis St. Laurent.

It was a gesture of considerable statesmanship for Pearson and St. Laurent to swallow their pride and send home the Queen's Own Rifles, replacing them with less glamorous — if more useful — service personnel. It could be, and was, made to look as though Canada had taken dictation from President Nasser. The opposition party in Parliament was never prepared to concede that Burns really had changed his mind and wanted administrative units, not infantry. In point of fact, he had. His decision is on record in writing.

CHAPTER IV

The Next Crisis

Putting a United Nations police force together from scratch in eight days is like visiting the Louvre in 15 minutes. It is better than not doing it at all—but that is about all that can be said for it. No one in his right mind would do it that way if he could help it.

Another time, if the UN is confronted with a crisis like that of November, 1956, the very least that would be useful would be a guide book, a distillation of knowledge and experience. In addition, the world organization would speak with more authority and act with more practical effect if it had at its fingertips a permanent police force, ready to do at least the limited kind of noncombatant duties that were assigned to UNEF.

Had such a force been available for use in Egypt, it is possible that the British-French invasion could have been forestalled altogether. Countries like Britain and France, sensitive to the moral judgment of mankind, require persuasive pretexts when they resort to force to gain their ends. Without such pretexts, they are unlikely to take action which the world—including many of their own people—will condemn. London and Paris scarcely could have announced to the world that they were attacking Egypt, and hence risking World War III, just to overthrow President Nasser and force internationalization of Suez. A government in Paris might conceivably have gotten away with such candor, given Egypt's aid to the Algerian rebels; but in London the cabinet would have been overthrown in 24 hours, and the party might not have regained power for a generation. The pretext that was, in fact, used—that because the UN was not in a position to act, they were going to separate the belligerents, halt the fighting, and protect the Suez Canal—would not have seemed persuasive, even to them, if a UN police force had been standing by, ready to perform those tasks. It is hard to see on what basis, then, the delegates of Britain and France could have vetoed a cease-fire order (as they did on October 30) if attached to it there had been, as part of the same Security Council resolution, a request to the Secretary-General to dispatch, or prepare for dispatch, a United Nations police force. Much as London and Paris might have wished to go ahead with their military action as planned, it would have been well-nigh politically impossible to do so. Sir Pierson Dixon of Great Britain and Bernard Cornut-Gentille of France had a hard enough time as it was defending their countries from a tidal wave of condemnation.

Assuming, however, that vetoes nevertheless were cast, and that the crisis thereupon reached the floor of the General Assembly, there is little question but what the story which then would have unfolded would have been substantially different. The time table of events could have been pushed forward by four to five days; the resolution which was passed the night of November 1-2 (the first call for a cease-fire) could have included all the basic ideas of the three police-force resolutions of November 4, 5, and 7. The force would not have entered Egypt until after a cease-fire, it is true; but Hammarskjold's negotiations with Cairo on the terms and conditions of its entry could have been begun as soon as the enabling resolution was passed. That would have been a time when President Nasser was in desperate danger from three adversaries, when bombs were raining on Port Said, when men influential with Nasser—such as Jawaharlal Nehru—were in greatest fear of World War III, and when the Soviet Union had not yet rallied to give Egypt all-out diplomatic support. It is obvious that, had Hammarskjold and the Assembly chosen to take advantage of these assets, they could have obtained more far-reaching terms from Nasser, and could have gotten them more easily. During this critical period, Nasser did in fact come forward in writing with an offer to settle the Suez Canal issue on better terms than Britain and France ultimately obtained. The foundations for peace-making in the Middle East might have been laid without infringing, or seeming to infringe, in the slightest on Egypt's zealously guarded sovereignty; Egypt's own view of her national interest might have been different. She might have wanted UNEF to occupy the canal zone, for example, to keep the British, French, and Israelis out.

Speculation on the probable course of events under different circumstances is always subject to pitfalls. It is conceivable that, even if a police force had been available, the General Assembly would have chosen not to make use of it until after some of the pressure on Egypt had lifted. The pattern of events might not have been different in any important respect. But to anyone who remembers the atmosphere of those extremely tense days, when every available tool for peace was being eagerly honed, this must seem highly improbable. At any rate, it is obvious that the General Assembly would have had a wider choice of possible courses of action if it had had a police force at its disposal.

On at least one other occasion in the recent past the existence of a UN force could have changed the pages of history. UN diplomats might have thought more seriously about sending a small force to Hungary before Soviet tanks crushed that unhappy land if a force had been readily available and a habit of using it had been established. To be sure, manpower was not the principal problem, by any means. The real reasons for inaction during the three critical days from November 1 through November 3, when Hungarian Premier Imre Nagy was appealing for UN help, were that diplomats were exhausted by all-night sessions and their attention was diverted by the Egyptian crisis; some were deceived by the façade of "negotiations" between the Soviet Union and the Nagy regime on "withdrawal of Soviet troops"; and cooperation between the principal western allies had broken down over Egypt, so that the UN's carburetor momentarily had spluttered and coughed. A police force on hand therefore might not have made any decisive difference. On the other hand, the existence of a tool does encourage its use; and if even as many as 25 or 50 men in UN uniform—a mere handful— had been flown to Budapest before November 4, it would have been much more costly for the Soviet Union to have terrorized Hungary. Not, of course, because of the physical power of the UN troops; for the UN to have made any military difference, even temporarily, at least a division (15,000 men), heavily armed, would have been needed. But a small detachment would have comprised a kind of political plate-glass window which Moscow would have had to shatter with a resounding crash before she could rob and despoil what lay behind.

It is easy to contend that such moral inhibitions would have no effect on a totalitarian power like the Soviet Union—easy, but not so realistic as it may first appear. Had some of the UN troops been Indian or Indonesian or Finnish or Yugoslav or Saudi Arabian, the political consequences to the Soviet Union of shooting them or even capturing and expelling them, would have been very substantial indeed. With one stroke, the Kremlin might have wiped out great pockets of neutralism in the world. Hundreds of millions of rubles' worth of propaganda would have been undone. These results would have been only a few degrees less dramatic in the (more likely) event that the UN troops had been drawn from western countries. All the consequences which in fact accrued to the Kremlin for its crime—defections from the Communist Party by the thousands, loss of influence among fellow-traveling parliamentarians and officials, setbacks everywhere, most notably in Asia—would have been multiplied manyfold if a UN team had been on the spot to be crushed, along with the Freedom Fighters, or to come out an dtell the world a vivid eye-witness story. Moreover, many of these consequences would have been fully apparent, in advance, to Kremlin policy makers. Since, according to an official UN study of the Hungarian tragedy, the Presidium in Moscow "may well" have been divided over whether to intervene, possibilities of this kind, entering into Soviet calculations, could conceivably have tipped the scales in the other direction and saved Hungary from a blood bath. The very existence of a UN police force, and the consequent possibility that it would be sent to the scene, would have been one factor which Moscow would have had to take into consideration. In the future if a similar uprising were to occur, the Soviet Union certainly would have to include a permanent UN police force in her calculations. It is safe to say that another time, there would be a lot less hesitancy at headquarters to answer an appeal like that of Premier Nagy.

Where else might the next crisis break out? Perhaps in Kashmir, the picturesque princely state which India and Pakistan have been contesting bitterly since 1947. The ostensible reason for the deadlock over a plebiscite to decide Kashmir's future is disagreement over the degree and rate of demilitarization to precede such a plebiscite. There is little apparent reason, at first glance, why a UN police force could not replace local armed forces and make possible any degree of demilitarization desired. The UN could then patrol the plebiscite and make certain the voting was free and secret. As early as 1951, Prime Minister

Robert Menzies of Australia proposed privately at a Commonwealth Conference of Prime Ministers that such a UN force, consisting of troops from Australia and New Zealand, be employed. India rejected the idea; Pakistan accepted it, and made it public in an obvious effort to bring pressure to bear on Prime Minister Nehru. Later, during behind-the-scenes negotiations in Paris at the 1951-2 session of the UN General Assembly, Dr. Frank P. Graham, UN Representative for India and Pakistan, brought up the idea informally. On learning India's position, he dropped it as outside his frame of reference, without having made it as a formal proposal. In 1957, following experience with UNEF in Egypt, the Pakistani government put it forward still again, in New York, with the same reaction from India.

The difficulty with this proposal is not that it would fail but, paradoxically, that it might succeed too well. In the present context, it is not a means of facilitating a negotiated and agreed settlement of the Kashmir problem. It is a means of imposing a settlement on India. India opposes a plebiscite for many complex political, psychological, economic, and religious reasons, including, no doubt, an awareness that in all likelihood Pakistan would win a majority if the vote were wholly free. Nehru agreed to the plebiscite at the height of the original crisis, and reaffirmed his agreement — under pressure from world opinion — in negotiations arranged by the UN. He and his aides are said to regret those decisions, and to have no intention of carrying them out if they can possibly help it. In these circumstances, a police force to facilitate a plebiscite obviously has no appeal for India. Its dispatch to the area would simply be a means of exerting political pressure on Nehru. Once it arrived, Pakistan could offer to meet India's terms on demilitarization, and Nehru might be hard put to find a persuasive excuse for further resistance.

There are a number of reasons why the world community hesitates to bring such pressure on India. One is that many states do not wish to set what they would consider an undesirable precedent by by-passing India's consent. Nehru refuses to agree to the stationing of a UN force in any part of Kashmir, all of which he contends is Indian territory. Few would contend that, in the eyes of the law, India has a right to bar a UN force even from the portion of Kashmir her armies now occupy, let alone the Pakistani-occupied zone, since—so far as the UN is concerned

—disposition of the whole territory has still to be decided. But as a practical matter, few UN member states, if any, would contribute troops to a force which might have to try to enter Indian-occupied territory against Indian resistance. Pakistan proposes only that the force be sent to her sector, where it would be welcomed. But it is highly doubtful that a two-thirds majority could be found in the Assembly for a recommendation that even that be done. India can rely on enough friendly votes from among the Afro-Asian and Soviet blocs to make the task very difficult; and the United States, which would have to lobby strongly for any such move if it were to succeed, does not wish to alienate the principal noncommunist power in Asia any further. The only practical result of an effort to pressure Nehru might be to give the Soviet Union an opportunity to befriend him—no doubt at a handsome price, which might inject Soviet influence deeply into India for a long time to come. The possibility that one day India might have to fall back on the Kremlin's veto in the Security Council, or its nine votes in the General Assembly, goes far to explain Nehru's policy of neutralism in the cold war. The United States hesitates to strengthen the motive for that policy. This, of course, leaves Washington in an anomalous position, because it has a military alliance with Pakistan; but diplomacy is full of just such anomalies. From time to time, considerable American pressure is understood to have been brought to bear on Pakistan to keep the Kashmir case quiescent.

By way of footnote, there are those who question whether the stationing of a UN police force in Pakistani-occupied Kashmir would serve even Pakistan's national interest. It might give her the plebiscite she wants so badly, but it probably would not prevent border crossings by Indian "peace brigades" (fanatic agitators and terrorists) determined to cow the electorate. Such agitators, it is said, might be able to frighten enough people to swing the outcome. A UNEF would be hard put to cope with undercover activities of this kind. There are many who believe that Pakistan is pressing for a police force primarily because she is confident India will continue to oppose it, and therefore continue to lose face with world opinion.

The Kashmir case has placed severe obstacles in the way of creating a permanent UN police force. The existence of a permanent force would simplify Pakistan's propaganda problem. It would then be an existing tool, not a potential one, which she would be proposing to use. The pressure on India would thus be correspondingly greater. Not surprisingly, India has consistently opposed, and Pakistan supported, a permanent force. Since India's voice is more influential, in terms of General Assembly votes, India's opposition is a serious matter. Mr. Krishna Menon has even bristled at the suggestion that UNEF's life be prolonged in Egypt, and has specifically criticized the idea that it might be regarded as "a kind of nucleus of a future force."

There are many other places where the next crisis could arise: Korea, Formosa, Indo-China, Algeria, Cyprus, Israel's unpatrolled borders, and the East-West frontier in Europe—notably that portion of it which passes through divided Germany. It is possible to imagine at least a theoretical role for a UN force in all of these areas, though in many cases the problem of consent would be insoluble, and in others, the political-military circumstances are such as to make UN intervention difficult.

In Korea, the UN is one side of the conflict. It is hard to imagine a UN police force patrolling an armistice line to separate UN troops from aggressor troops. To do so would be to imply that both parties were on an equal moral footing. No such force would be admitted onto the North Korean side of the line in any event; it would have to patrol solely on the South Korean side. But forces over which the UN banner is flying are already patrolling that side, and the world organization would not wish to imply that it ceased to regard them as UN representatives. The only visible use for a UN police force in Korea would be as reinforcements for the UN Command. But few countries would contribute soldiers for this purpose; on the contrary, those who did contribute have long since removed most of their men, feeling the emergency is past.

Would a patrol along the armistice line, consisting in part of Asian troops, help to inhibit a renewed attack from North Korea? No doubt it would, although a stronger deterrent surely is the physical power of the UN Command, plus the danger that such renewed aggression would lead to a war larger than Moscow and/or Peking may wish to fight. Conceivably the time might arise when the world community would want to restrain a South Korean government determined to renew the fighting. But if the

United States agreed, it could impose such restraint more effectively behind the lines, by withholding supplies and other means, than a UN plate-glass window could do along the 38th parallel. If the United States were not in favor of the restraint, no UN patrol could be sent, because the United States has enough close friends and allies in the General Assembly to block a two-thirds majority. In the Security Council, of course, the United States' own negative vote would be sufficient.

In Formosa, the political problems are even more difficult. Should the world community ever reach the point of wishing to impose a two-Chinas solution in the Chinese civil war, it might consider interposing a police force—presumably a naval force—between the antagonists. In point of fact, this is what the United States Seventh Fleet has been doing since 1950, except for a brief interlude of largely empty talk about "unleashing" Generalissimo Chiang Kai-shek. Would there be any advantage in turning this task of patrolling the Formosa Straits over to the UN—or in persuading the UN to designate the United States as its agent? From the American point of view, there would be considerable advantage (assuming, in the case of the non-American patrol, that it were done effectively). At the core, the United States' national interest lies in keeping submarine and air bases on the island of Formosa out of hostile hands. Those bases are within range of American lines of communication to the Pacific. With the UN's moral sanction added to the United States' physical power, or some equivalent, they could be insulated for many years to come. There would be protection against the consequences, not only of Red Chinese capture, but of a breakdown in American relations with Nationalist China, the possibility of which seemed to be foreshadowed in the anti-American rioting in Taipeh in the spring of 1957. A Nationalist China which had broken away from the American sphere of influence would not be a severe threat to the United States' chain of Pacific Ocean bases if it were effectively separated from the military resources of the mainland.

It is hard to imagine the UN General Assembly putting its stamp of approval on any such arrangement, and virtually impossible to conceive of the Security Council doing so. Both Chinas would fight it to the death; both consider themselves the rightful owners of all of China, including the island of Formosa. Nationalist China would acquiesce only if the alternative were imminent ejection from the UN and/or imminent capture by the mainland; and in either of those cases, Red China would scarcely wish to be deprived of the triumph she was about to win. Neutralist members of the Afro-Asian bloc, thinking of their own future relations with mainland China rather than the United States' strategic requirements, would not cooperate in imposing such a settlement; and some of the United States' closest allies, including Britain and much of the Commonwealth, would also resist, believing that greater strategic advantage could be won by seeking to split the Moscow-Peking axis than by withholding territory Peking covets, at the cost of solidifying that axis. Thus a two-thirds majority in favor of the plan would be a major diplomatic miracle. Even were it to be obtained, there might be bitter criticism in the United States from those friends of Nationalist China who would not wish to be deprived of the hope that one day Chiang might return in triumph to the mainland. A UN police force to separate the two Chinas does not seem a practical possibility.

An easier and no doubt more productive use for such a force would be to send it to Southeast Asia wherever a country on the borders of Red China felt in danger of attack. At the moment, Peking is not openly pressing its expansion to the south, and it may be that a UN majority would not wish to borrow trouble. But there would be no harm in having a police force in readiness to go to Viet Nam, or Laos, or Burma, or Nepal, or even — for that matter — India, should the time come when Peking and New Delhi ended their honeymoon. At one point in 1950, Tibet sent out an appeal to the UN for help which could have been met in part by dispatch of a police force. There are a baker's dozen of troubled borders in this general area; that between Pakistan and Afghanistan is another, and the one between Afghanistan and the Soviet Union could become troubled. Burma might be glad to enlist the help of a UN police force if Nationalist Chinese soldiers were again to become a problem in her remote northern territories, or if border disputes with Red China were to become acute.

One difficulty with UN action against Communist expansionism, however, is that the communists are more likely to use infiltration and subversion than they are overt armed attack.

UN police forces would have difficulty coping with this kind of challenge, since the world organization, of which they would be agents, has no jurisdiction over individuals. It may not arrest them, or try them in court, or put them in jail. The UN is not a government, and is not empowered to act like one. For it to become an adjunct to national police, helping keep domestic order, would be a very drastic departure, though perhaps, by special arrangement with the government involved, it might be possible. Duties not too dissimilar were proposed at one point for UNEF in Gaza.

Similarly, it would be a distinct novelty for UN troops to play any role with respect to another major source of world tension and turmoil, the struggle for self-determination waged by peoples under colonial rule. A UN force for Algeria might be desirable in order to keep order during elections to select the "true representatives of the Algerian people" with whom the French say they wish to deal. But in practice, the French scarcely would accept UN intervention into what they consider a domestic problem unless the nationalist rebellion got completely out of hand and Paris was desperate for a face-saving way out. In such circumstances, it is doubtful that the nationalists would want the UN to step in and limit their victory. Cooperation from both the French and the rebels would be necessary for the UN to succeed in pacifying the territory; without it, the UN would either be fighting a major war against France or else it would be trying to suppress a revolt which some 450,000 French troops had not been able to control. A long, bloody, and exhausting stalemate might perhaps bring both France and the rebels to the point of agreeing to a UN-policed cease-fire. France took one step in that direction when she offered to let "international" (though not UN) observers witness a national election.

Similarly in Cyprus, a UN policing operation almost certainly would be a last, desperate resort when all else had failed. If, however, the time came when Britain was prepared to pull out and a direct clash between Greece and Turkey seemed imminent, it is possible that UN troops could keep the island from becoming an international battleground. Turkey has intimated she would resort to force if necessary to prevent Cyprus from going to Greece. At such a time, some UN personnel along the Greco-Turkish border also might not be an unwise precaution.

In all this effort to project the "next crisis," and weigh the likelihood of a UN role in it, there is the danger that a diplomatic analyst — like the traditional military planner — will be mentally "fighting the last war instead of the next one." The time may not be far distant when land invasions over frontiers will be entirely outmoded. Future aggression may consist of the use of, or threat to use, missiles armed with mass-destruction warheads: nuclear explosives, chemical weapons, bacteriological devices, perhaps others not yet dreamed of. Nor may the great powers be the only ones to possess such lethal weapons. The problem of preventing small wars is certain to get more and more formidable as the word "small" progressively loses its meaning. One contribution a UN police force could make to world peace — perhaps its most important contribution — would be to stand watch over missile-launching platforms and other major weapons-delivery systems, such as strategic air commands, with enough communications equipment to alert a potential victim, if necessary, and thus set in motion retaliatory action. Were retaliation to be guaranteed, few aggressors would wish to strike the first blow. This, indeed, is the reasoning behind much disarmament negotiation under UN auspices. If and when a treaty is signed providing for inspection to guard against surprise attack, a UN police force could be used to assist in the task. Some of the inspectors, of course, would have to be highly skilled technicians, presumably civilians; but others could be foot soldiers — or if not infantry, then engineers, signal men, chauffeurs, and other service personnel.

One limitation on the usefulness of a UN police force is that at the present stage of world development, there is little inclination to use coercion as an instrument of peacemaking. The world community often has a perfectly legitimate and tangible interest in the removal of a serious source of friction, but few have suggested that this interest entitles the world community to insist upon what it considers a fair settlement, irrespective of the wishes of one or more parties to the dispute. The world may have to come to this, if it wants to rule out the use of force by nation-states at their own discretion. A state denied justice indefinitely is under tremendous temptation to take the law into its own hands. If the world community is to expect compliance with Article 2, Paragraph 4 of the Charter — "All members shall refrain in their international relations from the threat or use of force . . ." — then it clearly must make provision for "adjustment or settlement of international disputes or situations which might lead to a breach of the peace," as Article 1, Paragraph 1 obliges it to do.

One problem which long has cried for an imposed settlement is Palestine. The first effort at such a settlement, the 1947 partition plan, failed to stick. There were many reasons for this failure including, perhaps, the fact that no police force was available to see the plan through. (Colombia, New Zealand, and Guatemala proposed police forces, but nothing came of the suggestions.) Since then, most responsible diplomats have shied away from trying anew, perhaps not so much from lack of desire as from lack of confidence in the probable results. Cold-war politics has multiplied the difficulties. The West has not dared to bring adequate pressure on the Arab states, lest it drive them into total dependence on a Soviet Union awaiting them with open arms. And American domestic politics has inhibited pressure on Israel alone. Yet no solution produced without some pressure on both Arabs and Jews could hope to be equitable. If it were not equitable, it would not be lasting. As in Kashmir, as in Egypt in 1956, and as in so many other cases, cynical Soviet opportunism has tied the hands of the peacemakers — whether they seek to act through the UN or outside it. A UN police force might help cut through this dilemma, but clearly could not resolve it alone.

The approach the Secretary-General and other UN diplomats have adopted for Palestine is to try to achieve a period of tranquillity long enough in duration to permit old animosities to cool, bringing reason, rather than emotion, to bear on a negotiated settlement. An expanded UNEF, stationed all around Israel's borders, and given adequate authority, presumably could provide that tranquility. Some Arab diplomats say they have agreed to this measure on condition that UN troops be stationed on both sides of the armistice line; but Israel has refused to admit them onto her territory. One reason Israel refuses is that a UN police force would be more effective in deterring the large-scale, organized retaliation raids on which she depends than in preventing border crossings by small Arab fedayeen (commando) squads, usually consisting of five men. Thus Israel, in her view, could be pin-pricked to death while her hands were tied behind her. UN people reply that a no-man's land with barbed wire, land mines, and other obstructions could be made virtually impenetrable. Could it? In Germany, despite barriers of this kind, thousands of refugees were able to flee from the Soviet zone into the West every month. If Arab fedayeen had the same driving determination to get into Israel at any cost, they probably could manage it.

A second Israeli motive for resisting a UNEF along all her borders is fear that the UN some day will attempt an imposed peace settlement. Once a police force were ensconced around Israel, some Israelis say, the General Assembly might delineate new boundaries for a smaller state of Israel and order the force to close in to those boundaries, taking up stations on them. Those boundaries might be the original lines on which partition was made, for example, or some minor modification of them. If such a move were part of an equitable over-all settlement of problems such as refugees, water utilization, freedom for Israel's commerce, etc., there are many who would feel it was in Israel's long-range interest to have that done; but Israel is highly sensitive on the question of territory, and resists any suggestion that land be traded to the Arabs for concessions on other points. Desire to preserve every square foot of territory is another reason given by Israelis for refusal to admit a UN police force onto her side of the line.

Secretary-General Dag Hammarskjold has argued persuasively for a border patrol on both sides of the Egyptian armistice line. He was closeted with Prime Minister David Ben Gurion for long periods during a visit to Israel in the spring of 1957, but got nowhere because Ben Gurion said he did not wish to discuss the subject at that time. Judging from positions publicly taken, Israel would agree only if Egypt would abandon the theory and practice of belligerency — that is, would accept a *de facto* peace treaty with Israel on the basis of the *status quo*. This no Arab state, let alone Egypt, has been willing to do.

Thus the UN is faced with a problem so deep-seated that it is hard to see how it can be solved so long as the consent of the parties is regarded as an essential precondition to peacemaking at every stage. In order to by-pass consent, or extract it from unwilling governments, the Soviet Union would have to acquiesce; and her terms for so doing — reading between the lines of her diplomatic notes — amount to total withdrawal of western military influence from the area. That would simply be the prelude to a Sovietized Middle East. So the vicious circle is complete. All that can be done is to try to make UNEF so successful on the Gaza border that, in time, Israel will come to regard it as a contribution to her national security and hence an asset, rather than a liability. If and when that day comes, it may be possible to insulate Israel's other borders also.

In many ways the most dangerous of all the potential crisis areas is Germany. There the interests of the great powers come directly into contact, with the single most important prize in the cold war at stake. In official circles, there was a severe war scare over Germany in the winter of 1956-7, when it appeared that the East Germans might be rising up in revolt on the Hungarian pattern. In such an event, if the West Germans were to go to their assistance, and the Soviet Union were to intervene in full strength, how long would it be before NATO was drawn in? diplomats asked. The emergency passed, but no one really breathed easily. What if it arose again? Would a UN police force have a useful role? Not, it is clear, in sealing off the border between the two zones. It would be unthinkable to have the UN protecting Moscow's flank while it suppressed a freedom movement. It also would be ineffective; the Germans would pour through any such barrier. And it would be bad symbolically, in that it would stand for the division of Germany. But a UN force might have the same role in East Germany that it could have elsewhere in Eastern Europe: it could be inserted as a plate-glass window which it would be costly for the Kremlin to break. Such action might help to prevent the outbreak of trouble.

This *tour d'horizon* does not indicate that a UN police force would be a panacea. It could not automatically solve all the problems of the mid-twentieth century; they are far too complex for that. There are many to which it could not even contribute. But it would be one more useful tool in the hands of the peacemakers. In some areas, under some circumstances, it might represent the difference between success and failure.

CHAPTER V

The Long Road

The idea of an international police force is so logical, on the face of it, that it is a major mystery why — in all of human history — there have been so few serious attempts to establish such a force. Thinkers have pointed out the rationale since the time of ancient Greece. Just as a community organized in the form of a city or a state requires police to curb lawbreakers and protect the law-abiding, so the world community should have force at its disposal to use under law. The fundamental difficulty is that on a comparatively small scale, men often recognize a community of interest and are willing to trust a central authority to promote it; whereas on a world scale, rivalries, animosities, language and color barriers, and other differences obscure the community of interest, and prevent the creation of a central authority. Without such an authority, the use of force for common purposes is extremely difficult to organize. In a sense, the world in the mid-twentieth century has barely reached the stage of development of the American Wild West, when frontiersmen took the law into their own hands, or organized into posses to round up horse thieves and cattle rustlers.

The city-states of ancient Greece established what were perhaps the world's first prototypes of an international police force. Each state in the first Delian League, for example, (478-404 B.C.) contributed ships or money to a force designed to protect the League from Persia and stamp out piracy in the Aegean Sea. As soon as the danger from Persia passed, many of the "allies" in the confederacy — tiring of personal sacrifices — persuaded the governing synod to accept money, rather than ships, as contributions. Athens, providing most of the fleet, came to dominate the League, and soon it was an Athenian empire. The fleet, which had started out as an instrument of mutual defense, became a tool with which Athens imposed its will on the other member states.

The Achaean League, for its part, had a small standing army which served as a nucleus to which, in wartime, contingents from member states were added. Mercenaries also were hired on occasion. The Amphictyonic League elicited from members a pledge to take up arms and "utterly destroy" anyone who did violence to a member city; and the pledge was carried out.

Looking back through history one can find at least one example and a number of plans for what we today would call regional or world government. The Roman Empire was a government imposed on a large part of the then known world by troops recruited from many nations. This was scarcely a precedent for an international police force, though, like the Delian League, it may hint at one of the dangers implicit in the concentration of police power. In the late 16th and early 17th centuries, Henry IV of France (apparently in collaboration with Queen Elizabeth I of England) worked out a "Grand Design" for bringing peace to a Europe torn by religious wars. It was the most ambitious of several which had been put forward for the same purpose. There was to be a European Senate, with a combined army and navy — 270,000 foot soldiers, 50,000 horsemen, 200 cannons, and 120 ships — to enforce its decisions. William Penn, the Abbé de Saint-Pierre, and Rousseau also drafted plans for all-European governments, with police power. None, of course, was ever implemented.

In the 20th century, the first attempt at an international army was the allied force which entered China at the end of the Boxer Rebellion in 1900. It consisted of 18,600 men from five countries. But this was, strictly speaking, more of an *ad hoc* alliance than a true international police force. It did not even have a central command. A world police force must be drawn from, and be responsive to, an international organization which is universal, or nearly universal, in scope and purpose. President Theodore Roosevelt used the phrase "international police power" in 1904, but what he had in mind, at least for that stage, was "some combination between those great nations which sincerely desire peace and have no thought themselves of committing aggressions." Andrew Carnegie urged a similar course. These ideas were forerunners of the North Atlantic Treaty Organization more than they were of UNEF.

It was not until the years immediately preceding World War I that the idea of a genuinely international force came to the fore in the United States. It obtained expression in a joint resolution of Congress in 1910 which proposed that "a commission of five members be appointed by the President of the United States to consider the expediency of utilizing existing international agencies for the purpose of limiting the armaments of the nations of the world by international agreement, and of constituting the combined navies of the world an international force for the preservation of universal peace, and to consider and report upon any other means to diminish the expenditures of government for military purposes and to lessen the probabilities of war." The commission had not come into being when World War I broke out.

A number of ideas for banishing war sprang to birth during the fighting, as they always do at a time when the tragedy and futility of war are being seared into the public consciousness. The Covenant of the League of Nations, however, relied primarily upon economic sanctions to suppress aggression. If any member went to war in disregard of its pledges, the Council did have the power, indeed, the "duty", under Article 16, Paragraph 2, to "recommend to the several Governments concerned what effective military, naval or air force the Members of the League shall severally contribute to the armed forces to be used to protect the covenants of the League." But if the Covenant were interpreted strictly, an aggressor state, so long as it was a member of the League, could veto such a recommendation; only if the other members wished to take the drastic step of expulsion, or could find some other way around the veto, could they invoke this power.

The French pressed hard and repeatedly, both during the framing of the Covenant and thereafter, for establishment of stronger collective security machinery. While many other countries were seeking disarmament first, France — thinking primarily of the danger from Germany — demanded security first. Efforts were made to provide both. In 1922, the third Assembly of the League recognized that governments could not be expected to make "a serious reduction of armaments unless they received in exchange a satisfactory guarantee of the safety of their country." To provide such a guarantee, the Assembly suggested "a defensive agreement . . . binding them to provide immediate and effective assistance in accordance with a pre-arranged plan in the event of one of them being attacked, provided that the obligation to render assistance to a country attacked shall be limited in principle to those countries situated in the same part of the globe." In Europe, the principal effect of such an agreement would have been to pledge Britain to come to France's aid in the event of a new German attack. Out of the idea grew the 1923 Draft Treaty of Mutual Assistance, under which the signatories would have provided each other military aid in case the Council found that aggression had taken place, the Council deciding which countries should provide what aid. (In practice, since each contributing state could have vetoed the decision, the principle of consent was not to be by-passed.) A new Labour Government which came to power in Britain in 1924 declined to ratify the Draft Treaty, in part, no doubt, because — the United States not being a member of the League — there was little tangible military advantage involved for the Commonwealth and much obligation for it to undertake. Without Britain, the United States, Germany, or Russia as participants (the latter two also being non-members of the League at that time) the Draft Treaty would have been of little use, and it was abandoned.

A further effort was made in 1925 when the Assembly recommended a Protocol for the Pacific Settlement of Disputes (the Geneva Protocol). The principal innovation it introduced was a system of compulsory arbitration. A state refusing to arbitrate a dispute or refusing to accept the verdict of an arbitral process would be adjudged an aggressor, and each member of the League would be obliged to apply economic and military sanctions against her. So far as military sanctions — armed forces — were concerned, the contributing state would decide to what extent its "geographical position and its particular situation as regards armaments" would "allow" it to comply. This Protocol, too, failed of adoption, in large part because Britain and the United States were going through a period of isolationism; and efforts to build security thereafter were directed toward regional arrangements. The world was still not ready for genuine collective security.

During this period, there were several occasions in which an international police force was proposed, or used, for the entirely different purpose of preserving a peace which already existed, however precariously, or of assisting in measures for the peaceful settlement of a dispute. In the Polish-Lithuanian clash over Vilna in 1920-21, the League Council went so far as to prepare a police force of 1,500 to 1,800 men, consisting of one company each from Belgium, Denmark, Greece, Italy, the Netherlands, Norway, and Sweden, and two each from Britain, Spain, and France. The force was to keep order during a plebiscite to determine disposition of the province. It was to replace Polish troops which had seized the area in violation of a truce and in defiance of a Military Commission (consisting of one officer each from France, Britain, Italy, Japan, and Spain) sent to the area by the League to supervise a cease-fire line. Both Poland and Lithuania, in theory, accepted the plan for a police force and a plebiscite, but in fact, first Poland and then Lithuania put insuperable obstacles in the way. Protests by the Soviet Union finally torpedoed the scheme; the contributing states did not wish to send troops to an area when a neighboring great power objected. Further mediation failed, and Poland was left in *de facto* possession of the territory.

The war between Bolivia and Paraguay over the Gran Chaco, which began in earnest in 1932 and continued for six years, is a classic example of what happens when international peacemakers are unable to speak with authority. In this case, both belligerents suffered from the miseries of war and often wanted to make peace; fair and adequate settlements were proposed; but no face-saving way of accepting them was found. A small police force to occupy key forts and outposts in the huge, virtually uninhabited and largely unexplored Chaco plain, would undoubtedly have been enough to halt the bloodshed. At one point, Paraguay agreed to arbitration on condition that the fighting end and that steps be taken to prevent its starting anew. But no one proposed a police force to do that job. In part, this may have been because of divided responsibility between the Conference of American States and the League of Nations. The United States, which opposed action by the League, was able to keep primary responsibility in the hands of the Conference of American States for ten fruitless months. Thereafter, the League was no more effective. A peace of exhaustion finally was signed in 1938.

An "international" police force was employed to help solve

the Leticia dispute between Peru and Colombia which also began in 1932. The force was not in fact international; it consisted solely of Colombian troops, but it was under the control of a League Commission, and the pretense that it was "international" was the face-saving device that enabled Peru to accept it.

Peruvians, acting without the knowledge or approval of the government in Lima, seized the Colombian settlement of Leticia in a primitive jungle area of the upper Amazon. The government disavowed the action, but refused to permit Colombia to take the settlement back by force of arms, and the local Peruvian detachment would not withdraw. Problems of "face" arose; war fever developed in both countries. Peruvian airplanes bombed Colombian ships proceeding up the Amazon to the area. Just before full-scale war broke out, the Peruvian President was assassinated, and his successor accepted a plan of settlement which had been proposed by the League Council some time before. A League Commission administered Leticia for one year, assisted by an "international" police force consisting of Colombian soldiers wearing special arm bands. At the end of the year's time, the Commission pulled out as planned, and left Colombia in possession of the ground.

Perhaps the only occasion in which a truly international police force was employed by the League of Nations was in connection with the 1935 plebiscite by which the Saar basin was returned to Germany. Local police being inadequate to keep order before and during the voting, the League Council decided to constitute and send to the area an international force. Both the French and German Governments agreed to the plan. A total of 3,300 men was used, consisting of 1,500 from Britain, 1,300 from Italy, 250 from the Netherlands, and 250 from Sweden. The force was made up of infantry, auxiliary personnel, motor transport, and some armored cars. Its commander-in-chief, appointed by Britain at the request of the Council, operated under the chairman of the League's Governing Commission for the Saar. The voting took place in good order, and the result — overwhelmingly in favor of Germany — was implemented some six weeks later.

A considerable body of experience, therefore, was available to the framers of the United Nations Charter when they sat down to decide what force, if any, should be available to the new peace organization which was to emerge from World War II. Little, if any, attention seems to have been given to the formation of a modest police force to perform tasks short of combating aggression. Efforts were focused on a much more ambitious project: namely, giving the UN (or the UNO, as it was then known) the kind of power and authority France had sought so persistently and so fruitlessly for the League of Nations, and without which the League had been unable to meet any of the major challenges it had faced — Manchuria in 1931, Ethiopia in 1935-6, Spain in 1936-7, and Finland (the Russo-Finnish war) in 1939. Out of these efforts grew Chapter VII of the Charter, unquestionably mankind's most far-reaching blueprint for world collective security. Had Chapter VII become a reality, the UN would have had the "teeth" with which to enforce peace in all cases except those involving great powers.

Article 39 of the Charter, with which Chapter VII began, invested in the 11-nation UN Security Council the duty to "determine the existence of any threat to the peace, breach of the peace, or act of aggression," and in such a case, to take action to "maintain or restore international peace and security." It could take "provisional measures" of an unspecified character (Article 40); it could order economic and political sanctions (Article 41); and if these were insufficient, it could "take such action by air, sea, or land forces as may be necessary" (Article 42). In order that the latter provision — for military sanctions — should be meaningful, a key article, Article 43, required all member states to earmark elements of their armed forces and other "assistance and facilities" for use when the Council called for them. Article 43 provided, on paper, a world police force, consisting of quotas contributed by states (a "quota force"). It read as follows:

> 1. All members of the United Nations, in order to contribute to the maintenance of international peace and security, undertake to make available to the Security Council, on its call and in accordance with a special agreement or agreements, armed forces, assistance, and facilities, including rights of passage, necessary for the purpose of maintaining international peace and security.
> 2. Such agreement or agreements shall govern the numbers and types of forces, their degree of readiness and general location, and the nature of the facilities and assistance to be provided.

3. The agreement or agreements shall be negotiated as soon as possible on the initiative of the Security Council. They shall be concluded between the Security Council and Members or between the Security Council and groups of Members and shall be subject to ratification by the signatory states in accordance with their respective constitutional processes.

If the forces of a member state not represented on the Council were to be used in a crisis, it was given the right (under Article 44) to join the Council discussion in advance, but there was no provision, as in the League of Nations, for a veto by such a state. Special provision was made in Article 45 for air force contributions; and a Military Staff Committee was established, consisting of the chiefs of Staff of the Big Five, or their deputies, to "advise and assist" the Security Council and provide over-all "strategic direction" for the force (Article 47).

The Military Staff Committee met for the first time on February 4, 1946 and soon thereafter plunged into the task of planning the force. It was to be a long, difficult, and frustrating undertaking, ending in August, 1948 in total failure. The assumption on which Chapter VII had been based — namely, postwar cooperation among the Big Five — proved false; plans for a police force became swept up in the then-incipient cold war; and since the work was all done under the shadow of the great-power veto, great-power differences were fatal.

The principal point at issue was the size and nature of contributions to the force. The great powers, it was agreed, would contribute by far the most significant portion; but how should they divide the responsibility among themselves? The Soviet Union proclaimed a "principle of equality". No single great power, Moscow said, should contribute any more of anything — men, ships, rifles, planes, bullets — than any other great power. Otherwise there would be "advantages in the positions of certain states"; the police force might be used "in the interest of individual powerful states and to the detriment of the legitimate interests of other countries." The United States, Britain, France, and China felt, on the contrary, that each great power should contribute what it was best able to afford, and that the contributions (in the words of the United States delegate) could be "properly balanced and rendered roughly comparable without prejudice to the interests of individual nations."

In retrospect, it seems strange that this issue was allowed to become a major stumbling block. It was true, as the non-communist powers pointed out, that the "principle of equality" would have drastically restricted the size of the force, since none of the five could have contributed, for example, more planes than China, or more manpower than France. But in the light of present-day objectives — when a permanent force of even 6,000 men seems worthwhile — rejection as inadequate of a force that would have numbered over 100,000 men seems anomalous. Western negotiators, of course, were thinking in terms of a powerful fighting force, capable of meeting fairly large-scale aggression; they were not mapping out a UNEF to patrol and insulate an armistice line. Insisting on the former, they failed to get even the latter. The Russians, supporting a small fighting force, said what they had in mind was something in the nature of 12 ground divisions (presumably around 125,000 men), 600 bombers, 300 fighter planes, 5-6 cruisers, 24 destroyers, and 12 submarines. The United States wanted 20 ground divisions (some 300,000 men), 1,250 bombers, 2,250 fighter planes, 3 battleships, 6 carriers, 15 cruisers, 84 destroyers, and 90 submarines. It was a case where, as the French say, *le mieux est l'ennemi du bien.*

Had the free world accepted the Russian "principle of equality," it is entirely possible, of course, that the Kremlin simply would have used some other issue as a pretext for blocking agreement. Stalin's interest lay in turmoil and instability, not peace and order; communist parties, backed by the Red Army, were extending the Kremlin's sphere of power and influence in nearly every direction, especially in Europe. In fact there were important points of difference within the Military Staff Committee other than the size and nature of great-power contributions which could have served for such a purpose. One had to do with bases for the force. The Soviet Union refused to permit national contingents to be stationed outside their home territory when not in action. The West argued, on the other hand, that the contingents should be held in readiness wherever they were most needed. Perhaps the Kremlin foresaw something in the nature of NATO emerging under the UN's aegis. This, too, may be the reason why the Russians refused to agree that, under any conditions, a great power could provide supplies for another country's forces, professing to foresee opportunities for "political benefits and advantages" to the states doing the supplying. "The tendency of some powerful nations to supply and equip the armed forces of other states," said the Soviet delegate, "may be evaluated as seeking an opportunity to influence the policies of these states and thus to occupy a dominant position with regard to the armed forces to be placed at the disposal of the Security Council." Perhaps the men in the Kremlin had been reading the history of the Delian League, and did not want another Athens to come to dominate it by contributing most of the ships. It is also possible — and more likely — that the Kremlin did not want the UN to have any police force at all. If the Russians' objective was "indefinite expansion of their power and doctrines," as Sir Winston Churchill said in his celebrated "cold-war" speech at Fulton, Missouri in 1946 — and few would question this premise — then they had good reason to want the UN kept impotent.

History, of course, records that the free world went outside the UN and set up regional collective security organizations — ANZUS, NATO, the Rio Pact, SEATO, the Baghdad Pact — for protection against communist expansionism. Once again, as between the two world wars, efforts at worldwide collective security had broken down.

Had the UN been successful in setting up forces under Article 43, their use nevertheless would have been hampered by the veto. The world would not have had wholly effective police forces. The Security Council, their parent organ, could not have ordered them into action, or indeed, taken any other significant decision, unless all the great powers were willing. In order to have built a system of universal collective security in the midst of a cold war, some method would have had to be found to get around the veto. That is, it would have been necessary either to amend the Charter (itself an action subject to the veto) or to transfer the functions of the Security Council to the General Assembly, which makes its key decisions by two-thirds majority vote.

A method of circumventing the veto was in fact devised in 1950, in the wake of the Korean war. Logically, perhaps, this should have removed the final obstacle to a UN with teeth; but it did not, and the story of why it did not is one of the most interesting chapters in UN history.

The necessity for a world police force arose suddenly at 4:00 a.m. one Sunday in June, 1950, when North Korean armies drove a spearhead across the 38th parallel in what had been known, in legend, as "The Land of the Morning Calm." No police force existed; the UN had to improvise one. Largely because of a happy accident — the accident that the Soviet Union was boycotting the Security Council — improvisation proved possible. Many delegates fully expected Russia's stolid Yakov Malik to take his seat on that fateful Sunday in June and block action on Korea; but he did not. The Council therefore was able immediately to fix the blame, call for a cease-fire and a retreat to the 38th parallel, and recommend that all UN members "render every assistance to the United Nations in the execution of this resolution and . . . refrain from giving assistance to the North Korean authorities." Two days later, Malik still sitting it out, the Council observed that "urgent military measures are required" and recommended that member states "furnish such assistance to the Republic of Korea as may be necessary to repel the armed attack and to restore international peace and security in the area." It was necessary to *"recommend"*; there were no Article 43 forces to *order* into action. The United States and 15 other countries accepted the "recommendation" and carried it out; indeed, the United States acted on the basis of the first resolution, sending air and sea forces into battle some ten hours before passage of the second.

For many reasons, the UN's action in Korea fell short of a model international police action. An insufficient number of countries participated; the United States carried too large a share of the burden. (At least five countries in addition to the basic 16 offered troops, but for varying reasons were rebuffed by the United States, which acted as the UN's "Unified Command.") The "Command" was not truly "unified," except in a very limited sense; it consisted solely of Americans, with liaison officers from other countries. No one ever seriously suggested, of course, that the Military Staff Committee set up under Chapter VII should be assigned the strategic direction; it contained a distinct security risk in the form of Maj. Gen. Ivan A. Skliarov of the Soviet Union. But there could have been a joint command, including officers from some of the 16 contributing countries other than the United States. Efforts were made to persuade Washington to accept one, but without success. In the realm of political, as distinct from strategic direction, there was consultation in

Washington among the 16 UN allies, but it was begun somewhat belatedly and was not a true substitute for overall directives by an organ of the General Assembly. The arrangement was accepted because the United States in fact was bearing such a large share of the load. On the whole, these shortcomings were less important than the positive evidences of UN involvement: the overwhelming moral support, the 36,000 non-American fighting men, the non-military contributions by 21 additional states. The mental image of Korea as a UN "police action," rather than an American-led war of alliance, survived reasonably well; that is to say, the UN's moral "umbrella" remained largely intact. At least, it did until many Americans, frustrated by the absence of total victory and mistakenly blaming the UN restraints for it, began to rip the umbrella to shreds themselves. The new Administration which took power in Washington in 1953 also sacrificed some of the umbrella in eagerness for an armistice, agreeing to hold peace negotiations outside the UN (thus barring India) even though that meant accepting what had been, until then, a communist contention, namely, that the 16 nations — not the UN as a whole — constituted the non-communist side in the struggle.

Another time, there would be no assurance that the UN would be able to act at all. On August 1, 1950, Malik returned to his Security Council seat and gave no indication of ever abandoning it again. He obviously would be able to veto the next recommendation that forces be employed. The United States therefore came before the 1950 session of the UN General Assembly with a plan which, in effect, transferred from the Security Council to the Assembly the task of building and using a police force. There being no veto in the Assembly, if the world community really wanted a system of universal collective security, it could now provide one. A broad interpretation of the Charter was necessary to assign this kind of responsibility to the General Assembly; but constitutions are — or should be — living documents, capable of growth and adaptation. The Constitution of the United States has grown extraordinarily over the years through Supreme Court interpretation.

What the United States proposed was that all UN member states earmark troops for use, with the consent of the contributing state, when either the Security Council or (if the Council were hamstrung by a veto) the General Assembly so requested. The exact wording of the key paragraph was this:

> [The General Assembly] recommends to the States Members of the United Nations that each Member maintain within its national armed forces elements so trained, organized, and equipped that they could promptly be made available, in accordance with its constitutional processes, for service as a United Nations unit or units, upon recommendation by the Security Council or General Assembly, without prejudice to the use of such elements in exercise of the right of individual or collective self-defense recognized in Article 51 of the Charter.

The similarity between this idea and Article 43 of the Charter was obvious. There were, however, important differences. Instead of negotiating with the Security Council treaties which would pledge portions of their armed forces to the Council for use at the Council's discretion, nations would hold portions in readiness for use at their own discretion when the Council or Assembly asked for assistance. Cooperation was to be voluntary at all stages, except that there would be a certain amount of moral pressure on governments to heed an appeal in an emergency. But a country could always refuse. At first glance, this might seem to have vitiated the Charter plan, robbing it of its automatic character. As a practical matter, it did not. No plan would be automatic in fact. However binding a treaty might be in theory, a government could always disregard it, or invent a loophole, or simply tear it up. No government could be made to send its citizens to war against its will, or against what it considered to be its national interest. The United States would not be likely to send GIs to rescue Kashmir from an attack by Pakistan, for example, or Cyprus from an attack by Turkey, or — to take a much more far-fetched example — Red China from an attack, ten years hence, by the Soviet Union. A "binding" commitment would not in fact be binding in all circumstances. No doubt governments, in this 20th Century, should not "send to know for whom the bell tolls," but they do. Moreover, even if the United States had wished to propose a theoretically binding arrangement under the General Assembly, it could not have done so without offering something in the nature of the 1923 Draft Treaty of Mutual Assistance. Power to issue orders — as distinct from recommendations — is clearly not available to the Assembly under the Charter.

As it proved, governments were unwilling to set aside troops even with all the safeguards and qualifications which were built into the American proposal. The United States itself got cold feet when the time came to act. The resolution — known at the time as the Acheson Plan, and since then, by its official name: the "Uniting for Peace Resolution" — was passed 39 to 5, with only the Soviet bloc voting "no" and 11 countries abstaining. A Collective Measures Committee set up to carry it out invited all 60 member countries to tell the committee "as a matter of urgency" what they planned to do. Seventeen did not bother to respond at all. Two sent polite acknowledgments of the query, without answering it. Twenty-one ranged in tone from negative to wholly noncommittal. That left only 20 replies which could be considered friendly, even in tone. Some of these — Canada's, for example — appeared at first glance to be commitments, but on closer study were carefully hedged. Only four — those of Denmark, Norway, Greece, and Thailand — actually set aside any forces then in existence without a great many strings attached. (Uruguay offered two destroyer escorts.) The four offers of infantry added up to a total of about two regiments, that is, six battalions or about 6,000 men — half of them from Thailand, and roughly 1000 each from the other three countries. That would have been an excellent start toward a non-fighting force of the UNEF type, but it did not take the UN very far along the road to universal collective security.

The United States' reply was a model of skillful obfuscation. It appeared to be responsive, but in fact was not. It said that "in appropriate circumstances, pursuant to the [North Atlantic] Treaty and the Charter," and "in accordance with due constitutional processes," American forces "maintained in furtherance of the Treaty" could "participate in collective military measures to maintain or restore peace and security in the North Atlantic area in support of United Nations action." In other words, if the United States chose to go to war in the NATO area, its NATO troops would be happy to let themselves be called UN troops. But the United States would decide when the "circumstances" were "appropriate." As soon as American manpower was no longer needed in Korea, the question of troops for the UN would be "reviewed." One explanation for this decision to abandon the effort for collective security through the UN — for that is what it was — was that the State Department had lost a long, running battle with the Defense Department, which had not wanted the Uniting for Peace Resolution proposed in the first place and which, therefore, did not want it implemented. Defense did not believe the UN could or should be relied upon, even in part, for United States security; was fearful that the United States might lose its friendly majority in the Assembly; wanted no action which could lead to de-emphasis of the United States' regional alliances; and did not want its hands tied, even morally, in respect to the future use of any specific element of the United States armed forces. Other opponents, not confined exclusively to the Defense Department, argued that the whole American military establishment would be available to support a UN police action, if we thought the action wise, and that therefore to earmark any specific portion would be to weaken rather than to strengthen the UN. The contrary point of view — that the United States should earmark specific forces — steadily lost ground within the government, though it was vigorously presented. The United States' response would set the pattern for many other states, it was pointed out. At least a token designation of land, naval, and air forces would stimulate other countries to take the same step. If no troops were earmarked by the United States, few would be forthcoming from other countries. These warnings proved only too accurate. The United States lost its ability to influence other UN members, and Washington found itself in the extraordinary position of having formally urged a course of action in the Assembly, won approval for it, and then been unwilling to take that action itself. The decision was reviewed in the government a year later, and reaffirmed.

The basic reasons for failure of this effort to give the world community a system of peace enforcement could be summarized as follows:

1. United States policy. In the face of the Soviet threat, the United States was not prepared to shift its reliance from regional alliances to universal collective security, and did not believe the two security systems could be set up effectively side by side. The United States' friends and allies followed this lead.

2. The cold war. Many neutralist states hesitated to earmark

forces lest they appear to be promising to assist the United States in the event of war with the Soviet Union or one of its satellites. They did not want to "take sides" in the cold war, fearing involvement and provocation.

3. Unwillingness to "fight other people's wars." Nearly all states wished to retain complete freedom of action for the future. Their national interests might not be involved in any given case, or might be involved on the opposite side from the UN majority. Being unable to foresee the specific circumstances, and not recognizing a need for common action in the general interest, they were unprepared to commit themselves in advance, even with the reservations written into the Uniting for Peace Resolution. Some countries cited obligations to contribute to hemispheric or other regional self-defense; some wished to judge their own capacity to contribute when the time came; others cited needs of internal security; and all refused to venture outside their established constitutional processes.

4. Lack of confidence in the General Assembly. Like most large deliberative bodies, the Assembly normally is slow, cumbersome, and unwieldy. At that time, in 1950, the United States had a wholly reliable two-thirds majority, made up of its friends and allies in Latin America, Europe, the Commonwealth, and elsewhere; but a large number of new countries, many of them neutralist in sentiment, were seeking admission. Some men foresaw — accurately, as it proved — that entrance of these countries would drastically reduce the United States' influence. Though it would not remove the United States' power to block actions (Washington could always muster more than one-third of the votes), it would deprive the United States of affirmative control over policy and action, and it might not therefore be wise — from a strictly selfish American point of view — to give the Assembly too much power. So it was argued. This viewpoint overlooked many opportunities for the United States to retain and solidify its position of leadership by constructive statesmanship. It took counsel, instead, of fears and defeatism.

As an over-all effort to strengthen the UN's capacity to meet aggression, the Uniting for Peace Resolution was not a total loss, by any means. One plus factor was establishment of a Peace

Observation Commission, whose job would be to send teams of observers to trouble spots before a crisis arose. The observers would supply the UN with accurate information if and when the worst happened. A special commission which had been sent to Korea for a different reason had been of immense help in identifying the guilty party when war broke out and hence in facilitating political decisions at headquarters.

In the field of collective security, the Collective Measures Committee spent many months plowing the field to receive any seed that might one day be sown. It planned command arrangements, offered ways for countries to support military action effectively without contributing troops, tackled legal and administrative problems, mapped economic, political and other sanctions short of war, and did a great deal of other important paper work which one day could be taken down off the shelves of the UN library, dusted off, and put to use — if the will to do so were found. The General Assembly expressed its appreciation of the Collective Measures Committee's work and urged governments to study its recommendations carefully.

One of the more interesting and novel ideas the Committee examined was a proposal that the UN supplement its prospective police force with units of individual volunteers. In a sense, this idea dated back to June, 1948, when the then Secretary-General, Trygve Lie, disheartened over the failure to implement Article 43, and believing (as he later explained) that "even a small United Nations force" could have "saved many lives . . . in Indonesia and Palestine," proposed what he called a "United Nations Guard Force" of 1,000 to 5,000 men. It could be used, Lie suggested, "for guard duty with United Nations missions, in the conduct of plebiscites under the supervision of the United Nations, and in the administration of truce terms. It could be used as a constabulary under the Security Council or the Trusteeship Council in cities like Jerusalem and Trieste during the establishment of international regimes . . . ." When 1,000 to 5,000 men struck some delegates as too many, he reduced the estimate to 800, of whom 500 would be held in reserve at home. He estimated the cost at $4,000,000 a year.

The idea ran into stiff opposition in the 1948 General Assembly. Soviet delegates professed to see in it a plot to establish the nucleus of a fighting force under the Assembly, thus by-passing the Security Council (and the Soviet veto); they charged that it would be dominated by the United States. In vain did Mr. Lie protest that it would be strictly a "non-military" group. Other delegates objected to the cost; France called it "an expensive and useless luxury." Difficulties in integrating personnel diverse in language, religion, and training were cited; so were divided loyalties, differing standards of efficiency, and the possibility of quarreling inside the Guard, as between Russians and Americans. There would be morale problems if the Guard were inactive for any length of time. South Africa even questioned the value of "patrol duties in neutralized zones, and supervision of elections," claiming that "the exercise of these two functions might encourage a tendency to regard the United Nations Guard as a body which bore the responsibility for the execution of the recommendations of the Organization." This, the South African delegate felt, was a "danger". The United States, always influential, was lukewarm; supporters were few; and the upshot was that the idea was referred to a committee — a favorite way of tactfully burying an idea. It later emerged and was approved in a totally changed form as a "Field Service," that is, a team of unarmed international civil servants to assist field missions in various ways, including the operation and maintenance of vehicles and communications equipment. The Field Service was a useful project, but it was not a police force. At that stage of UN history, Lie commented in his book, *In the Cause of Peace,* "an internationally recruited force was too radical an idea for many governments."

That was in 1948-49. Later, in the context of the Uniting for Peace Resolution, the atmosphere seemed sufficiently changed to justify a new effort. Hence Lie placed before the Collective Measures Committee a blueprint for a "United Nations Legion" (later called a "United Nations Volunteer Reserve") of 50,000 to 60,000 men. Unlike the Guard, the Legion was to be a fighting force, or rather, a contribution to one. It was conceived of primarily as a way in which small countries, unable to provide large fighting units, could offer manpower which would supplement — i.e., fight or work alongside — units earmarked by larger states. If one small country could not supply enough men by itself, several countries could pool their personnel. A group of the smaller Latin American states, for example, might make up a Spanish-speaking battalion. The men could volunteer for the duty and would be held at home, in their own country's armed forces, until needed by the UN. States would pay to recruit, equip, and train the men, and when they were not assigned to UN duty, could use them in the same way as any other of their soldiers. Mr. Lie even provided that if the home government wished, it could refuse to let the men fight for the UN when the UN called for them. The states were to have full control over the use of the units thus organized.

Nevertheless, the idea did not catch on. It seems to have died from lack of interest, rather than serious or deep-seated opposition, though there was some of that. Several countries feared that political refugees would find a haven in such a force. The name "Legion," suggesting the French Foreign Legion, evoked negative reactions from some who thought that what was being proposed was a force made up of individuals under direct UN control, stationed at an international base, and ready for use at the UN's discretion. The Secretary-General and his staff considered this idea, and discussed it with members of the Committee, but finally dropped it. It raised far too many problems of cost, integration, command, law, and politics. "The creation of any supranational, self-contained standing force, internationally recruited for a fixed period of full-time service and subject, not to the control of any national government, but to a self-contained United Nations Command," said Lie, is "administratively, financially, and militarily impractical at the present time." And the Collective Measures Committee agreed.

Neither did anyone seriously consider asking member states to contribute units of their armed forces to a fighting force which would be stationed at an international base and placed under UN control. No country was prepared to relinquish control over its citizens to the world organization. Moreover, some countries seriously doubted that the General Assembly would have power, under the Charter, to organize and employ a force of this kind.

By 1952, therefore, efforts to give the UN "teeth" had come to a dead end. John Foster Dulles, in presenting the Uniting for Peace Resolution to the Assembly's First (Political) Committee, had said the UN's reaction "may determine, perhaps decisively and finally for our generation, whether or not the nations of the world really want an effective, as against a paper, system of collective resistance to aggression . . ." If so, the answer was that they did not. But perhaps this need not prove to have been the last word in the matter.

CHAPTER VI

Can The UN Enforce Peace?

Because it never has been politically possible to establish a permanent international police force, it does not necessarily follow that it never will be possible, or even that it is not now possible. There were many, including at first the Secretary-General of the United Nations, who thought UNEF was beyond reach. It was not; the UN now in fact possesses, at least temporarily, a force to maintain peace. One step has been taken along a road mankind has sought to tread for centuries.

There are indications that public opinion in the United States would be prepared to take still a further step. In the spring of 1957, after UNEF had been on the job for about six months, the American Institute of Public Opinion (the Gallup poll) asked a representative cross section of Americans the question: "Do you think the UN should have its own permanent armed forces, including troops from the United States, which it could use to enforce UN decisions — or would that be giving too much power to the UN?" The results, published May 7, 1957, were as follows:

>   Yes, should have........ 53%
>   No, should not......... 23%
>   Can't say 24%

The results of this poll were almost identical with those of an earlier one (February, 1957) taken by *Fortune* (Elmo Roper). In this instance, the question asked was, "Would you favor or oppose a permanent UN police force with American troops in it?" The results:

>   Favor 57%
>   Oppose 22%
>   Don't know 21%

Over a period of years, opinion has fluctuated, but has generally shown a substantial majority in favor of the idea of an international police force. William Buchanan, Herbert E. Krugman, and R. W. Van Wagenen made a study of various polls on the subject taken between 1939 and 1953. Their findings were published by the Princeton University Center for Research on World Political Institutions. The following table is taken from that interesting study:

Question 1 (Peacetime): Would you like to see the United States join in a movement to establish an international police force to maintain world peace?

	August 1939 (AIPO)	April 1947 (NORC)	July 1953 (AIPO)
Yes	46%	75%	56%
No	39	17	30
No opinion	15	8	14

Question 2 (Wartime): Should the countries fighting the Axis set up an international police force after the war is over to try to keep peace throughout the world?

	July 1942 (AIPO)	March 1943 (OPOR)	April 1943 (AIPO)	Oct. 1943 (OPOR)	April 1944 (OPOR)
Yes	73%	80%	74%	79%	77%
No	16	12	14	11	13
No opinion	11	8	12	10	10

Question 3: Would you be willing to give the United Nations Organization the power to call out American troops, along with those of other countries, to help stop an aggressor?

	Nov. 1948 (NORC)	Nov. 1949 (NORC)
Yes	62%	58%
No	26	32
Don't know	12	10

Note: AIPO—American Institute of Public Opinion (Gallup Poll)
NORC—National Opinion Research Center (University of Chicago)
OPOR—Office of Public Opinion Research (Princeton University)

The authors point out that many qualifications are necessary in interpreting the results of these polls. Not everyone questioned, by any means, had the same idea of what was meant by an "international police force to maintain world peace." On one occasion, in 1943, nearly half of those polled (48%) gave no answer when they were asked to define the phrase. On another occasion, the responders split equally in three directions when asked whether the force should be larger than the armed forces of the United States, smaller, or about the same size. There is a "suspicion," the authors say, "that many of the respondents favorable to an international police force were endorsing the *goal* of an IPF — world peace — rather than endorsing the police force as a mechanism for achieving that goal."

Nonetheless, it seems clear that the general idea is attractive to many Americans. Early in 1957, two U. S. Senators (John J. Sparkman (D) of Alabama, and Ralph E. Flanders (R) of Vermont) and two Representatives (Peter Frelinghuysen Jr. (R) of New Jersey and A. S. J. Carnahan (D) of Missouri) introduced into the houses of Congress similar resolutions endorsing it. The Senate resolution reads as follows:

> Whereas the United Nations Emergency Force, created pursuant to resolutions of the United Nations General Assembly of November 3 and 4, 1956 (A/RES/391 and A/RES/394) has made an important contribution to international peace and security in the Middle East; and
> Whereas the need for such a force appears likely to continue; and
> Whereas such a force could be an important instrument for the maintenance of international peace and security not only in the Middle East but also in other areas of the world: Therefore be it
> *Resolved,* That the Senate welcomes the establishment of the United Nations emergency force.
> Sec. 2. It is the sense of the Senate that —
> (a) a force of a similar character should be made a permanent arm of the United Nations;
> (b) such a force should be composed of units made available by members of the United Nations: *Provided,* That no such units should be accepted from permanent members of the Security Council;
> (c) consideration should be given to arrangements whereby individuals would be allowed to volunteer for service with such a force: *Provided,* That individuals who are nationals of permanent members of the Security Council should not be acceptable;
> (d) equipment and expenses of such a force should be provided by the United Nations out of its regular budget.

Within the United Nations General Assembly, there appears to be a considerable nucleus of opinion which is favorable — at least in principle — to the establishment of a force. Several delegates put that view on record in December, 1956:

Canada:
If our experiment [with UNEF] works . . . it may be that the United Nations might usefully consider some means of having units of armed forces of the smaller countries made available at short notice for such supervisory duties, on the call of the United Nations.

Chile:
We are therefore in complete accord with those who have expressed here the hope that the United Nations will organize a permanent armed force ready to step in whenever its services may be required to deter aggression by any State which forgets the commitments undertaken upon its entry into this world Organization and send (sic) its troops outside its own frontiers.

Greece:
The following are the measures which I think we should take: (a) Progressive disarmament . . . ; (b) Creation of a United Nations police force, capable of ensuring international order. (The present Middle East experiment is a small step in the right direction); (c) Monopoly of atomic weapons to be held by the United Nations.

Iran:
[UNEF] is not the international army which was envisaged by the Charter. The Organization does not yet have an army which is capable of making its decisions respected, because the permanent members of the Security Council have been unable to reach agreement. It is none the less true that the creation of this international police force marks a great step forward and will make it easier, later on, to organize that international army without which the Organization can never enforce its decisions completely, in spite of its great moral influence.

Ireland:
The United Nations Emergency Force, created under the able and imaginative guidance of the Secretary-General, may prove to be a turning-point in the history of the Middle East and of the world. We all hope so, and we hope that this device of a multi-nation police force, implementing a resolution of this Assembly, may prove its worth in other critical areas. I do not, of course, refer to situations in which a large-scale military effort may be required, as in Korea, but to situations calling for a limited police action. However, it is difficult for certain countries, even when they would like to give effect to a resolution of the Assembly, to participate in such actions at short notice. There are sometimes legal, as well as administrative difficulties to be overcome. I should

like to support the suggestion . . . that member states might consider placing some units of their defence forces on such a footing that they could quickly co-operate in an action of this kind. There would, of course, be no obligation on any member to supply such a contingent, but it would be useful if members generally were in a position to do so in cases where their Governments wished to act following a resolution of this Assembly.

Laos:
. . . we can only welcome the recent creation of the United Nations Emergency Force under the high authority of our Secretary-General. We hope that it is only a first step, and that this nucleus of a world police force will develop into an effective instrument of action, a real armed force in the service of peace.

Nepal:
I regard the creation of the United Nations Emergency Force as a very bold and great step in the direction of perfecting the world body. This Force, created as it is to supervise the cease-fire and the withdrawal of foreign troops from Egyptian territory, has strengthened the faith of the smaller nations in the efficacy of the United Nations. Their feeling is that if they find themselves in a similar situation, they can count on similar assistance from this Force.

New Zealand:
It is a gain that the situation should have provided the stimulus for the creation of a United Nations Force, perhaps the first step towards investing the United Nations with the practical means to make its decisions effective.

Norway:
The establishment of the United Nations Emergency Force in the Middle East constitutes a momentous new institutional development. . . . It would . . . seem worth considering the establishment on a permanent basis of United Nations forces in readiness for emergencies such as the one with which we are now faced. Such forces would not, in the proper sense, constitute an international police. They might, however, be considered an international fire brigade, available for use in situations where there is reason to fear that existing international tension might result in brush fires.

These statements were made during the UN General Assembly's 1956 "general debate," an annual ceremony which consists of unrelated, or distantly related, statements of national policy and sentiment, normally lofty in tone, broad in scope, and

— like much election-campaign oratory — not intended to be taken too literally. Few countries would wish to be held strictly to every ringing platitude they utter at that time. Nevertheless, the fact that countries as disparate as Greece and Iran, Laos and Ireland should have gone on record as favorably inclined toward a permanent police force indicates the idea has begun to take root.

What exactly is meant, however, when one refers to a "permanent police force"? Laos, for example, spoke of "an effective instrument of action, a real armed force"; Greece, of "ensuring international order"; New Zealand, of "the practical means to make [UN] decisions effective." In these cases, a fighting force seemed to be what the delegate had in mind. Canada, however, spoke of "supervisory duties"; Norway, of an "international fire brigade"; Ireland, of cooperation in an action of the UNEF kind. These delegates clearly were referring to something more modest than a fighting army.

Should a permanent police force be able to meet aggression? If so, aggression of what size? Should the force be made up of national contingents, contributed by member states (a "quota force"), or should it consist of individual volunteers directly recruited (an "international force")? Who should command it? Should it exist on paper, in the form of pledges by member states, or should it be "in being," at an internationally operated base or bases? If the latter, where would the base or bases be located? All these questions, and many more, would have to be answered by anyone planning a permanent police force.

Suppose it were decided that the force should be designed to meet aggression — aggression of any size, by whomever committed. Suppose its function, in short, was to guarantee peace in the world, and to impose settlements of disputes before they became wars. Such a force obviously would have to have more power than any single country or group of countries — more than the Soviet Union and its satellites, more than the NATO countries combined. Unless the great powers could be persuaded to disarm, this would mean an international police force costing tens of billions of dollars a year. Obviously this would be impossible on top of present defense budgets. But how to persuade the great powers to disarm? Must the force await a successful outcome of disarmament negotiations? If so, it would wait a long time. Indeed, it would never be possible to be sure the atomic powers had wholly disarmed; nuclear scientists know of no way to detect hidden stocks of atomic and hydrogen bombs. The bomb casings are complete shields for radiation; since none of it penetrates, none can be detected. Nor can fissionable materials produced in the past be traced with sufficient accuracy. No matter how uninhibited a team of inspectors might be, therefore, it would never be able to state with assurance that a country had complied with an order to destroy its nuclear weapons. Pending a solution of this baffling scientific problem, an international police force equipped to meet great-power aggression would have to have an atomic capability of major proportions, to guard against the possibility that a future aggressor had secreted away at least a few score, or a few hundred, H-bombs. The cost of a force with that much firepower obviously would be prohibitive, even if the problem of basing it could be solved; and any single individual or group of individuals given control over such a force would have more power than most thoughtful persons would wish to give them.

Perhaps, then, it would be decided that the international police force should be large enough to meet any aggression except that committed by a great power. It would be hard to draw a clear distinction between "big" and "small" aggression, because there might well be a lesser aggression (as in Korea) which was supported by a great power. But say the planners hit upon a force of 500,000 men — surely a minimum — stationed at strategic points around the world, and supplied through an elaborate logistical network which provided food, clothing, vehicles, spare parts, etc. The United States has found that it costs roughly $6,000 per man per year (not including research and development of weapons and retirement costs) to keep such a force in being. By drastically lowering standards of pay, housing, insurance, family allowances, etc., this sum might perhaps be cut in half. Even so — even if that were feasible — it would still cost the UN $1,500,000,000 a year to maintain a force of 500,000 men. The present budget of the UN is roughly $50,000,000 a year, or one-thirtieth that amount.

Divide the size of the force by ten; predicate a mere 50,000 men — scarcely enough to interfere with a serious attack by a state the size of Israel — and the cost would still be out of reach.

for all practical purposes, unless the United States wished to carry most of it. It would be a good investment in American security to use $100,000,000 or $150,000,000 a year for this purpose, especially if the United States could be sure the force would be used wisely on all occasions. But the only way to guarantee this — that is, the only way to guarantee that the United States would think the decisions wise — would be to give the United States full control over the force, either indirectly through control of its logistics, or directly by weighted voting in the UN General Assembly. The latter would require an amendment to the Charter impossible to obtain, and the former probably would not be reliable enough to satisfy Congress the money was being safely spent. It certainly would not be enough to satisfy the United States Department of Defense, which has fought against a UN police force for years.

Would atomic weapons provide the answer? Thorough-going inspection can prevent countries that do not now possess them from building them in significant numbers; that much is scientifically feasible. If it could be guaranteed that the UN police force would never be attacked by atomic weapons, the possession of such weapons by the UN might give it adequate power on a financial shoestring. (It would have maximum "bang for a buck.") But even supposing that all small countries would be willing to forego nuclear weapons and accept UN inspection — a very questionable assumption — who could guarantee that the next Korea would not find a Soviet satellite army with atomic artillery which had simply been smuggled across the border? And if the aggressor did not have atomic weapons, would the UN really be prepared to use such weapons against him? What of destruction to cities and civilians in the territory of the victim state, where the aggressor's armies had penetrated? Can anyone seriously conceive of the UN General Assembly announcing to, say, Israel that unless its armies were withdrawn from Egypt by a certain date, Tel Aviv or Jerusalem would be atom bombed by a UN air force? And then following through if the order were defied? A peace organization depending on weapons of mass destruction would be such a drastic departure as to be almost a contradiction in terms. The only practical result of giving the UN an atomic capability, in all likelihood, would be to persuade all potential aggressors to match it — and thus make all small wars atomic.

If these alternatives are to be ruled out, and the world nevertheless wishes to establish a permanent UN police force, what remains? A small, mobile force of 5,000 to 50,000 men with light to medium conventional weapons — that is to say, a permanent force on the model of UNEF, ranging in size from that of the present UNEF (6,000 men) to one which would be about eight times as large. Such a force would not, by itself, be able to stand up to an aggressor for very long, even given the maximum size. It would not be able to invade hostile territory against organized resistance; therefore it would not be able to enforce UN decisions, in the literal sense. If the world community wanted an enforcement agency, it would have to face up to the problems of a larger, more heavily armed force.

What a police force of 5,000 to 50,000 men could do would be to prevent border crossings by small, unorganized, or irregular forces (such as Arab fedayeen); act as a strip of insulation, or a tranquilizer, between hostile and fearful states — separating them and preventing unplanned clashes; patrol cease-fires and armistices, and by its very availability for the task, help diplomats to obtain the cease-fires; perhaps enforce arms embargoes or other interruptions of commerce or communications; and do a host of miscellaneous jobs. (UNEF, among other things, restored the Port Said water supply and helped break up a narcotics ring in Sinai. A Bedouin tried to persuade a UN officer to buy hashish; the officer pretended to agree, but paid in marked money and later lured the leaders of the ring into a desert rendezvous which was a trap. The leaders were all captured together with an opium cache valued at $500,000.)

Such a police force could be used as an international "trip wire." It could be placed in the path of an aggressor together with a warning that if it were attacked, member states would come to its rescue. If these promises of reinforcement were seriously intended, and clearly made, an aggressor would have to reckon not merely with the force immediately confronting him — force which he certainly would be able to overcome — but with the power which it represented. States which were serious in their intention to deter aggression could use this means of doing so. Less effective, but perhaps adequate in some circumstances, would be a decision to put the force in the path of an aggressor without any clear indication of the consequences if it were attacked. The aggressor at least would think twice before risking the possible consequences, even though those consequences might consist solely of the moral condemnation of the world community. A small, mobile UN police force would also be of use in the twilight zone between peace and full-scale, organized aggression. It could have played an important part, for example, in the Greek civil war (1946-1949), helping seal off the Greek borders to bands of communist rebels based in neighboring satellite states. Such a force might actually have been able to halt that war.

This alternative type of force, then, is worth detailed study. Suppose, at the outset, that the target were set at a modest level: a lightly armed infantry brigade of about 7,000 men. The troops could be directly recruited, as individual volunteers; or they could be borrowed from UN member states; or there could be a directly-recruited headquarters establishment, forming the nucleus, and troops from member states could make up the body of the force. There are so many practical difficulties in the way of a truly international army of individual volunteers that it would be unwise to attempt to form the whole force in this manner. It would cost the UN a lot more than a quota force; all the burden of salaries, pensions, hospitalization, equipment, etc., would fall on the world organization, instead of being shared with contributing states. It might be difficult to screen out undesirable personnel. There would be legal problems involving possible loss of citizenship for some of the individuals; court martial standards would have to be overhauled (some crimes are serious in one army and trivial in another); language difficulties and other problems of coordination would have to be solved. States would have a less immediate interest in paying for, and rescuing from attack, a force with which they did not feel as closely associated as they would one which included units of their own armed forces. A prospective host state might object to some of the personnel on grounds of nationality, religion, etc.; and the objections might have to be honored, however improper they would be in principle.

Many of these problems, indeed most, could eventually be surmounted, given a willingness by governments to take on the job and a bit of enthusiasm from public opinion to spur them on. At first, however, it would seem best to limit the directly-recruited portion of the force to the headquarters unit, if indeed it should include volunteers at all.

Such a force ideally should be assembled at a base, given training as a unit, and kept in readiness for use on short notice. It should have, or plan to obtain, a small air arm consisting of transport and reconnaissance planes, and perhaps helicopters; it should have armored reconnaissance vehicles and communications equipment; it might usefully have a few small naval vessels for patrolling water boundaries; for psychological reasons, it might have some paratroops. All this would require a considerable logistical "tail," i. e., supply pipeline. Standardization of equipment would be one early desideratum.

Troop contributions from member states could be stationed at the base for periods of from six months to two years; thereafter, they could be replaced by contributions from other states. Training would consist primarily of instruction and practice in sealing off borders, in patrol and surveillance, communications, riot control, and combat against small, irregular hostile forces. Troops which returned to their country of origin after training would have a valuable store of knowledge and experience which could be tapped by considering them a "ready reserve" for a period of at least one or two years.

The choice of a commander should be made by the General Assembly. He and the Secretary-General could build a staff of officers for the force headquarters by drawing on UNEF personnel, by borrowing members of the UN's truce-supervisory teams in Palestine and Kashmir, and by direct recruitment. If there were enough high-quality men with military experience who wanted to make UN service a career, direct recruitment would be the ideal plan. To combat boredom and stale thinking (always a problem, military men say, if a man is kept at the same assignment too long), the officers could be rotated to truce-supervision teams already in the field. Indeed, these teams might — and any others set up in the future certainly should — become an integral part of the UN police force, so that all peace-supervision activity would come under its aegis. Should it prove impossible to obtain enough headquarters officers by direct recruitment, they could always be borrowed for limited terms from the armed services of member states (as the Palestine and Kashmir observers now are obtained).

In addition to a Commander and his staff, headquarters of the force in the field should consist of about six companies of enlisted personnel (perhaps 1,200 men) for purposes of administration, logistics, and maintenance. These men could be troops obtained from member states, or they could be volunteers, depending on how strongly the spirit of pioneering was running in the General Assembly when the force was established. But if they were "quota forces," their tour of duty might usefully be longer than that of the trainees, so as to provide maximum continuity. Ideally, the headquarters unit should remain permanently in position.

In addition to headquarters of the force, there should be a small staff of officers in New York, at UN headquarters, advising the Secretary-General and making long-range plans. And the Assembly of course would also wish to establish a subordinate body of its own, similar to the Peace Observation Commission or the UNEF Advisory Committee, to work with the Secretary-General.

One of the principal problems in setting up such a force would be to obtain a base or bases. At the outset, one base unquestionably would be all the world organization could afford; indeed, if it had to be built from scratch, even one would probably be more than the UN could swing. An adequate base for 7,000 men, including barracks, training grounds, airfield, depots, hospital and recreation and communication facilities, would be likely to cost in the vicinity of $65,000,000. As a practical matter, the UN almost certainly would have to rent or buy, on advantageous terms, a base already in existence, and this would mean finding a member state which was willing to dispose of one of its own. The United States has a number of suitable ones; Britain and France have a few; but there are not many other countries with facilities which would be adequate and which would be likely to be available. In all probability, the ability of the UN to obtain a base would depend upon the willingness of the United States to supply one at considerably less than the original cost.

Maintenance and servicing of such a base would be a major item. It undoubtedly would run to $1,000,000 a year. Countries contributing troops to the UN Force would have to supply the original equipment; otherwise, to equip a force of about 7,000 men with light arms, vehicles, and other standard equipment would cost from $12,000,000 to $20,000,000. If, say, 21 modern jet transport planes were included for deployment, the cost would skyrocket; it would go up by $120,000,000. Logistics are difficult and costly, even for infantry, let alone for aircraft and naval vessels. Labor, spare parts, and fuel for aircraft are especially expensive items. It would cost $13,000,000 a year to maintain the 21 transport planes, assuming they were in the air an average of one hour a day (a minimum for economical upkeep). Twenty-two small reconnaissance planes and 28 helicopters, estimated to be approximately the requirement for a force of 7,000 men, would cost nearly $3,000,000 to buy and about $2,000 an hour to maintain and operate. Arrangements with commercial airlines to charter aircraft in an emergency, or with member states to contribute them, might be necessary in view of these costs, despite the obvious disadvantages — notably the fact that the needed planes might be in use and hence unavailable on short notice.

Cutting all the corners possible — arranging to charter the aircraft, assuming no cost at all to the UN for the base or the original equipment, depending on contributing states to carry all the expenses they assumed in the UNEF operation — it might be possible to keep the annual budget for a 7,000-man force down to $25,000,000 when it was not in action. This is probably an optimistic estimate; and if the force were committed, the figure certainly would increase.

It is easy to argue that the world community should be willing to undertake an expense which is, by comparison with many national budgets, minimal. The cost of a single Forrestal-class aircraft carrier, for example, is $200,000,000. The United States recently abandoned the XC-99, a troop and cargo-carrying aircraft, which cost $15,000,000 to build and $1,100 an hour, or some $9,600,000 a year, to maintain and operate. Logically, the various nations' share of a UN police force should be considered a good investment — a great deal of additional security for a comparatively small cost. But the unfortunate fact is that there is almost no chance whatever of the UN General Assembly spending $25,000,000 a year merely to keep a police force in being, without any immediate task for it to perform. There is great reluctance to spend a similar sum — approximately $27,700,000 — for the first 14 months of UNEF, and UNEF is performing a useful task in a critical area. Every effort is being made to persuade the United States to assume a large share of this cost, and the United States has been resisting. The Senate and the House of Representatives draft resolutions endorsing a permanent force both speak of paying for it out of the UN's regular budget. That would mean limiting the United States' share to one-third, or less. If that is the most Congress will contribute, there is little or no hope of establishing a permanent force that costs $25,000,000 a year or more, because the other states are not willing to shoulder the other two-thirds. An item of $25,000,000 would add nearly 50% to the UN's budget.

Nor is this the only severe hurdle to be faced. Where would a base be located? To place it in North Africa or the vicinity of the Mediterranean might be to suggest that UNEF as such was being made permanent, or that the UN was preparing to impose a Palestine peace settlement, or that the newly-won sovereignty of the states of that area was being compromised, or that a new form of colonialism was being devised. These reactions would be irrational and unjustified, but that would not make them any less real, and they might be strong enough to deny the UN the necessary permission. If the base were located on the territory of one of the great powers, or a close ally of a great power, there would be suspicions that it would be dominated by that power —suspicions which might have some foundation. (The United States, for example, would never wish to see it located in a Soviet satellite.) To put the base in South Asia would arouse vigorous opposition from India, and would rule out a site in any of the several Asian states friendly to her. The force could not be too far away from civilization — an isolated Pacific island, for example — nor could it be located in an area where the climate was difficult, for reasons of morale, health, etc. Service in the force should be made a prize, not a hardship. A spot such as New Zealand or Formosa, if available, would have certain advantages, but would be remote from such possible trouble spots as Palestine and Eastern Europe.

Then there would be knotty problems connected with command of the force. The General Assembly was prepared to give

Secretary-General Hammarskjold wide discretion with UNEF because it had great confidence in him and because the emergency demanded unusual measures. But would it be equally willing to make him, or some other Secretary-General, in effect the commander-in-chief of a permanent army without severe restrictions? It would be understood, of course, that the force would not be sent into operation by anyone but the Security Council or General Assembly, and that when in operation, the Council or a committee of the Assembly would be kept constantly abreast of day-to-day developments. But what exactly would be the division of responsibility between the Secretary-General and such a committee? Where would the Secretary-General's discretion end and the committee's authority begin? A Secretary-General might be happy to be relieved of all responsibility, happy to see it given to the committee, with him simply its agent. But would this be good for the force? Some types of command decisions cannot wait while diplomats debate, contact their home governments for instructions, and vote. At least, not in an emergency.

Where would the political responsibility at UN headquarters end and the military authority of the commander in the field begin? And who would be on the headquarters committee? That group might become as significant an organ as the Security Council, perhaps more significant; and if so, the scramble for representation would be a sight to behold. Some delegates might have legal qualms about creating a permanent body which would preempt some of the duties of the Security Council, since under the Charter, the Council is the organ with primary responsibility for maintenance of peace and security.

All these considerations mitigate against a force permanently in being. None of the problems is necessarily insoluble, given an impelling desire to solve it and a conviction that a standing police force is essential to peace. But such desire and such conviction do not today exist on a sufficient scale. The momentum from UNEF is considerable, but not that great; it is not enough to carry governments past the obstacles involved. Public support for measures to strengthen the UN's peacemaking power should be harnessed to something more modest, and for that reason, more easily attainable at this time.

CHAPTER VII

What Can Be Done—Now?

If a force in being, stationed at a strategic base, with planes, ships, and vehicles to take it wherever it is needed is not now feasible, must it necessarily follow that nothing can be done? Must a permanent UN police force become, like peace with justice, the rule of law, self-determination, and the virtues of the newly elected Assembly President, something to which verbal obeisance is paid in the UN's annual "general debate," thereupon to be forgotten until the following year?

A case could be made for the contention that in an emergency, a police force could be set up again *ad hoc,* as it was in November, 1956. Despite all the mistakes and wasted motion which inevitably accompany improvisation, the first 45 men of UNEF were delivered in Capodichino by November 10, three days after passage of the final enabling resolution. By November 12, there were 150; and by November 14, 649. By November 14, there were also 111 tons of equipment, and the buildup of both men and equipment was faster thereafter. If a few transport planes had been available from small countries, so that it would have been politically feasible to locate the staging area in Egypt, there would have been no reason why the same number of men and the same equipment could not have been at the scene of action in virtually the same length of time, Egypt willing.

This might or might not be fast enough in another emergency. It was good enough in Egypt; it probably would not have been fast enough in Hungary. But there is no need to trust wholly to improvisation a second time. Without spending more than a few hundred thousand dollars, mostly for salaries, the General Assembly could set up on paper a permanent peace force similar to the one described in Chapter VI. That is to say, the Assembly could make all the necessary plans to call a peace force of that size — or any size — quickly into being. States could set aside troops for use as UN units, and a staff of officers at UN headquarters could coordinate the pledges. If without advance planning UN troops could be mobilized in days, with careful planning it could be done in hours. A pledged force might be made almost as readily available as one in being. Indeed, under some circumstances, it could even be more readily available. Troops earmarked by Yugoslavia, for example, and held in readiness near Belgrade, might get to a crisis area in the Middle East faster than UN troops stationed in New York. Such a force would be more flexible, more easily adapted to circumstances, than one in being.

The advance preparation, however, would have to be careful and thorough. UNEF experience has taught many invaluable lessons in this respect, and should be used as the starting point. In the early days of the Egyptian crisis, it would have been extremely useful to have known, for example, where armored reconnaissance troops could be found; which countries had large transport aircraft capable of ferrying not only men but vehicles across the Mediterranean Sea; where a staging area like Capodichino could be had on short notice; which Asian countries (known to be particularly acceptable to Egypt) would be prepared to contribute infantry; where engineers, ordnance men, medics, etc. could be found, and how many would be needed; how large an over-all force would be required to do the job envisaged — insofar as any precise job was envisaged at that stage; and a hundred and one other important things. With such information at hand, Hammarskjold and his staff could have planned out a force that would have been well balanced — from both the political and military points of view — before contributing countries were approached or made public offers, committing their prestige. It also would have been possible to sound out Egypt privately at an earlier stage and find out what troops would be acceptable. Steps such as these might have avoided the whole fiasco of the Queen's Own Rifles, and would have saved some severely ruffled feelings in New Zealand, Pakistan, and elsewhere. Such preparation also would have smoothed over many other practical and political problems, and could probably have cut in half the time required to get UNEF on the ground in Egypt.

Admittedly, it is not a simple matter to get advance promises of cooperation from governments. Few, if any, are willing to pledge themselves to send their men anywhere the UN General Assembly may ask, at any time, for any purpose the Assembly may consider wise, even if the men are not likely to have to fight. Countries making such a commitment might find themselves, when the time came, faced with the alternatives of reneging on their promise or taking action they considered against their own national interest. For example, suppose Canada and New Zealand — two of the most internationally-minded of countries — were to pledge a certain number of troops to the UN for use as the UN General Assembly saw fit. Suppose then that a leftist government of Indonesia were to send armed forces into Irian (West New Guinea) to make good its claim to that territory, and Australia — fearing for its security, to march westward from its half of New Guinea to drive the Indonesians out. If the UN Assembly were to recommend a police force to separate Australia from Indonesia, and thus in effect protect the Indonesian forces, it is doubtful that either Canada or New Zealand would wish to take part. They would not be happy if their hands had been tied in advance. In 1954, the United States and its friends would not have wished to help insulate the frontiers of Guatemala until after the revolutionary armies based in neighboring Honduras had succeeded in overthrowing the leftist-inclined regime of President Jacobo Arbenz Guzmán. The world community has not yet reached the point (despite high-sounding phrases in the UN Charter) where all use of force, for whatever purpose, is regarded as necessarily bad. Before that point can be reached, there must be more adequate provision for peaceful settlement of disputes. It may well be that in this respect the world has not yet awakened to the implications of the atomic age; but it is a fact, nonetheless, and so long as it is a fact, states will not be prepared to pledge themselves to help check any and all use of force under any conditions.

A substantial number of governments, however, might be willing to promise that if they agreed with an Assembly recommendation dispatching a peace force, they would contribute a certain number of troops for certain kinds of duties, and that meanwhile they would hold them in readiness for such a purpose. A headquarters staff of officers, believing that the UN might need manpower of a type not yet pledged, could so inform states and suggest that they earmark it for UN use; and with the necessary reservations, some member states undoubtedly would be prepared to do so. It is true that an effort to persuade governments to set aside forces for UN use failed in the early 1950's; but what was then involved was establishment of a reservoir of fighting forces to resist an aggression like that in Korea. A similar effort today, on the understanding that the troops would be used for patrol, observation, and police duties of the UNEF type, not for fighting, might get different results.

It would be easier to get many countries to earmark troops if they knew, in advance, what their gesture of international-mindedness might cost them in cash. The specific nature and dimensions of a crisis, of course, could not be forecast, but the division of financial responsibility between the UN and the contributing country could. The precedents being set by UNEF undoubtedly will be a guide, but it would be very helpful if a set of principles could be outlined and endorsed by the General Assembly. Broadly speaking, if the Assembly wanted to maximize contributions, the principle could be laid down that the contributing country would pay only such expenses as it normally would incur in maintaining its troop contribution on home territory. Just what such expenses would include might usefully be spelled out. For example, what about replacement of equipment? Most equipment would have to be replaced anyway; but no doubt it would wear out somewhat faster than it would have at home. What about such things as insurance, leave, special pay bonuses, and non-service disabilities? Suppose a country were obliged to set up a special battalion, or to maintain one in service longer than it otherwise would have done. Suppose the dispatch of a unit for UN duty meant that additional troops had to be called up at home to replace them. Who then pays? Such questions have arisen with UNEF, and have given trouble.

Another, related, subject which it would be useful to clarify, if possible, would be the formula for division among member countries of the UN's share of the costs. These costs should be shared by everyone on the same scale as the regular UN budget; but for any operation the size of UNEF or larger, the United States and a few other countries may well have to bear more than their normal share, because many small and/or underdeveloped countries simply could not afford to add substantially to their present UN contribution. The real questions would be: How much more would the richer countries have to carry? Could and should their special contributions be in some different form? It may be that it would prove impossible to obtain from the General Assembly in advance, any decision at all in this area. Too many governments might wish to see the specific circumstances before committing themselves. Some, for example, might be willing to contribute financially to a UN force for Egypt, but not to one for Hungary or Kashmir. Some would be ready to contribute on one basis to a comparatively small and inexpensive force, but would wish freedom to escape from the obligation if the costs went beyond a certain limit. Any clarification which was possible, however, would unquestionably prove useful.

An area in which detailed advance planning certainly could be made is logistics. It should not be necessary another time for Mr. Vaughan to telephone around the world seeking berets which can be dyed blue, or for vital rations to depend so largely on the accidental proximity of American supply depots. Those organizing the force should either have food and uniforms on hand, in rented depots, or should know where these things could be found and transported quickly. It would be useful, too, to know — for example — that Indian troops do not like Egyptian rice, and that Indonesians do not have winter clothing as part of their regular equipment. An Indonesian offer of troops for UNEF was put aside—and actually forgotten—for several weeks when Jakarta said its men were not equipped for winter in the desert. UN headquarters did not know where wool uniforms of suitable design could be found on short notice.

There should be experienced men available to the Secretary-General who know answers to the key logistical questions: where air and sea transportation for manpower can be had; where food, uniforms, vehicles, spare parts, weapons, and all other kinds of supplies are available, and how they can be transported where they are needed; where staging areas can be set up quickly; what kind of food troops of various countries want, and what their other special needs are; and many other important details. A certain amount of elementary strategic and tactical planning also would be desirable, even though there would be no thought of a police force having to fight against organized opposition. Non-secret maps and data on climatic conditions, for example, could come in handy. How should a police force have been equipped for use in Tibet in 1950 — and how could it have best gotten to the scene? Very little time would have been available to find out after a call for help.

There should also be advance provision for a headquarters and commander. It was a happy accident in November, 1956, that a commander for UNEF, with a ready-made staff, was available in the immediate crisis area. The next crisis might not be so happily located. A small pool of trained personnel ready to be flown to a danger spot immediately might also serve a highly useful purpose. A very few — a comparative handful — might be enough. In the early days following the cease-fire in Egypt, ten officers from General Burns' Palestine Truce Supervision Organization were rushed to Port Said, with Egypt's permission, to patrol no-man's-land and help preserve what was then a very precarious truce. Tempers were at white heat, and a single incident of the wrong kind could have revived full-scale fighting. The physical presence of the ten observers, with UN insignia, flags, armbands, etc., had a remarkable psychological effect, according to eye-witnesses, calming the atmosphere and giving promise of fuller UN intervention to come. The men also helped keep the enemy forces physically apart. Anyone who has been in a combat area can testify to the value of this kind of thing.

UNEF has proved that there can be a severe problem of morale with men whose duties are routine and who are stationed far from normal entertainment. The glamour of a UN armband can wear off very quickly for a man who has to patrol a barren desert in 100-degree heat and sandstorms, and has nothing to look forward to when he is off duty except poker and shooting craps on a blanket in his tent. Some of the UNEF troops found beaches; a few soccer balls and chess sets occupied others; but it was nowhere near enough. Officers discovered that the men were fraternizing with Israeli WACs across the demarcation line, a practice which could have undesirable political as well as other implications. A leave center ultimately was set up in Beirut, and men rotated to it once every six months. Professional show people from the United States and elsewhere were enlisted, on a volunteer basis, to come and entertain. But it was all begun much too long after the men arrived; the Golden Gate Quartet, first on the scene, was not there until the spring of 1957, and it was summer before the first sultry redhead, Abbe Lane (Mrs.

Xavier Cugat) set out. It simply had not occurred to UN headquarters that redheads and baseball bats were essential parts of a peace force operation.

In addition to areas in which it is clear that advance planning would be desirable, there are other fields in which it might well be better not to outline the course of action too closely, but to leave the General Assembly — or Security Council — ample scope for decision in the light of the circumstances. One such field is that of the political control over a force. If a Secretary-General in office at the time a crisis arose enjoyed as nearly universal confidence as Hammarskjold, no doubt the Assembly would wish to entrust him with the key decisions, subject only to consultation with an organ such as the UNEF Advisory Committee. In other circumstances, the Assembly might wish to give the Committee powers of decision, and make the Secretary-General merely its agent. Or the Assembly might wish to revive the Peace Observation Commission, set up in 1950, and entrust it with the powers of advice or control. Much could be said for the desirability of strengthening the P.O.C. and giving it specific tasks to perform.

It might or might not be useful to try to formulate in advance the rules that should govern dealings between the world community on the one hand and the countries contributing troops on the other. What obligations would a contributing state be undertaking when it offered troops? How much control, if any, should it retain over them? Under what conditions could it withdraw them? To what extent, if any, should it expect to participate in deciding the disposition, functions, duties and length of stay of the troops in the host country? Some countries contributing to UNEF insisted on a considerable say in these matters; others made their offers with no strings attached. Later, a standard agreement was drawn up providing, for example, for withdrawal of contributions after "notification" of the Secretary-General. Hammarskjold would have preferred advance "consultation," but some contributing countries would not accept this word. For the future, it would seem useful, if it were possible, to solve — or at least to clarify — such problems in advance.

As for the "host" state, what rights does it possess beyond the elementary right of deciding whether or not the force should be admitted to its territory? Could or should this right ever be waived or modified, and if so how and by whom? To what extent should the host state expect to participate in the selection of troops to be admitted? in determining where they will be stationed, and the duties they will perform? in deciding when and under what conditions they should withdraw? These are all highly controversial and, indeed, politically explosive issues. The very act of raising them might rend the delicate fabric of cooperation with Egypt. What about a "host" which is not generally recognized as a state — for example, North Korea or Red China? Would dealings with it constitute recognition? Must its consent be given equal weight? How much difference is there when a territory is not an undisputed portion of the host state, e.g., where control is provisional or the very object of the dispute?

It is hard to envisage the General Assembly reaching an agreed consensus in advance of a specific set of circumstances. Indeed, it might not even be desirable to do so; the greater the obscurity, it could be argued, the greater the flexibility. If moot points were decided in advance in favor of the world community, troop contributions might dry up and prospective host states, for their part, might accept UN help only as a last resort. If, on the other hand, decisions went in favor of national sovereignty, the world community might find itself hamstrung in an emergency.

There are dangers, however, in avoiding decisions of this kind. If there were no accepted plans and blueprints to serve as a guide, the world community's freedom to act in a crisis would depend entirely on the amount of military and political pressure brought to bear on the "host," as it did in the case of Egypt. If such were the case, there would be a powerful motive for aggrieved states, or states believing themselves aggrieved, to bring pressure to bear on their adversary. In some circumstances, the aggrieved state might be tempted to commit, or threaten, aggression in order to extract from the adversary consent to UN peacemaking. Moreover, the aggrieved state would have few reasons to halt its action and turn over the job of peacemaking to the world community (as Britain and France did in November 1956) until the desired consent were forthcoming. An additional incentive for the use of force might thus have been created.

Some leaders, therefore, such as Pearson and United States Secretary of State John Foster Dulles, have sought to pioneer in a more advanced concept of consent, interpreting international law to give the world community greater scope for its peacemaking. Others have attempted to argue away the necessity of consent, contending that when a danger of atomic war is involved, old concepts of sovereignty are outdated. Such opinions, however, have not gained wide acceptance in diplomatic circles and have been uttered, one suspects, more with a view to helping establish a new state of affairs than to describing an existing one.

Pioneering in the field of consent is made especially difficult by the impossibility of predicting future conditions. A victim state might command such universal sympathy that no one would wish to by-pass its consent (though this seems unlikely in a world where few issues, if any, are wholly black and white in every spectator's eyes). The victim might have been reduced to desperation before the world community could act, or chose to act, and in this case, too, no problem of consent would arise. But what of a case where both the victim and the aggressor were considered equally to blame for the state of affairs which led up to the aggression? or where the victim was considered more at fault, before the actual outbreak of violence, than the aggressor? Would it be equitable to condition all peacemaking action on the consent of the victim, and thus enable him to use the world community to enhance his relative bargaining position? Would this, or would it not, be too great a penalty to exact from the aggressor for the use of force under conditions of great provocation? What, also, of the case where an undoubted victim, such as a Soviet satellite under Red Army attack, was speaking with two voices — one of them calling for help, the other rejecting all "interference"? If the latter authorities in fact controlled physical access to the territory, should the world community attempt to force its way in to respond to the call from the former? The number of possible permutations is so great as to argue powerfully against any attempt at codification of the law of consent. The effort might well be as fruitless as defining the term "aggression" has proved to be. The best line of approach might be to attempt to set desirable precedents with UNEF, and let them be the pattern for the future. This is, in fact, what Hammarskjold and his aides, within the limits in which they have had to work, have tried to do.

CHAPTER VIII

Conclusions

The General Assembly could set in motion the machinery for a permanent UN peace force in a resolution which, among other things, would:

Note the outstanding contribution which the United Nations Emergency Force has made to peace and security in the Middle East, and express gratitude to those who have assisted or are assisting in that operation;

Point out that UNEF is a temporary measure designed to serve a limited purpose;

Recognize the widespread desire that similar facilities to keep the peace be made permanently available to the United Nations for use in other emergencies;

Request member states, other than the permanent members of the Security Council, to designate elements of their armed forces for use, with the consent of the states concerned, in a United Nations Peace Force which would do observation, patrol, and other similar duty in response to a request by the Security Council or General Assembly for assistance in maintaining and strengthening peace and security;

Direct the Secretary-General to establish, within the Secretariat, a permanent staff of officers, headed by an Adviser to the Secretary-General, whose task would be (a) to plan the organization, transportation, supply, and command of such a Peace Force in advance of its use; (b) to consult with the states concerned on the equipment, training, and state of readiness of designated personnel; (c) to make such other plans as would also facilitate the effective employment of the Force on short notice; and (d) to undertake, under the direction of the Secretary-General, the supervision of an Observer Corps provided for in the following paragraph;

Establish, as part of the Secretariat, an Observer Corps consisting of (a) officers like those serving the Truce Supervision

CONCLUSIONS

Organization in Palestine, and (b) enlisted personnel similar to the headquarters guard force;

Request the Secretary-General to recruit a limited number of such officers and enlisted personnel for duty with the Peace Force and to hold them in readiness for instant use at the call of the Security Council or General Assembly;

Request the Peace Observation Commission (perhaps with different membership), or a committee specially created, working in conjunction with the Secretary-General and the permanent staff of officers, to study such further steps as would facilitate the usefulness and availability of the United Nations Peace Force, and report to the next session of the Assembly;

Request the Advisory Committee on Administrative and Budgetary Questions and other organs of the United Nations to assist the Peace Observation Commission (or special committee) in the performance of this task.

One element of similarity between such a resolution and the Uniting for Peace Resolution of 1950 is immediately apparent. Both call upon member states to earmark elements of their national armed forces for use as a United Nations unit or units. But whereas the purpose in 1950 was to help restore peace through "collective measures including . . . the use of armed force when necessary" — that is, to meet aggression head on — the purpose today would be to keep a peace which already existed but which, without the UN force, would be dangerously unstable.

Contingents earmarked for UN use would not expect to have to fight, certainly not against the organized forces of a state. Their job would be to prevent fighting. If they did any shooting in anger, it would be against individual marauders or small bands. Their power would lie less in their rifles than in their armbands; they would represent the moral authority of the United Nations. Their very presence in a danger zone would help to prevent trouble. Any state which attacked them and either captured them or wiped them out would take upon itself an overwhelming burden of world condemnation. No one, of course, could *guarantee* that their tour of duty would be pacific, but this would be the intention.

It would be well to keep this distinction between a fighting force and a peace force clearly before world opinion and before governments. Not only would a clear picture help to maximize troop contributions, but it would guard against false hopes and consequent disillusionment. Twice before — in 1945 and in 1950 — the world was led to think the United Nations was being made into an organ of genuine collective security, only to find that governments were not yet ready, in fact, to create such an organ. It would be disastrous to appear to try a third time, and fail.

This is one principal reason for issuing a new appeal for troops, rather than reaffirming the appeal which is already on the books in the form of the Uniting for Peace Resolution. To reaffirm the 1950 appeal might be to appear to seek fighting forces, however much were said to the contrary. It should be clearly specified in the new appeal that the troops requested would do "observation, patrol, and other similar duty" in "maintaining and strengthening" (not "restoring") peace and security.

Choice of the Peace Observation Commission, rather than the Collective Measures Committee or some other group, to work out details and thus become a kind of godfather to the force, would also help to clarify the role envisaged for it. The very name of the Peace Observation Commission suggests one of the duties of the force. To be sure, a permanent United Nations peace force would not be merely a uniformed subcommission of the P.O.C., because it would do more than merely observe and report. But it would be so similar in its over-all objective that the mental image would be worth cultivating. Mr. Pearson, in an article in the April, 1957, *Foreign Affairs*, has referred to such a force as "an extension in space of the Peace Observation Commission and the subordinate bodies it was expected to produce." This may be underselling the peace force a bit, but it would be better in the long run to undersell it than oversell it. World opinion will quickly give it its full stature if it is a success.

How would such a peace force fit into UN peaceful-settlement work? First, before a crisis arose, a subcommittee of the Peace Observation Commission could be sent to the scene. Observation and reporting in an area of tension might be sufficient to prevent an outbreak of fighting, either by clearing up genuine misunderstandings or by denying to a potential aggressor the cloak of confusion and falsehood under which he had planned to act.

If this were not sufficient, dispatch of the peace force by the Assembly or Security Council could be the next step, and might

CONCLUSIONS

add the dimension required. It would not be necessary to wait until after the event to send UN troops. Had a force been sent to the Egyptian-Israeli armistice line prior to Oct. 29, 1956, for example, it probably would have inhibited the invasion of Sinai, whereas the presence of observers (the Truce Supervision Organization) did not.

If despite all precautions, or before adequate precautions were taken, fighting broke out, the problem would become one of restoring — rather than preserving — peace and security. It would then, so long as the fighting continued, be beyond the scope of the peace force envisaged in this book. Should the world community wish to suppress the aggression by force of arms, it could always act under the Uniting for Peace Resolution. That resolution remains valid, and could be implemented on comparatively short notice. Much of the logistical and other planning done for a non-fighting peace force might be quickly adapted to the broader purpose.

Once a cease-fire had been obtained — through diplomacy, political or economic pressure, or military action — the pattern would revert to that of UNEF in Egypt. Taking a leaf from the UNEF experience, the first step after the firing stopped might well be the immediate dispatch of a few men to patrol no-man's-land and try to calm trigger-happy front-line troops. These trouble-shooters might have to be available without any delay whatsoever. This is the reason for asking the Secretary-General to recruit and hold in readiness a limited number of additional military observers and guards as an Observer Corps within (or on loan from governments to) the UN Secretariat. One hundred would probably be enough; even 50 might do. It is their presence, not their numbers, which would be important for the job they would be doing.

The principal problem would be to give them useful employment when they were not on duty in a crisis. In the case of the observers, this could be solved by rotating them with existing UN armistice missions — the Truce Supervision Organization in Palestine (which could use extra personnel) and the United Nations Military Observer Group in India and Pakistan (i.e., Kashmir). A portion of the whole observer team would always be kept at headquarters; when there, the men could be assigned to the permanent staff of officers whose job it was to do detailed planning for the force. They would stand ready either to be flown to a crisis area themselves or to replace men in the field who were so dispatched. The guard personnel (enlisted men, as distinct from officers) could be added to the staff of Secretariat guards, who now number between 125 and 150. With a total of 175 or 200, some 25 or 50 could always be spared for emergency duty in a crisis area. It would be useful to have a pool of perhaps 200 to draw from, since at any given time some nationalities and some religions might not be welcome in a host state. One could not send Jews to Egypt, or Egyptians to Israel, for example, despite the fact that all men employed in the Secretariat should be regarded as impartial international civil servants.

Exclusion of the Big Five — the United States, the Soviet Union, Britain, France, and China — from a permanent UN peace force would be wise, at least at the outset. When great powers take part in an operation such as this, they dominate it; the smaller countries are window dressing, make-believe. Great powers would have special interests in many trouble zones which would limit their freedom of action. To the extent that the great powers gear their armed forces to atomic weapons, these armed forces would become less suitable for a peace patrol. Obtaining the consent of a host state to the admission of great-power troops might involve special problems; some host states, for example, might have deep-seated fears of "imperialism." And there would be other factors complicating the preliminary negotiations, such as prestige and political "balancing."

Moreover, from the point of view of the United States, it would be essential to keep the Soviet Union out of many areas where the peace force might operate, and the only convenient way of excluding the Soviet Union is to bar all five. Were the United States to contribute troops in a crisis, the Soviets probably would insist on doing so too (despite their contention that the whole undertaking is "illegal"). And it would be very awkward for the Secretary-General or the control organ to refuse such a demand. Soviet satellites would not be excluded by banning the Big Five, it is true; but this would not necessarily enable Russia to participate by proxy since satellite troop offers would not have to be accepted. Czechoslovakia and Romania offered men in the case of UNEF, but they were not used. If, for some reason, it were considered expedient — as in Indo-China — to let communists take part in supervising an armistice, the damage to the operating effectiveness of the force would be less severe if they were satellite personnel than if they were Russians. The Canadians and the Indians have found they can work with the Poles in Indo-China. They simply out-vote them. (In Korea, where the Swiss and Swedes cannot out-vote the Poles and Czechs, there is complete paralysis.) But no one out-votes the Russians. They carry a veto around in their shoulder holster, as it were. In Berlin, where they are outnumbered three to one by the Americans, British, and French, they have made trouble for more than ten years. The difficulties can be overcome, as in Vienna, but prestige and firepower add a new dimension to the challenge whenever the great powers rub elbows.

Exclusion of United States troops might cost the force a certain amount of support from American public opinion. Congress might more willingly appropriate funds if GIs were included — though the corresponding inclusion of Russians would more than counteract any such advantage. If the force were given a difficult task, such as patrolling the Formosa Straits, it would be useful to have American firepower, though no doubt the Canadians and some others could do the job if they were willing. American logistical support would be virtually essential in most cases when the force went into action — at least, it would until an elaborate UN supply network were established; and that might be such a costly undertaking that it would never be attempted. But American logistical support could be had without American troops. It has been available for UNEF without troops on the spot, and could be made available again.

One indication that a permanent peace force would be an asset to the free world is the fact that the Soviet Union is strongly opposed to the idea. Soviet delegates have attacked UNEF, its prototype, as "illegal" and resisted paying their share of the cost. Their contention is that the General Assembly, under the Charter, has no power to take "action" (Article 11, Paragraph 2), but must defer entirely to the Security Council. Setting up a peace force and recommending that it be sent to a crisis area, the Soviets say, is "action" within the legal meaning of the word. Western delegates contend that this is too strict an interpretation of the Charter, and point out that (under

Article 22) the Assembly may "establish such subsidiary organs as it deems necessary" and (under Articles 11 and 12) may make recommendations to states on "any questions relating to the maintenance of international peace and security brought before it," so long as the Security Council is not at that time "exercising" its "functions" with respect to the problem. This argument was settled years ago, in the eyes of the Assembly majority, by passage of the Uniting for Peace Resolution, but the Soviet Union continues to dispute the legality of that resolution. (Not bothered by consistency, the Soviet delegate in the Security Council voted in favor of invoking the Uniting for Peace Resolution on October 31, 1956 in the Egyptian crisis. Many would say Moscow thereby irrevocably acknowledged its legality, and having done so, can scarcely claim to be on firm ground in challenging the much less drastic step of establishing a noncombatant police force.)

It would be important to make clear, in setting up a permanent force, that there was no intention of making UNEF itself permanent, as such. This is why an enabling resolution should point out that UNEF is a "temporary measure designed to serve a limited purpose," and that the facilities being made permanently available to the UN were for use in "other emergencies." During the winter of 1956-7, the United States delegation considered proposing a permanent force, but eventually dropped the project. The decision not to press ahead was motivated in part by fear that Egypt — jumping to the conclusion UNEF was being made a permanent army of occupation — would order the force out of her territory. Much of that danger has passed, now that UNEF has benefited Egypt and hence proved popular with the Egyptian government and people; but in all likelihood there would still be a sharp reaction if Cairo were to get the impression UNEF was to stay, indefinitely, on her side of the line. Some contributing countries, too, would resist any suggestion, however unintended, that their commitment was being made permanent, especially if it came to appear that the principal function of UNEF was to protect Colonel Nasser. There need be no misunderstanding, however; there would be no relationship between UNEF and the permanent force except that the latter would draw on the experience of the former and perhaps take over some of the personnel of General Burns' headquarters. General Burns himself would be an excellent choice for the Secretary-General's military adviser, as soon as he could be spared from his job in Palestine.

The task of planning the development of the force could be done by the Peace Observation Commission, or by some committee specially set up for the purpose. One reason for selecting the P.O.C. would be to revive that almost-forgotten bit of peace machinery and transform it into an active, useful part of the UN picture. When it was established, in the Uniting for Peace Resolution, the P.O.C. was popularly hailed as the future "watchdog" of peace in the world, the "eyes and ears" of the UN. But except for a very minor role in Greece, it has never been used. Given the new duty of planning for a peace force, the Commission might well take a new lease on life. The possibility that the force would be needed in a trouble zone might become apparent during its planning work; if so, it could recommend to the General Assembly or the Security Council that a P.O.C. sub-commission be sent to that area to explore the need. In time, the P.O.C. might be given authority to send out sub-commissions on its own initiative — always assuming, of course, the consent of the state to which the sub-commission was to be sent.

The Assembly, in setting up the P.O.C., provided for a body "which, *for the calendar years 1951 and 1952,* shall be composed of fourteen members, namely: China, Colombia, Czechoslovakia, France, India, Iraq, Israel, New Zealand, Pakistan, Sweden, the Union of Soviet Socialist Republics, the United Kingdom of Great Britain and Northern Ireland, the United States of America, and Uruguay." (italics added.) There is no legal barrier to a change in this membership, or even in the number of countries represented; the Assembly is a wholly free agent to constitute a new P.O.C. as it wishes. If the P.O.C. were to be reconstituted, there would be both advantages and disadvantages in keeping the Big Five on it. It would not be dealing with any secret military information which would have to be withheld from the Russians (or from anyone), nor would there be any veto power, so the United States might well feel that continued inclusion of the Soviet Union was not too great a price to pay for an American seat. On the other hand, if the great powers are not to participate in the peace force, it might be wiser and more logical not to put them on the group which is to do the planning for the force. Should the United States, Britain, and France be prepared to have smaller countries act as architects of the force, but want to retain seats on the Peace Observation Commission because of its other duties, there would have to be two different organs — that is, the Assembly would have to set up a special committee to build the force.

There are many things the P.O.C., or a special committee, could do to weld the force into a useful organism. There are, in the first place, fundamental political decisions to be threshed out for action by the General Assembly. One such decision has to do with the financing of the force. Which costs can reasonably be left to the contributing countries, and which should be assumed by the UN as part of a common international budget? How should the common costs be allotted among member states? (The P.O.C. might wish to delegate this task, in the first instance, to a group of budgetary specialists such as the Advisory Committee on Administrative and Budgetary Questions; but it should itself have the responsibility for recommending broad principles to the General Assembly, because these principles will directly affect the availability of troops from contributing countries, the circumstances in which the force might be used, its supply problems, etc.)

Then the P.O.C. might also usefully tackle the whole range of problems which come under the heading of consent — that is, the consent of contributing countries to the use of their manpower, and the consent of the host state to the force's activities on its territory. To what extent should the terms and conditions of a troop contribution be spelled out in advance, so the contributing state would know what kind of things it would be asked to do when the crisis arose, and the UN would know what it could expect? Would a model agreement be useful, perhaps along the lines of the one negotiated with UNEF contributors in the spring of 1957 (when the first six-months tours of duty ended)? If the P.O.C. thought so, it could very well draft one.

To what extent would it be helpful to spell out in advance the matters on which consent of the host state would be required? Would it be desirable to draft a model agreement on the privileges, immunities, and general status of a peace force in a host state similar to the agreement negotiated with Egypt for UNEF? In addition, would it, or would it not, be useful to draft a treaty or treaties under which states would oblige themselves to admit a UN peace force for certain kinds of duties under certain conditions? These are questions the P.O.C. could consider. There may be serious doubt about the desirability of a treaty granting consent in advance or modifying the requirement of consent to any considerable degree. The very effort to draft one might be counterproductive. But if there were some other way (perhaps a General Assembly resolution) in which the rights and obligations could be spelled out, and agreement reached, without unnecessarily restricting the world community's freedom to act, the P.O.C. certainly should consider doing so. (It might wish to delegate the spadework for this task, too; but again, the final decision clearly should be a political one, recommended to the Assembly by the P.O.C.)

Still another broad range of subject matter for the Peace Observation Commission would be ways to assure the effectiveness of a force made up of disparate nationalities, languages, practices, and standards of training. Many logistical and other details could be left to the permanent officer corps. But the Commission could and should be concerned with such things as whether — in order to standardize practices and help unify the force — there should be a command and general staff school for commanding officers of the national contingents and their staffs; whether to hold joint mobilization and training exercises; and what steps, if any, should be taken to jog the memories and consciences of countries which had failed to earmark troops.

By the terms of the basic resolution, the Security Council or General Assembly would have ultimate control over a peace force in action. But who would exercise day-to-day operating control in such a case? This is another question the P.O.C. could study. In the case of UNEF, the task was given to the Secretary-General, who was to have the help of an advisory committee. Without knowing who the Secretary-General might be in some future crisis, the Commission might not wish to commit itself too firmly to this arrangement. Indeed, the Commission's final recommendation to the Assembly might be that it was the better part of wisdom not to decide this point until an emergency arose. When the time came, a control organ could be chosen and its relationship with the Secretary-General could be defined. The amount of discretion given the Secretary-General might turn, not only on the individual, but on the nature of the crisis and the composition of the control organ. That organ could be a UNEF-type advisory committee set up *ad hoc;* or it could be the Peace Observation Commission itself. The P.O.C. might come to be regarded as the logical choice; it would gain a considerable body of expertise and a familiarity with the special problems involved. In any case, the Secretary-General could be given as much or as little freedom of action as the Assembly thought wise.

Is such a peace force feasible at this time? Or would the idea start like a skyrocket, only to fizzle out the way the 1950 effort did? Would a substantial number of countries earmark troops, or would they simply reply, when asked, that they approved of the idea in principle, and would be happy to consider contributing if the need arose? In the latter case, the UN would not be much further ahead than it was before the Egyptian crisis. No fewer than 24 countries, however, offered troops for UNEF; some, in fact, were eager to serve and not a little put out when they were not permitted to do so. The opportunity was considered a distinction; it was a domestic political asset to many governments. Logically, a number of these same countries, and others which were discouraged from volunteering for UNEF, should be prepared to cooperate in setting up a permanent force.

Within reason, there would not need to be any limit, upper or lower, on the size of troop-elements earmarked; anything from a company to a division would be suitable, and the person or UN committee organizing the force could pick and choose. In practice, no more than a battalion (about 800-1000 men) would probably be accepted from any one contributor. (In the case of UNEF, contributions ranged from 250 men from Finland to 1,180 from Canada. During the first two six-month periods, the total force consisted of some 5,790 men from ten countries, making the average contribution about 600.) Some countries might have to amend their laws or constitutions to permit contributions in the future; if so, it would be better to take this action in advance than to wait for a crisis. Changes in basic law rarely can be made overnight.

It should be made perfectly clear that the country earmarking troops would have full freedom not to serve, if it wished, when the occasion arose. The "consent of the states concerned" would be necessary, and this would mean their consent as well as that of the host state. There would be no need of evasive action and heavy qualifications in the original response. Once governments and public opinion fully realized the importance of intelligent, informed advance planning — planning that could not be done without specific earmarking of at least specific kinds of troops, if not the troops themselves — there should be a satisfactory response.

Designation as a UN unit might well come to be a coveted honor within the contributing nation's armed forces, an honor to be competed for and won through outstanding performance in the field and in training camp. There would have to be incentives — special items of uniform, perhaps additional pay, perhaps the prospect of joint maneuvers at some climatically attractive site, perhaps a trip to UN headquarters with time off in New York City. Other incentives also could be devised. The contributing government would benefit from such competition. It would raise the level of performance throughout the service.

Should this plan not appeal to a government for any reason, an alternative would be to accept volunteers for a special United Nations unit or units on the understanding that volunteers would serve for a given length of time in the national armed forces. It has been proved repeatedly that there are thousands of idealistic young people eager to help promote world peace. They have volunteered by the scores of thousands, for example, for labor in work camps designed to raise the standard of living in other lands.

There is every reason to think that troops could be obtained. Mr. Pearson is one who believes so, and he undoubtedly knows the UN as well as any diplomat alive. "Even if governments are unable to give the United Nations a 'fighting' force ready and organized to serve it on the decision of the Security Council," he wrote in *Foreign Affairs*, "they should be willing to earmark smaller forces for the more limited duty of securing a cease-fire already agreed upon by the belligerents. We might in this way be able to construct a halfway house at the crossroads of war, and utilize an intermediate technique between merely passing resolutions and actually fighting."

If the experience of UNEF is not built upon, he said, "we shall only go back again to the situation in which we found ourselves last November [1956] when everything had to be improvised, when there was no precedent for making units available, no administrative and financial procedure, and no organization to which the Secretary-General could turn in the task given him by the Assembly of putting a United Nations force into a dangerous and delicate situation.

"We improvised successfully then. We cannot reasonably expect the same degree of success a second time."

CHAPTER IX

Looking Ahead

In an age of hydrogen bombs, intercontinental missiles, jet planes and napalm, it may seem child's play to talk about police forces patrolling borders with rifles and flashy armbands. Surely, the skeptic would say, such toys can have no relevance to the basic issues of our time. Make the UN a world government; give it a monopoly of military might; disarm the great powers, and enforce the peace — this, some would contend, is the only solution. Junk the UN; silence the meaningless clackety-clack; depend for security on more and better weapons; and the rest of the world be damned — this, say others, is the realistic approach.

Truly realistic thinking, however, must start with the world as it is, not as it may be 50 years from now or as it was before Hiroshima. There is today no conceivable way of persuading either the Soviet Union or the United States to disarm and entrust its security to a world government. Not when atomic scientists have shown it to be a technical impossibility for either side to be sure the other has, in fact, destroyed its nuclear weapons. There being so such thing as "enforceable" total disarmament, the most that can be expected from any future East-West detente is a moderation of the arms race, an easing of major political issues (such as the unification of Germany), and inspection machinery to minimize the danger of surprise atomic attack. Stockpiles of nuclear weapons will continue to exist, together with ever-improving means of delivery. As far as anyone now living can see into the future, the fundamental strategic fact will continue to be a capacity for mutual annihilation in the hands of both the United States and the Soviet Union. Unless there is some dramatic breakthrough in the field of defense, neither great power will be able to survive the outbreak of a major nuclear war.

This might not be an unacceptable state of affairs if, out of this nuclear stalemate, there emerged an era of stability. But the bipolar world of the years from 1949 to 1955 is fast breaking up, and with it, even the precarious form of stability known as a "balance of terror." Neither the United States nor the Soviet Union is fully in control of the issues of war and peace within its sphere of influence. In the Soviet sphere, there is turmoil and unrest nearly everywhere. Poland seems to be following Yugoslavia out of Moscow's iron grip, and Hungary has tried to escape and failed. Red China has asserted ideological independence. It is by no means clear that the Kremlin could determine when, or if, large-scale war should break out over Formosa. In the Western world, the British-French action against Egypt in defiance of American wishes demonstrated that Washington had lost its control over events — or more precisely, that voluntary cooperation inside the Western alliance, under American leadership, had temporarily broken down. Neither the United States nor the Soviet Union ever had full control over events in the no-man's-lands of the Middle East, South Asia, and Africa; and these areas are constantly increasing in importance. Thus to some extent the survival of both the great nuclear giants has come to depend on decisions and actions which neither can control. Small wars can break out which could lead to a big war without their being able to prevent it — or daring to intervene directly, themselves, to stamp it out, lest such intervention itself precipitate a major war.

Thus both the United States and the Soviet Union have an interest in an effective international organization which could prevent, moderate, and/or halt small wars in the atomic age. The Soviet Union does not recognize, or acknowledge, this interest, in part because effective peacemaking would cramp its style in some areas and in part because Moscow has no hope of controlling the machinery of peacemaking. The United States, which through imaginative diplomacy and sound leadership could regain control of that machinery, does recognize its interest in effective peacemaking, acknowledge it, and seek spasmodically to make the UN an effective instrument for the purpose.

One method of increasing the UN's peacemaking prowess would be to provide it with a permanent police force. If this force were strong enough to stamp out small wars, and if the courage and wisdom to use it were available, a great, gaping hole in the world's structure of security would be filled. The United States Government would be relieved of an agonizing problem which has hung over its policy planners for years: whether to gear the military establishment entirely to atomic war, or to maintain in addition, at great cost, a capacity to fight small wars with non-atomic weapons. If the anguish of the possible "small" war with all its consequences really could be lifted from Washington's shoulders, the savings in money alone would be enough to justify an investment of hundreds of millions of dollars in a UN force.

Nor would the United States be the only one to benefit, by any means. Because of the financial burden of simultaneous atomic and conventional capabilities, the tendency in both the United States and Britain is toward sole reliance on atomic weapons; and there are indications that the Soviet Union is following the same path. Carried to its logical conclusion, this would mean that all future wars, however small at the outset, would become atomic as soon as they involved the great powers or their atom-armed allies. All nations — great and small — therefore have a mounting interest in preventing small wars, or if this is not possible, in preventing great-power involvement.

The motive for a new look at the whole problem of a UN police force thus now exists, and is likely to get stronger as years go by. Such a force would have to be financed in large part by the great powers — that is to say, by the United States — because there is no other place where sums of money in nine and ten figures may be found. It could not include great-power personnel, because it would be precisely in order to avoid great-power involvement that the force would be created. Such a force could not very well have atomic weapons, because one of its principal purposes would be to obviate their use. It would operate under the UN General Assembly, not because the Assembly is an ideal instrument — far from it — but because the Assembly is the only workable instrument likely to be available to this generation.

All this, no doubt, is an ideal solution to the small-war problem in the atomic age. But wishing will not make it so. Such a force is not today feasible, nor are the courage and wisdom to use it readily apparent. Nearly all nations want collective security in theory, but shrink from it in practice; they want to benefit from the protection it might afford, but will not make sacrifices so that others may benefit; they are prepared to make ringing speeches at the drop of a gavel, and will even vote for high-sounding resolutions, but are not prepared to carry them out. Money is one major obstacle. No government enjoys taxing its people; the people demand immediate, tangible results, and a UN police force would not provide them. Its value might lie entirely in wars which never happened. Sovereignty and national interest are other obstacles. There is little sense of community as yet on a world scale, and much tendency to ask, "Am I my brother's keeper?" Lack of adequate provision for peaceful change is still another major obstacle. Nations are reluctant to render force impossible until they can be confident that means short of force will succeed in removing injustice. There is today no such assurance.

Meanwhile, however, though ideal solutions may be beyond reach, no one need despair of strengthening the instrumentalities for peace which do exist. It is only necessary to set one's sights on that which is feasible, to attempt short steps which can be taken rather than long ones which will not. UNEF has demonstrated that a peace force unable to fight — at least, unable to fight against organized opposition — can nevertheless be a highly valuable instrument. It is by no means an "expensive and useless luxury," as was said of Trygve Lie's "United Nations Guard." It can stabilize precarious armistices, deter aggressions, supervise plebiscites, help administer disputed territory, and do a hundred other jobs which could all be classified as helping prevent small wars. It can do this by harnessing a power the possibilities of which the world has scarcely begun to exploit: the power of world opinion, the moral judgment of mankind. Few, if any, governmental leaders choose to stand up for very long against this force. Even the men in the Kremlin have begun to show themselves sensitive to it, though by no means in the same degree as popularly-elected rulers. This power is the essence of the United Nations' peacemaking potential at the present stage of world development and anything which helps to channel and dramatize it strengthens the UN to a measurable extent.

Establishment of a small, permanent peace force, or the machinery for one, could be the first step on a long road toward order and stability. Progress cannot be forced, but it can be helped to evolve. That which is radical one year can become conservative and accepted the next. Once nations have earmarked troops for use in a peace force, they might wish to set up a base to which the men could be sent for a cycle of training and joint maneuvers. Having a suitable instrument at hand, the UN Assembly might wish to use it to nudge statesmen toward just solutions of dangerous problems. The force, in short, might become an instrument of peaceful change. Over a period of generations, as concepts of sovereignty were modified and the nature of the cold war changed, a UN peace force could grow to have a collective security function. Or it could become the backbone of an arms-control system. It could evolve in many directions, depending on the growth and needs of the world society.

No one can look with assurance ten, twenty years ahead into the developing atomic age; but one thing is certain: old patterns of thought, old prejudices, old limitations are vanishing. Anyone who is discouraged at the snail's pace of this development need only recall that the United States Senate is still wrangling over states' rights more than 150 years after the United States of America ceased to be a loosely-knit confederacy and became a federal republic. It should not be too surprising that the world community, still in the pre-confederacy stage, should be unwilling to permit any rapid inroads into national sovereignty. On the contrary, it is surprising that so many small inroads have been made. Anything which hastens the process of awakening to the atomic age should be welcomed, encouraged, and built upon — because no one can know how long the world will have in which to grow to maturity.

A permanent UN peace force would be one such instrument of awakening.

APPENDICES

PAUL H. NITZE — President, Foreign Service Educational Foundation; Chairman, Advisory Committee, School of Advanced International Studies, Johns Hopkins University; formerly Assistant Secretary of State for Economic Affairs, 1948-49; later, Director, Policy Planning Staff, Department of State.

RICHARD L. PLUNKETT — Graduate student, Department of Public Law and Government, and the Russian Institute, Columbia University; Ford Foundation Fellow, in Soviet and East European Studies program for 1954-55, 1955-56; author of "China Views Her Soviet Tutor" (*Far Eastern Survey*, July 1953).

CHARLES P. NOYES — Consultant to Rockefeller Brothers Fund; formerly Department of Defense representative, Senior Staff, National Security Council, 1951-53; Member of staff of U. S. Mission to the United Nations as advisor on Security Council and General Assembly Affairs, 1946-51; U. S. Deputy Representative on Interim Committee of the U. N. General Assembly.

LT. COL. CHARLES A. CANNON and LT. COL. AMOS A. JORDAN — faculty members of the Department of Social Sciences at the United States Military Academy, West Point, New York. Lt. Col. Jordan is Deputy Head of the Department.

LELAND M. GOODRICH — Professor of International Law and Government, Columbia University; Chairman, Board of Editors, *International Organization;* Member International Secretariat, U. N. Conference on International Organization, 1945; co-author (with Edvard Hambro) of *Charter of the United Nations* (Rev. ed., Boston: World Peace Foundation, 1949) and co-author (with Anne P. Simons) of *The United Nations and the Maintenance of International Peace and Security* (Washington: The Brookings Institution, 1955).

STEPHEN M. SCHWEBEL — International lawyer associated with New York law firm of White & Case; author of *The Sceretary-General of the United Nations: His Political Powers and Practice* (Cambridge: Harvard University Press, 1952).

WHERE AND UNDER WHAT CIRCUMSTANCES MIGHT A UNITED NATIONS POLICE FORCE BE USEFUL IN THE FUTURE?

by Paul H. Nitze

The thoughts contained in this paper are at best tentative and preliminary. No research or extended analysis has been given by the author to the problems involved. The suggestions offered by the paper are only for the purpose of stimulating further consideration and discussion.

It will be the intention of the paper first to offer some comments on the general strategic situation within which the possible usefulness of a United Nations Police Force may be considered. It will then discuss certain specific types of situations in which such a force might play a role. And, finally, it will offer some general comments on the relationship of such a force to the general reduction of international tensions, to fostering the objectives of the United Nations Charter, and to supporting the aims of United States foreign policy.

I.

Strategic Framework

It is assumed that there will be a further development of both Western and Soviet nuclear capabilities; that the offense in nuclear warfare will continue to offer greater possibilities than the defense; and that it will be possible for both sides to maintain sufficient warning, dispersal, cover or concealment to deny to the other side the possibility of achieving a one-sided victory through initiative and surprise. In other words, it is assumed that the general strategic situation as to nuclear weapon systems, while not absolutely stable, will not be characterized by gross inherent instability.

Under such conditions it should continue to be to the interests of the great powers, as well as of the lesser powers, that the world situation not degenerate into general war.

But what happens with respect to those issues and conflicts which individually, and in themselves, do not offer the prospect of a decisive shift in the world balance of power but which as part of a general trend might presage such a shift if the trend were not eventually reversed? Such issues would not in themselves seem to justify general war for either side. But if there is no apparent way of reversing an adverse trend once it begins there will be those who take a different view.

Many on the Western side have thought that the Soviet leaders would be able to command vastly superior manpower and conventional military forces and that once the Western nuclear superiority was balanced off by Soviet nuclear capabilities, then the Soviet leaders could be expected to show great boldness in using or threatening to use those conventional forces while deterring our nuclear deterrent with their nuclear counter deterrent. After the Hungarian developments it is not entirely clear that the Russians have an effective manpower superiority today and it is certainly doubtful whether it is necessary that the West concede them such a superiority for the indefinite future. Russia has a population of 200 millions. Western Europe and North America have a population of some 450 millions. The Eastern Satellites are hardly an asset to Russia. The Russian birth rate is not high. Chinese manpower is of dubious help to the U.S.S.R. except in the Far East.

Even though there may be no basic physical reasons making it necessary to concede manpower superiority to the U.S.S.R., there are political difficulties to be met in expanding or even in maintaining Western non-nuclear defenses. They are expensive both of money and manpower. As a result there is a strong tendency for military policy to follow the line suggested by the British White Paper. This involves increased reliance on nuclear weapons and missile systems and a decreased reliance on conventional weapons and delivery systems.

It is therefore prudent to look ahead to a period, which may be extended, where the main emphasis of Western military preparation is concentrated on building the forces and weapons necessary to deter the Soviets from using, or being politically effective in their threats to use, nuclear weapons; where the West maintains a certain non-nuclear capability but one which is not clearly superior to that maintained by the Soviets; where the underlying and basic competition and hostility between Soviet leaders and the West continues; and where tensions may rise and may fall but can never be ignored and forgotten about.

Within such a general strategic situation what role might conceivably be played by a United Nations police force of the general size and nature contemplated by the Carnegie Endowment Study?

II.

Types of Specific Situations Which May Arise

In analyzing the types of situations in which such a United Nations police force might be useful, two main categories of consideration come to mind. One set of considerations is the nature of the conflict; overt aggression, threatened aggression, civil war, subversion, suppression of anti-colonial agitation, territorial or boundary disputes, violation of treaty obligations, arbitrary or discriminatory action in the economic field, or violation of human rights and basic equities. Another set of considerations is the degree of great power commitment in the conflict. Considerations related to this latter group include the geographic locus of the conflict, particularly in relation to the great powers, and the ease with which they could bring their own forces to bear upon the conflict. And perhaps equally important to geographic location is the degree of great power interest, involvement, and political support to participants in the conflict.

The easiest case to consider is one where the nature of the conflict involves the danger of overt aggression and where it is to the interest of both major powers (for the purposes of this paper it is assumed that only the U.S.S.R. and the United States fully qualify for the role of major power) that the aggression not take place. This is the situation on the borders of the Gaza strip today. Furthermore, neither Israel nor Egypt desires, under present circumstances, to be free to undertake aggressive action or to threaten it. The Israelis have tried it once and been forced by international pressure to withdraw. The Egyptians, having been soundly defeated, can hardly be under any illusion that they have the military strength to tangle with Israel. The role of the United Nations Emergency Force is consequently merely one of assuring that what everyone wants to happen does happen and that border incidents, misunderstandings and frictions do not create a situation which can get out of control.

It is conceivable that similar situations may arise in the future and that a United Nations force similar to the one now on the Gaza strip can play a similarly useful role. It is, however, not likely that a new situation would correspond in all details with the Gaza strip situation. Furthermore, the purpose of the Carnegie Endowment Study is to explore the possibility that an expanded and differently organized United Nations force might play a useful role in more complex situations.

It is therefore appropriate to explore various conceivable variations on the Gaza strip situation.

The first variation might be to assume that the nature of the conflict is basically unaltered—that the situation is still one of possible but not actual overt military aggression across a recognized border or armistice line—and that the great powers still do not wish the aggression to take place, but that one of the local powers desires to aggress or threaten aggression. Let us assume that some years have gone by and Egypt is now in a position where it is militarily stronger than Israel and wishes to bring pressure on Israel. Can a United Nations force play a useful role in such a situation?

The first question would be whether Egypt could make the continued presence of a United Nations force intolerable. It would seem unlikely that world opinion would today support the maintenance of United Nations forces in Egypt against Egypt's will. The United Nations is not a world government and it can be argued that any attempt by the United Nations to station forces in a sovereign country's territory contrary to its will would be an invasion of that country's sovereignty. It is doubtful whether either the United States or the U.S.S.R. would welcome the precedent which any such action would establish.

However, United Nations forces, at the request of Israel, could be stationed on the Israeli side of the line and serve as observers, a trip wire, or even as combatant forces to assist Israel in repelling an invasion, provided the necessary decisions were made by the United Nations. On our assumption that both the United States and the U.S.S.R. did not want the aggression to take place, it is conceivable that the necessary decisions could emerge from the Security Council without veto.

A second variation would be to assume the situation as above but with the further assumption that the U.S.S.R. did not wish to oppose and might in fact favor the threatened aggression. In this contingency a veto in the Security Council could be anticipated and the issue would have to follow the procedure of the Uniting for Peace Resolution.

The question would then arise as to whether two-thirds of the General Assembly would support action against Egypt and in defense of Israel, even though the threatened action was overt military aggression across the armistice line. On a clear and blatant set of facts it is possible that such a majority could be obtained. It is more probable, however, that Egypt, possibly with Russian guidance, could so obscure and fuzz up the apparent equities of the situation that friendships and loyalties rather than considerations of principle became the main motivating factors among members of the Afro-Asian bloc. Substantial support of Egypt by Arab states and the Communist bloc would make the achievement of a two-thirds majority impossible.

A capability and willingness on the part of the United States to intervene promptly and effectively in support of Israel in the event United Nations action is blocked in both the Security Council and the General Assembly and aggression then takes place may tend to reduce the chance of this contingency actually arising. The greater the prospect of effective direct United States intervention the more unlikely it may be that the U.S.S.R. would encourage a chain of developments which would lead to United States direct intervention. These considerations would not operate, however, if the United States either did not have the capabilities for effective intervention or if the political situation were such that any intervention by the United States, even if militarily successful, would have undesirable political repercussions in the general area.

A third variation in our assumptions arises if we assume that hostilities have already broken out and the contemplated United Nations action is to enforce a call for a ceasefire. Here again sub-variants arise depending upon whether both great powers and both sides of the local conflict desire a ceasefire or whether they do not. The most difficult of these sub-variants arises when one of the local contestants does not desire a ceasefire and is backed by one of the great powers, say the U.S.S.R. On these assumptions it would probably be preferable from the standpoint of United States policy to back an attempt by a United Nations force to restore the situation and obtain a ceasefire than to intervene ourselves. It is improbable, however, that a two-thirds vote could be obtained in the General Assembly or that neutral countries such as Sweden or Switzerland would contribute forces to such a United Nations effort even if called for by the General Assembly.

A fourth variation would be provided by the assumption that the conflict was of an internal nature rather than a conflict across recognized borders or armistice lines. Let us assume that a coup is attempted in Jordan, that most of the army remains loyal to King Hussein, that the city mobs under communist guidance rise against the King and army, that the King requests outside assistance and the United Nations considers that a threat to the peace exists because of the possible spreading of the conflict to the Middle East generally. Could a United Nations force play a useful role in such a contingency?

Again it would appear that from the United States point of view it would be preferable to back a United Nations intervention than to intervene directly with United States forces. It would seem highly unlikely that a two-thirds vote could be obtained in the General Assembly for such intervention. In all probability neither the United Nations nor the United States would intervene in such a situation and the issue would have to be fought out on the basis of indigenous forces given merely clandestine support by the various interested powers.

As one contemplates variations still further removed from aggression across boundaries the prospect that the United Nations would authorize the intervention of United Nations forces becomes less and less likely. Treaty violations, nationalization actions, discriminatory actions, violations of human rights as in South Africa, would all seem to fall outside the category of conflicts with respect to which United Nations authorization could be obtained for intervention.

Another class of conceivable situations deserves analysis and comment. These are situations in which one of the great powers, say the U.S.S.R., is seriously and vitally interested but where the overwhelming body of world opinion disapproves of the action which is being taken. The Hungarian crisis was such a situation.

It is conceivable that roughly similar situations could arise with respect to Poland, East Germany, Yugoslavia, or even Finland or Afghanistan.

One's first reaction is to assume that United Nations force could play no role in such a situation where the vital interests of a great power are involved. This may be true for the basic reason that it is extremely difficult to visualize two-thirds of the General Assembly being prepared to face up to an issue involving Russia's vital interests if facing up to it may involve something more than mere words. But two-thirds of the General Assembly did condemn Russia's actions in Hungary and it is not certain that had practical measures been available to affect the Hungarian situation support could not have been found for them.

It can be argued that the availability of United Nations forces, ready and able to move were the United Nations to authorize their movement, would in itself be a factor which the Russians would have to take into account in estimating the correlation of forces in any particular situation. We are apt to look at a situation such as the Hungarian situation and say that to intervene in any way would be to take a certain degree of risk of starting World War Three. Our quite justifiable reluctance to take any substantial and avoidable risk in that direction causes us to shy away from the action. It is by no means certain that the Russians are any less anxious to avoid avoidable and substantial risks of bringing on a general war. An important object of policy for the West is to find ways in which the situation in Central Europe can be nudged in the direction of greater independence, justice and freedom for the people of the area while keeping control over those factors which might bring on a general conflict.

Let us assume that a United Nations observer unit were in being with the necessary air transport to take off on a few hours' notice. Let us assume that the necessary preparatory work had been done so that if Gomulka requested the presence of such a unit authorization could be gotten through the United Nations in a matter of hours. It would not be necessary in advance to decide what degree of backing such a unit would be given in the event it was challenged by Russian force. If challenged it might very well be the part of wisdom not to back it up. The Russians, however, would be put in a position where they would have to decide the degree of risk and the degree of exposure to world opprobrium they were willing to run rather than permit an evolution of the situation in Poland toward greater independence.

If in addition to an observer unit a United Nations military force of limited but substantial size were available for rapid deployment, a further increase in the risk which the Russians would be forced to face up to might be provided.

The point which I am trying to make and which seems to me to be worth further exploration is that the existence of United Nations tools of the type under study can create possibilities for action which the Russians must take into account in their planning. The use of these tools and the degree to which they are in fact backed up can be tailored so as to bring a certain degree of pressure on the Russians while the degree of pressure is controlled so as to reduce the probability of bringing on general war to proportions commensurate with the objectives for which the risks are taken.

The type of situation just discussed edges over toward the class of situations which include major overt aggression. If Russia were to move against Iran or Communist China against Burma, it would be far better from the standpoint of United States policy to back a United Nations response than to react directly ourselves. If the aggression were blatant and overt, it is probable that a two-thirds United Nations majority could be found in spite of the very great risks involved to everyone. The objective would in all probability be to repel the aggression and restore the situation without having it degenerate into general war. The commitment of United States forces and perhaps the use of atomic weapons might be necessary to stem any serious and determined effort. The existence of a United Nations force to spearhead the riposte would be of the utmost political importance both from the standpoint of providing a political rallying point behind which an adequate effort could be mobilized and from the standpoint of maximizing the possibility that general war can be avoided. Once massive United States forces become involved the prestige of both major powers will be fully committed and it is difficult to see how any limits on the contest can be long maintained. The commitment of United Nations forces, even though militarily of inadequate strength, would have maximum political effect while efforts to find a solution or limitation to the conflict are in progress and while more massive forces are being mobilized.

Finally it is conceivable, even if unlikely, that something comparable to the security arrangements originally contemplated by the United Nations Charter based on the assumption of great power agreement may be worth renewed exploration with the Soviet government. The Russians in the atomic energy field have indicated an interest in the so-called fourth power problem. The risks of general nuclear war in a world in which the U.S.S.R., the United States and Britain possess nuclear weapons is great enough. They may very well be still greater if a large number of countries possess them. If United States and U.S.S.R. interests coincide in wishing a limitation on the possession or production of such weapons and on local conflicts whose spread might involve their use, the basis may have been created for a re-exploration of certain of the security measures originally contemplated by the Charter and within which a United Nations force had its appropriate place. If certain areas of common security interest with the U.S.S.R. are found to exist, something could perhaps be done about them without improvidently permitting the recognition of those areas of common interest to obscure the continuing conflicts of security interest that persist between the U.S.S.R. and the United States.

III.

General Comments

The foregoing analysis suggests a number of points about a United Nations military force.

The first and most important point is that such a force might be committed in a given situation with less danger of the conflict then spreading into a world war than if United States or Russian forces were committed in the same situation.

The second point is that the political impact of such a force would be considerably greater than its mere military power by virtue of the world political consensus necessary to authorize its use.

The third point is a corollary of the second. The fact that such a force can only be committed if a world political consensus has authorized its use drastically restricts the issues on which it could have a bearing. Neither the United States nor any other country could count in advance on the use of force being authorized on issues which it considered vital.

Related to this third point is the question of the degree to which votes in the United Nations are governed by the merits of the particular issue in the light of the principles of the Charter, the facts of the situation, and past precedents or by the more strictly political alignments, commitments and pressures bearing on the particular state called upon to vote. Certainly Poland is today not going to vote contrary to the U.S.S.R. on any issue in the United Nations no matter what the Polish government's views on the merits of the case may be. She has much too important issues immediately at stake with the U.S.S.R. herself and is too immediately threatened by direct Russian military presence to take any such risk. On the other hand, the merits of an issue do affect the way countries vote. The overwhelming vote against the Russian intervention in Hungary is not explicable on any other assumption.

One is left then with the general proposition that such a force might well be useful in a number of conceivable situations but that it is doubtful whether its commitment in just and necessary instances can be counted on.

The decision as to whether to press for such a force or not would then seem to depend in large measure on whether more reliable and hopeful alternatives are available.

I take it that the United States does not propose to relax in any way its efforts to keep constantly in readiness the capacity for massive atomic retaliation. The deterrent effect of such a force is undoubtedly necessary. No one suggests, however, that the actual use of this force would be other than disastrous for the United States as well as for the rest of humanity. It does not therefore constitute an alternative to a United Nations military force.

The alternative, if it exists, is the capability of the United States, with or without allies, to intervene militarily in limited war situations.

The British-French experience in Suez demonstrated both the military difficulties in training, mounting and transporting the forces necessary for prompt and politically effective intervention in such a situation, and also the political hazards involved in undertaking such an action without a world political consensus behind one.

It may be that, taking everything into account, the alternative of direct United States intervention in limited war situations is just as difficult to prepare for, more hazardous, and no more certain of finding the world political support which would be a prerequisite to its success, than is United Nations intervention.

Prudence would seem to suggest that in the short run we strive to be prepared for either alternative.

In the long run it may well be that there will be a growing realization of the changed strategic situation in the world brought about by modern technology and weapons systems. As the destructive power of the weapons systems possessed by the major powers approaches the absolute, these systems cannot be invoked except in support of absolute and unlimited objectives. Any involvement of the forces of the major powers, even limited forces in support of limited objectives, may involve an intolerable risk that the objectives and means employed will spread as a result of the military and political interaction of a war situation. The risks involved are of vital concern not just to the major powers but to the world as a whole. A growing realization of this situation among the politically effective masses of mankind can in the longer run lay a foundation on which the necessary political consensus which is the pre-condition for a functioning United Nations force can be expected to arise.

To the degree that such a development takes place a developing harmony between the purposes stated in the United Nations Charter, the consistent long run aims of United States foreign policy, and world opinion may arise which will find its political expression in a growing body of precedent and experience in the United Nations and its military instrument in a United Nations military force.

A UNITED NATIONS FORCE: ITS USEFULNESS IN THE RESOLUTION OF VARIOUS CRISES

by Richard L. Plunkett

I. *Introduction*

This paper examines the uses to which a UN Force might have been put, had one existed, in connection with international crises in Greece, Indonesia, Kashmir, and Palestine. Thus, this is a speculative, "iffy" analysis of what might have happened had a United Nations Force been in existence, and had such a force been used in these crises.

We are interested in two basic questions:

1. How might an international force have been used to help stop the fighting?
2. How might an international force have been used after the fighting stopped?

We are dealing with many questions of an "iffy" character, such as the effect of the *prior existence* of a United Nations Force upon the decisions taken in the Security Council and on the actions of the parties to the dispute, as well as with questions which are a matter of historical record. Some of these questions can be avoided by relying on events as they actually occurred up to the point where we assume that the Force would have been used. Beyond that point the analysis becomes speculative, one "what-might-have-happened" among many possibilities.

Many considerations should be taken into account in evaluating the effectiveness of a United Nations Force in these crises. Such political questions as the willingness of the parties to abide by decisions of the United Nations, to accept UN jurisdiction or good offices, to negotiate with each other, to accept and maintain a cease-fire, are as important to the functioning of the Force as technical considerations, such as the size of forces engaged in the fighting, their disposition, access to the area of hostilities, its topography, etc. The effectiveness of direct intervention by the United Nations Force cannot be separated from either aspect, political or technical. The Force cannot operate without clear instructions from the Security Council or General Assembly; in each of these crises the political developments which lead to the UN decision are as much a part of the resolution of the crisis as the technical questions involved in the use of the Force.

However, to speculate about the political elements in the use of a force would inescapably run the risk of rewriting, and falsifying, history. In some of the cases, the record strongly suggests that, in fact, a decision to employ a UN force would have been difficult or impossible to reach or that, if such a decision were possible, it would have been unnecessary. Therefore, this paper will not attempt to speculate about these important political considerations. In order to examine the uses to which a force might have been put, if the political climate had been favorable, such a political climate will be arbitrarily postulated.

For the purpose of this analysis, therefore, certain basic assumptions about the Force and its use must be stated.

The first assumption is that it would have been politically feasible to employ an international force in each situation. This assumption immediately involves the question of *timing*. We must postulate the point in the development of each crisis at which the Force was to be used. In reality, this decision would depend on the information available to the organ concerned, the Security Council, or the General Assembly assuming that the latter could take such action before the Uniting for Peace Resolution of November, 1950.

The question of *access* by the UN Force to the scene of the fighting is also involved in that of political feasibility. We must assume access to the fighting through the territory of the disputants. Here the problem in reality would have been whether there had been sufficient political clarification so that the Force would be granted access to the area of hostilities. The need for clarification on such problems is seen in the experience of the Commission for India and Pakistan, denied access to Kashmir until a late stage of negotiations by the government of India. Another example was the action of the British Government as Mandatory Power in denying the Palestine Commission access to Palestine.

The second basic assumption describes a United Nations Force for the purposes of this paper. The Force would be an expanded and strengthened UNEF with heavier armament, and a military capacity to perform patrol duties, to protect borders against incursions, to supervise armistices and troop-withdrawals, to enforce embargoes on certain kinds of merchandise and communications, to carry out civil affairs duties, to supervise elections and plebiscites. The Force would not be capable of resisting a full-scale military attack, but would be able to hold its own in minor fighting and skirmishes. In keeping with its duties, it would be specially equipped in radio and other forms of field communications. In size the Force would range between 6,000 and 50,000 men, excluding logistic support. Budgetary and logistic considerations probably would hold the size well below the upper limit.

Given the Force as described, several conclusions follow from the stated assumption. The Force would not be used to stop large-scale hostilities by its own efforts, but must follow, as a minimum, an agreement for a cease-fire which would allow the Force to take a position between the parties. It is most unlikely that the Force would be used to hammer its way between both parties, or even that it would be militarily capable of such action.

The third assumption is that there will be some kind of stand-by commitment from nation-states to come to the assistance of the Force if it should be attacked. This commitment would allow the UN Force to operate in situations where it lacked full military capability in its own right, as compared to the armed forces of the disputing parties. On the other hand, this assumption probably would limit the use of the UN Force in cases where the danger of a large-scale conflagration is very great. Thus the use of the UN Force would be unlikely in direct conflicts between the Soviet bloc and the Western nations, since the chance of spreading the conflict into a full-scale engagement might be too great.

II. *United Nations Action in Greece*

The problem of the situation along the northern frontiers of Greece during the second communist rebellion, 1946-1949, is perhaps the simplest and clearest of the four crises examined in this paper. The Greek case is the only one of the four to involve a direct conflict between the Soviet bloc and the Western nations; the problem is easily stated, the lack of agreement as to the basic issues is sharply drawn between the parties, and despite Soviet use of the veto power in the Security Council, the assumption that the UN might have taken strong action is not totally unreal.

We cannot assume any real cooperation or acceptance of the UN decisions on the part of Greece's northern neighbors, Albania, Yugoslavia, and Bulgaria. The direct historical evidence in this case and the lessons of the postwar decade rule out such an assumption. But we can assume that the detailed findings of the UN Commission of Investigation and its Subsidiary Group and the determination of the Western nations to take effective action led to a decision to use the UN Force, by action of the General Assembly in late autumn, 1947, to strengthen the border observation already in effect, and, within the limitation of free movement only on Greek territory, to seal off the frontiers against leap-frog incursions of rebel bands, and against passage of military assistance to the rebels from Albania, Yugoslavia, and Bulgaria.

The development of the Greek crisis and of the United Nations' response to the situation indicates a definitely limited role for the UN Force here where there is no possibility of agreement as to the accepted functions of the Force. That a role exists for the Force despite such a stalemate indicates the flexibility of the United Nations and the usefulness of the Force under most adverse conditions.

On 3 December 1946, the Greek Government, acting under Articles 34 and 35 of the Charter, requested early consideration by the Security Council of a situation which was leading to friction between Greece and her northern neighbors, Albania, Bulgaria, and Yugoslavia. The Greek charge that guerilla movements in Greece were receiving training, support, and foreign assistance was detailed in a memorandum[1] submitted to the Security Council.

After debate, the Security Council on 19 December 1946 established a "Commission of Investigation" (UNCI) under Article

---

[1] United Nations Doc. S/203, December 4, 1946, pp. 1-34.

34[2] to ascertain the facts relating to the "alleged border violations" along the northern frontier of Greece. UNCI, composed of a representative of each of the members of the Security Council, aided by a twenty-seven man Secretariat, was given authority to investigate where it considered necessary, to call on governments, officials, and individuals, and to make proposals as well as prepare a report to the Security Council. The Commission eventually totalled over 150 persons, traveled to Greece, held ninety-one meetings, conducted thirty-three field investigations, heard 238 witnesses, and gathered testimony to fill a three-volume report.[3]

In its lengthy report, UNCI presented massive evidence that the three northern neighbors of Greece had encouraged, assisted, trained, and supplied the Greek guerillas in their armed rebellion. On the basis of these facts the Commission came to the conclusion, by a vote of eight to three, that "Yugoslavia, and to a lesser extent, Albania and Bulgaria, have supported the guerilla warfare in Greece."[4] The Soviet Union and Poland supported a different conclusion.

The Commission made a number of proposals, among them a recommendation that the disputing governments establish good-neighborly relations, establish new frontier arrangements along the lines of the Greco-Bulgarian Convention of 1931, and that a small Commission or a single Commissioner be appointed to maintain continued frontier observations, to investigate complaints of violations, etc. The Commission was explicit in its belief that

> ... future cases of support of armed bands formed on the territory of one State and crossing into the territory of another State, or of refusal by a government in spite of the demands of the State concerned to take all possible measures on its own territory to deprive such bands of any aid or protection, should be considered by the Security Council as a

---

[2] "The Security Council may investigate any dispute, or any situation which might lead to international friction or give rise to a dispute, in order to determine whether the continuance of the dispute or situation is likely to endanger the maintenance of international peace and security."
[3] United Nations Doc. S/360, May 27, 1947.
[4] *Ibid.*, Vol. 1, p. 167.

threat to the peace within the meaning of the Charter of the United Nations.[5]

As the summer progressed, reports of continued border violations from the Subsidiary Group added immediacy to this conclusion.

While Security Council debate went on throughout the summer, talk of conciliation continued. The growing sense that the situation was highly explosive was supported by reports from the Subsidiary Group, with headquarters in Salonika, set up by UNCI under the terms of a Security Council resolution of 18 April, 1947.[6] Soviet obstruction prevented Security Council agreement on any course of action. As the situation worsened, Greek appeals for action under Chapter VII encountered the growing deadlock in the Council. The U. S. position had stiffened considerably, as seen in the following passage:

> It is the view of the United States Government that Greece is in grave peril. This peril results from the guerilla warfare now being waged against the Greek Government by communist-led bands actively supported by Albania, Bulgaria, and Yugoslavia and by the Communist Party of Greece. . . .[7]

While seeking the support of the Council for an Australian draft resolution providing for action under Chapter VII, the U. S. stated that the Greek problem must go to the General Assembly, if blocked by another Soviet veto. After the Australian resolution and a similar U. S. proposal were defeated as a result of Soviet vetoes, discussion in the Security Council was ended, and on the next day, 20 August 1947, the United States requested the Secretary-General to place the Greek question on the supplementary agenda of the General Assembly.

Despite the immense detail of the work of UNCI, the Security Council was not able to reach a decision in a debate which lasted nearly two months. Enforcement action had not been considered; but even efforts to extend the investigation of the border violations had met in failure, although the Subsidiary Group still existed and continued its work under the terms of the April resolution of the Security Council.

---

[5] *Ibid.*, p. 248.
[6] United Nations Doc. S/AC. 4/223, April 21, 1947.
[7] Security Council, Official Records: 2nd Yr., No. 74, 180th Mtg., August 12, 1947, p. 1908.

At this point we depart from the historical record to assume that a United Nations Force would be sent into the area of hostilities by action of the General Assembly, with the acceptance and cooperation of Greece, and the loudly expressed non-cooperation of Albania, Bulgaria, and Yugoslavia.

Two functions could be performed by a United Nations Force in the Greek situation, beginning in the late fall of 1947. The first would be border observation, which was actually carried out by observer teams under the United Nations Special Committee on the Balkans (UNSCOB), established by action of the General Assembly on 21 October 1947.[8] As this system was developed, the more than 500 miles of Greek frontier, often in mountainous territory, was covered by between 30 and 40 military observers, operating in teams of six. This function could have been taken over very easily and expanded in scope, by a United Nations Force.

The second function would be to seal off the frontiers, thus isolating the rebels from their training camps, medical facilities, and their sources of military aid and depriving the rebel bands of their ability to "leap-frog" over the frontiers when pursued by the Greek army. This is a vastly more difficult operation and would take a sizable contingent of the UN Force. The major difficulty is the topography of the Greek frontier combined with the lack of roads and transportation facilities.[9] To combat the approximately 13,000 rebels within Greece,[10] there was the Greek Army, numbering about 100,000 men (seven divisions) plus a gendarmerie of 30,000 men.[11] This Greek army, while effective in open combat, could not use its heavy armaments in the mountainous country in which the guerillas made their bases. The task of a United Nations Force would have been to hold a narrow strip along the northern frontier, often in mountainous country difficult of mechanized access, in order to seal off the rebel sources of supply. Use of the UN Force in this manner would not in-

---

[8] U.S. Dept. of State *Bulletin*, Vol. 21, No. 533 (September 19, 1949), pp. 407-31.

[9] For a summary of road, transport, and economic conditions in the summer of 1947, see K. M. Smogorzewski, "The Greek Tragedy," *World Affairs* (published under the auspices of the London Institute of World Affairs), Vol. 2, No. 1 (January 1948), pp. 62-79.

[10] See testimony of Dean Acheson, U.S. Dept. of State *Bulletin*, Vol 16, No. 409A (May 4, 1947), pp. 107-08; and United Nations Docs. S/AC. 4/100, 116, 130 and 137, March 7, 10, 12 and 14, 1947.

[11] Smogorzewski, *op. cit.*, p. 67.

clude direct UN action against the Greek rebels, except as they used the international frontier to carry out strategic maneuvers in pursuit of the rebellion. By using the international force to separate the regular units of the Greek army from those rebel units encamped in Albania, Yugoslavia, and Bulgaria, the possibility of an explosive frontier incident might be reduced. Rebel tactics reported by the military observer teams of UNSCOB, such as firing upon Greek army units from Albanian or Bulgarian territory, using foreign territory to turn the flank of Greek forces, and the supplying of the rebels with arms and military supplies, could probably have been reduced by a contingent of the United Nations Force properly equipped for operations in mountainous areas.

The military situation at the time we posit for the intervention of the United Nations Force had deteriorated because Greek troops had been diverted from large-scale offensive action against the rebel-held massifs in order to defend the villages. This resulted in an all-over worsening of the military situation by September 1947. At that time the United States found "reliance must be placed on the creation by the UN General Assembly of a commission which can effectively seal the Greek border against assistance to the guerillas from Greece's northern neighbors."[12]

Assuming the non-cooperation of Albania, Bulgaria, and Yugoslavia, the operations of the UN Force would have been limited by topography on the Greek side of the frontier. It would not have been possible to seal off all rebel movements in these areas without very large commitments of UN forces, but a significant effort in this direction could have been made by the employment of several mobile units backed on the southern flank by units of the Greek army. The area of the Albanian frontier would be particularly difficult, because the mountainous areas held by the rebels straddled the frontier along a considerable sector, supported by a road network on the Albanian side only.

Resolution of the Greek crisis might have been speeded by the use of the UN Force to strengthen the observer network and to attempt to seal off the northern frontiers. As it was, the major

---

[12] U.S. Dept. of State, *1st Report to Congress on Assistance to Greece and Turkey for the Period ended September 30, 1947*, Publication 2957, Near Eastern Series II (Washington: U.S. Govt. Printing Office, 1947), pp. 14-15.

turning point came with the Tito-Stalin break in the spring and summer of 1948. But it was not until September 1949 that UNSCOB could report the virtual elimination of guerilla warfare along the northern Greek frontiers.

Assuming action by the General Assembly in October or November 1947, contingents of the UN Force could have reached positions along the frontier by March or April 1948, ready to occupy higher ground after the spring thaws. A loose estimate of the numbers needed would be 8,000 troops equipped for mountain fighting, with special attention to radio communications and mobility of reserve forces, and another 1,000 troops to expand the function of border observation and facilitate the efforts of the larger task group.

Successful operations by the UN Force might have speeded the processes of peaceful settlement by convincing the three northern states of their frontier obligations and of the necessity of peaceful relations with Greece. Even without such change or agreement on the part of Greece's neighbors, the Force could have substantially eased the threat to Greece. In the Greek case as in any crisis, the United Nations Force could have acted only within the terms of instruction of the General Assembly or Security Council; this could have been a not ineffective, if limited, role.

III. *The Indonesian Crisis*

Effective intervention of an international force during the Indonesian crisis poses very different considerations from those raised by the Greek case.

The Indonesian case is vastly more complicated. For one thing, it did not lead to the same possibility of determined political decision, except for the Communist states, that the Greek case did, until a very late stage in the crisis. The Security Council's competence was challenged by the Netherlands argument that the matter was within its domestic jurisdiction and therefore not subject to Security Council action. Hesitance of other colonial powers to support steps which could become precedents for future action against them also played a limiting role. Although United Nations action eventually contributed to an acceptable solution to the crisis, the records of the Security

Council to the time of the second Dutch "police action" in December 1948 show an unwillingness to take strong or effective measures, a hesitance to deal with or even discuss the substantive issues, and a pattern by which the Security Council in each instance settled upon the lowest common denominator of actions demanded of it, in each instance the maximum action it could take because it was the maximum acceptable to the Netherlands.

In view of the Security Council's hesitancy the assumption that a United Nations Force would have been used in the situation is entirely arbitrary. Such a decision would have required acquiescence of the colonial powers in the Security Council. If they had been willing to countenance so strong an action, the use of a UN Force would probably have been unnecessary. If France, Britain, Belgium, and the United States had been willing to maintain strong diplomatic pressure on the Netherlands in support of a strong position in the Security Council, the course of events would have been vastly different.

By the time the Security Council took up the Indonesian question on 31 July 1947, at the request of India and Australia, the Indonesian archipelago had been a trouble center for almost two years. The immediate cause of the Security Council's involvement was the Dutch police action of 20 July and the failure of subsequent efforts to bring about a cease-fire negotiated by the parties. But, before then, there was a history going back to 1945 of bloodshed involving, at first, the British occupation forces, and then the Dutch as the returning colonial power, and the newly formed Republic of Indonesia.

As early as January 1946 a Ukrainian resolution calling the situation in Indonesia to the attention of the Security Council was rejected as an attempt to divert attention from Soviet activities in Iran. There were a series of attempts at negotiation including an agreement reached at Linggadjati in Java in November of 1946, but signed on 25 March 1947 only on the basis that each side retain its own interpretations. The "premature agreement to agree"[13] at Linggadjati broke down because its vagueness provided no real basis to stabilize the situation. At root, the ob-

---

[13] William Henderson, *Pacific Settlement of Disputes: The Indonesian Question* (New York: Woodrow Wilson Foundation, 1954), p. 10.

jectives of the Dutch and the Indonesians were irreconcilable, and mutual distrust mounted throughout this period.

On 20 July 1947 the Dutch launched the first "police action" which included the movement of nearly 100,000 troops attacking at a score of points. Ten days elapsed before the large-scale hostilities in Indonesia were brought to the attention of the Security Council. By then Dutch troops had already plunged deep into Republican territory in a number of columns which cut off large pockets of Republican troops. By 26 July Acting Governor-General Van Mook had claimed the virtual completion of the first phase of military operations. The pattern established in this police action was to continue in the fighting during the next eighteen months: Dutch troops drove up river valleys, occupied the lines of communication, roads, railroads, major ports, and established bases in the major cities; Republican forces fell into defensive positions in the interior and in isolated areas and made preparations for a long-range guerilla warfare, relying immediately on a diplomatic offensive.

The need for speedy action by the Council was urgent. By couching the resolution in terms that avoided the constitutional issues, particularly by not specifically defining its competence to act under the Charter, the Council was able on 1 August to call on the parties, among other things, to cease hostilities and settle their disputes by "arbitration or other peaceful means." At this time, and subsequently, until the second Dutch police action in December 1948 completely altered the atmosphere, the Council could act only in ways that the Netherlands accepted as not infringing its sovereignty. Thus, it was not until the Council acted in response to the second police action that a UN Commission for Indonesia was established, with limited powers to intervene; until that time, the Council was represented in the field, at first, by a Consular Commission with power only to report on events and then by a Committee of Good Offices which was free, in effect, to help the parties maintain contact with each other but not, under its mandate, to make proposals to them or bring pressure to bear.

Although both the Netherlands and the Republic notified the Council, within several days after the 1 August Resolution, that cease-fire orders had been issued to their forces, the cease-fire in subsequent months was honored as much in the breach, as the observance. Broken by sporadic clashes, the cease-fire existed on a tenuous, day-by-day basis for the next months, with constant threats of renewed large-scale fighting owing to different interpretations of the cease-fire. The Dutch contended that the cease-fire line included all territory within a line drawn across the spearheads of their advance; the Indonesians resisted Dutch "mopping up" operations of these enclosed pockets by guerilla raids and occasional large-scale battles.

In this situation, the Consular Commission was woefully undermanned for even the limited duties it had to carry out.[14] A UN Force would have been useful as an adjunct to the Consular Commission in performing its limited reportorial responsibilities. In the circumstances that existed, more extensive use of a UN Force would clearly have been out of the question. Assuming the impossible, however, it might have been highly desirable to have a UN Force in the field to assist in separating and disentangling the opposing forces and, thereafter, in patrolling the cease-fire lines. For a UN Force to have been effective would have required several conditions that did not exist: a) willingness of both parties to accept use of the Force as a means of maintaining a cease-fire they wanted to preserve; b) a clear mandate to the Force setting forth the tasks it was to assume and the principles it was to pursue; and c) willingness in the Security Council to back up the Force with clear directives to the parties, supported by diplomatic and other necessary action.

As events actually unfolded, the basic reluctance of the Security Council to come to grips with the substantive issues of the Indonesian crisis limited the field organs, the Consular Commission and the Committee of Good Offices, to ineffectual roles and eventually contributed to the resumption of the so-successful Dutch "police action." The field organs could not do more than the Council, and the Council itself was not in a mind to advance real solutions to the issues with which the Commission and the Committee were struggling.

The Committee of Good Offices began to function slowly. Created by a resolution of 24 August 1947, it did not reach Batavia to offer its services until 27 October. It soon found that

---

[14] J. Foster Collins, "The United Nations and Indonesia," *International Conciliation*, No. 459 (March 1950), p. 135.

the Netherlands refused to accept suggestions on any substantive questions on the grounds that this lay beyond the function of a good offices committee. Despite such handicaps, the Committee eventually succeeded in drafting a compromise known as the Christmas Draft Message,[15] whereby the Republic was asked to accept the Van Mook demarcation line which linked all the Dutch spearheads in exchange for a promise of a fair and peaceful settlement of the political questions.

The draft message provided that troops would be withdrawn behind demilitarized zones on both sides of the demarcation line under supervision by UN observers who would continue to assist implementation of the agreement. It also provided that within three months of the signing of a political agreement the Republican civil administration would be restored and Netherlands troops withdrawn from the territories occupied under the police action.

This Christmas Draft Message went much too far for the Dutch; the counter proposal of 3 January omitted the restoration of Republican civil administration and withdrawal of Netherlands troops. The function of UN observers was weakened, and provision for termination of the agreement was included. Although this counter proposal meant surrender on many points, the Committee of Good Offices urged the Republic to accept it, under heavy pressure from the Dutch who issued a veiled threat on 9 January that their "police action" would be renewed unless the Republic accepted all the Netherlands conditions.

With the private but non-binding assurances of the Committee of Good Offices that the UN would continue to maintain interest in the peaceful settlement of the Indonesian crisis, the Republic yielded to the unequal bargain which was the Renville Truce Agreement, signed 17 January 1948, with additional principles on 19 January 1948.

At this point in the history of the dispute, employment of a UN Force would again have been useful. Such use would have required the Security Council to go much further than it was in fact willing to do. Rather than merely "accepting" the Renville Agreement, the Council would have had to agree to implement its provisions by introducing contingents of the UN

---

[15] For text, see United Nations Doc. S/649, Feb. 10, 1948, pp. 70-75.

Force into Indonesia beginning in the spring of 1948. Small units of the Force would assist in the observation of the truce, assist in troop withdrawals, patrol the cease-fire line, and assist in the implementation of other provisions.

The Renville Agreement would have provided adequate terms of reference for the UN Force, i.e. a basic political agreement sufficiently clarified to give instructions to an international force which itself could not decide political issues.

An alternative to assuming that the UN Force could have been dispatched to Indonesia following the conclusion of the Renville Agreement, would be the dispatch of the UN Force to Indonesia at the time of the second Dutch "police action" in December 1948. This would be a rather hopeless gesture, since the assumed size and composition of the international force would be insufficient even at maximum strength to deal with large-scale military operations of the scope of the Netherlands "police" action, which involved the bulk of the 120,000 men in the NEI armed forces, included paratroop assaults, tank attacks, full-scale amphibious landings, full air cover including use of heavy bombers, and a naval blockade.

Given the introduction of the UN Force into Indonesia after the conclusion of the Renville Agreement in January 1948, and resolute determination on the part of the Security Council to accept responsibility for a peaceful settlement, such as the determination evidenced in January 1949 after the second "police" action, the process of settlement in Indonesia might have been facilitated. Under the Renville Agreement the Force might have assisted in the withdrawal of over 25,000 Republican troops from the "pockets" enclosed by the cease-fire demarcation line accepted under the truce agreement. With the evacuation of the pockets of resistance, the Force might have been able to seek a minimal pullback plus the demilitarization of zones near the line, in order to allow the Force to patrol the line of demarcation and to effect an actual physical separation between the military forces. A further function, perhaps requiring more UN troops, would have been to assist in the implementation of the provision for a plebiscite contained in the Six Additional Principles incorporated in the Renville Agreement. The plebiscite was to determine whether the people of Java, Madoera, and Sumatra wished to be part of an independent Republic of Indonesia or to be incorporated in the federal United States of Indonesia contemplated by the agreement. The plebiscite was to be held from six months to a year after the signing of the agreement, and was to be supervised by the Committee of Good Offices if either the Netherlands or Indonesia requested its services.[16]

The pattern of UN Force involvement would be the initial dispatch of small units, in the neighborhood of one or two thousand men, for the initial supervision of the withdrawals from the pockets, with the dispatch of additional forces to take over the function of patrolling the demarcation line and creating a physical separation between the parties. A total UN Force of 10,000 to 15,000 troops could probably perform the necessary patrol functions, if backed by a determined Security Council and a strong Commission on the scene.

Given the presence of a United Nations Force, probably about 15,000 strong, exerting pressures for progress toward a peaceful settlement on the basis of the Renville Agreement, given a Commission for Indonesia with power to act in implementation of the provisions of the Renville Agreement, and given the expressed determination of the Security Council that the Indonesian situation was not to be resolved by further resort to arms but on the agreed basis reached under UN auspices, the gradual breakdown of the Renville Agreement that actually occurred might have been prevented. The presence of a UN Force might, in any event, have deterred the Netherlands from its second military adventure, the "police" action of December 1948. The United Nations Force would, of course, have been gambling that it would not be subjected to a full-scale military attack. The Force could not have resisted an attack such as that launched by the Dutch in December 1948, nor would its equipment have included the necessary heavy naval and air support to resist such an attack. But the existence of the Force would have been a factor with which the Netherlands would have had to reckon before launching a military action, not because of the military capacity of the Force itself but because of what it represented in terms of political decision and possible support in the Security Council and among other UN members.

---

[16] See *ibid.*, p. 97.

IV. The Kashmir Dispute

The dispute over Kashmir would have presented a good opportunity for the use of the United Nations Force in the process of peaceful settlement. India and Pakistan reached, at least nominally, an agreed basis for settlement of the dispute very early in the development of the crisis. In this case, the Security Council accepted its responsibility to deal with the situation, sent a Commission to the scene, and, over the past nine years, has made a long series of attempts to implement the agreed basis in the face of continued Indian obstinacy. To assume that a UN Force might have been used to break the stalemate over demilitarization of Kashmir, necessary before the holding of a plebiscite in Kashmir so that the people could choose between India and Pakistan, is not totally unrealistic.

The dispute was precipitated when some two thousand tribesmen from Pakistan invaded Kashmir in October 1947. Kashmir, under its Hindu Maharajah, thereupon acceded to India, following the procedure adopted by most of the princely states in joining either India or Pakistan in the partition of the sub-continent. Indian troops were rushed to the defence of Srinagar, the capital, and the battle was joined. At this stage, the army of Pakistan, under the command of General Sir Douglas Gracey, did not support the tribesmen.

In the first days of the dispute there were public statements from both sides that a free and impartial plebiscite had to precede a final solution of the conflict.

The insistence of Lord Mountbatten, Governor-General of the new Indian Union, that Kashmir's accession to India was provisional, to be followed by a plebiscite, was accepted by Prime Minister Nehru, and the principle was spelled out in Mountbatten's letter of 27 October 1947 to the Maharajah of Kashmir.[17]

On 1 November the Pakistan leader Jinnah made a proposal which is tragic because it so closely foreshadowed the basis of formal agreement to be reached after a full year of fighting. Jinnah proposed (1) an immediate cease-fire including a warning

---

[17] Josef Korbel, *Danger in Kashmir* (Princeton: Princeton University Press, 1954), p. 83.

to the recently-proclaimed Azad ("Free") Kashmir movement, (2) mutual withdrawal of all non-Kashmir troops, and (3) a plebiscite under the joint supervision and control of the two Governors-General.[18]

It soon became evident, however, that between statement of the principle and its acceptance in practice there was a large gap. In a message to the Prime Minister of Pakistan on 21 November, Nehru expressed determination to clear the tribesmen and vocal pro-Pakistan elements out of Kashmir before proceeding with any plebiscite plans.

By 1 January 1948 when India, charging that Pakistan had committed an act of aggression, submitted the Kashmir dispute to the United Nations under Articles 34 and 35, more than 200,000 Muslims had fled into Pakistan from Kashmir to avoid massacres of the pro-Pakistan civilians. The bloody communal fighting which had taken over a half million lives in the Punjab threatened to engulf all Kashmir.

From the first day of debate in the Security Council, India argued on the narrow grounds that Pakistan committed an act of aggression against India by permitting the tribesmen to invade Kashmir. Security Council calls for a cease-fire were not successful; Indian army movements, tribal attacks and local massacres of the Muslim population continued. Despite a resolution of 20 January to set up a United Nations Commission for India and Pakistan (UNCIP), no members were named and the Commission was not dispatched. Discussion, repeated exchanges of charges, and the fighting all continued apace. By May, regular Pakistani forces had joined in the hostilities although this was not known in the UN. India continued to maintain the validity of the hurried accession, thus justifying the presence of Indian troops, and to charge Pakistan with aggression. Pakistan denied the validity of the accession and claimed that the Muslim majority (61% in Jammu and 93.7% in Kashmir)[19] would vote for Pakistan if given a free election. Both parties agreed to the principle of a free election, although India insisted that her troops should remain, that they were legally present and could conduct a free plebiscite since the state of India overlooked religion as a basis for community.

---

[18] *Ibid.*, pp. 88-89.
[19] *Ibid.*, p. 6.

In a resolution of 12 April 1948, the Security Council instructed the parties to settle the dispute by peaceful means through a free and impartial plebiscite, with the aid and good offices of a UN Commission which would make arrangements for the plebiscite and arrange a cease-fire. Both governments objected to this decision, India mainly to the withdrawal of Indian troops on grounds that this would endanger the security of Kashmir, Pakistan to the lack of firm guarantees on the conditions for the plebiscite. But the UN Commission for India and Pakistan was ready to take on the job of achieving a quick peace and a solution in Kashmir. In the face of many obstacles, UNCIP managed to bring about an agreement on the means of settlement and a cease-fire on 1 January 1949.

Among other things, the agreement visualized: (1) a cease-fire in the State of Jammu and Kashmir at the earliest possible date; (2) a truce on the basis of the withdrawal of Pakistan troops and tribesmen, and the temporary administration of the evacuated area by the Azad movement, with the withdrawal as well of the "bulk" of the Indian Army and retention of the minimum of Indian forces necessary to assure law and order in Kashmir; and (3) political settlement involving a plebiscite to be administered by a Plebiscite Administrator of high international repute, nominated by the Secretary-General of the UN and UNCIP.

These terms, embodied in UNCIP resolutions of 13 August 1948 and 5 January 1949, were the foundations of settlement, a basis accepted by both parties, but little further agreement or actual implementation of the plan has been possible in the eight years since 1949, largely because of India's obstruction on the question of the demilitarization of Kashmir. Implementation has foundered on the meaning of the "bulk" of the Indian forces to be withdrawn. There was a further complication, i.e., the arming of the pro-Pakistan Azad Kashmir forces to form an irregular army of 32 battalions, or between 25,000 and 30,000 armed men. India's fear that a general evacuation of forces would leave the area defenseless is supported by Kashmir's geography, with 400 miles of frontier with Sinkiang, 450 with Tibet, 700 with Pakistan, perhaps 20 miles with the Soviet Union, 160 miles with Afghanistan, and 350 miles with India, nearly all mountainous and not determined by international agreement. In this situation a United Nations Force could have played a very helpful role.

The cease-fire of 1 January 1949 was assisted by the efforts of military observers, as provided in the Security Council resolution of 21 April 1947. The Indian Army in Kashmir at the time of the truce numbered some twelve brigades or three divisions, the Pakistan Army had six brigades in Kashmir, plus the Azad Kashmir force of six brigades or 32 battalions. These forces maintained a very uneasy cease-fire until a fixed cease-fire line was negotiated under UNCIP auspices in Karachi on 27 July 1949.[20] UNCIP initially requested forty military observers; the observer contingent has varied between thirty and forty officers plus assistants over much of the subsequent period. The military observers stopped many local incidents from spreading, dealing directly with the local field commanders, reporting through a network manned by civilian radio technicians, and using transportation supplied by each side as needed to cover the truce line which measured more than 500 miles through primitive and mountainous areas. One commentator concludes that the military observer groups were a "most useful tool for preserving a semblance of peace. . . ."[21]

All subsequent efforts to bring about demilitarization, by UNCIP, by UN Representatives Sir Owen Dixon and Dr. Frank Graham who succeeded UNCIP, in the meetings of Commonwealth Prime Ministers, have been unable to overcome Indian resistance. Pakistan accepted all resolutions of the Security Council, the resolutions of UNCIP, all but one of Sir Owen Dixon's draft proposals, and most of Dr. Frank Graham's recommendations, and was willing to submit the problem of demilitarization to arbitration. India refused on nearly every occasion to permit any reasonable demilitarization, which she viewed as the prior step or precondition to the holding of the plebiscite. India's obstinacy has held firm over the years, complete to the recent incorporation of Kashmir into India despite specific Security Council requests to the contrary, and Nehru's attitude has hardened to the point of refusing any possibility of foreign troops in Kashmir.

---

[20] United Nations Doc. S/1430, Annex 26, July 29, 1949.
[21] Sylvain Lourie, "The United Nations Military Observer Group in India and Pakistan," *International Organization*, Vol. 9, No. 1 (Feb. 1955), pp. 19-31.

In this situation, the use of a United Nations Force would have been of maximum benefit. A military intervention during the fighting, which involved forces totalling nearly 100,000 regular and irregular troops, would not have been likely, considering the limited size of a UN Force as sketched in Section I, the difficulty of access to the area of fighting, and the Security Council's reluctance to invoke Chapter VII of the Charter. Existence of a UN Force might have strengthened UNCIP's hand in the negotiations and thus brought about an earlier cease-fire, but it is doubtful the Council would have called for a large-scale intervention in the fighting, which until the UNCIP arrival on the Subcontinent was considered to involve only the Pathan tribesmen on the Pakistan side.

Let us, however, assume that the UN Force would have been used to implement the UNCIP resolutions of 13 August 1948 and 5 January 1949 which provide the political basis for the settlement. These resolutions would have furnished the basic terms of reference to the UN Force in its activities in Kashmir. The timing of the dispatch of the UN Force to Kashmir is not crucial, since the cease-fire held firm under the assistance of the Military Observer Groups. From the past record of the Security Council we may assume that the Council would have pursued its attempts to reach agreement on demilitarization and the holding of the plebiscite, as was actually the case until Indian intransigence became inescapably apparent. Let us assume that, with the failure of Sir Owen Dixon's efforts to reach agreement on the terms of demilitarization in the spring and summer of 1950, the Security Council would have decided to make use of the UN Force in Kashmir. This assumption is arbitrary; it ignores political obstacles including a possible veto by the U.S.S.R.

The report of Sir Owen Dixon and the reports of Dr. Frank N. Graham indicate some of the ways in which a UN Force might have been used in attempting to bring about demilitarization. One solution might have involved the Pakistan Army closing the frontier against further incursions of the tribesmen; similar disposition of the Indian Army might have closed the border with India. Within Jammu and Kashmir Provinces, a UN Force of 5,000 to 10,000 troops could have been aided by a civil authority recruited for local control against outbreaks of lawlessness, commanded by UN officers. The first phase of the operation would have been demilitarization, guarding and directing a staged withdrawal of the armed forces to the frontiers, and directing a partial disarmament of the Azad Kashmir forces as well as the pro-Indian civil militia organized by the Kashmir interim government. The second phase would have involved creating the preconditions of law and order necessary for the plebiscite. The cooperation of Pakistan in closing the frontier and guarding Kashmir against further attacks by the unruly tribesmen of the Northwest Provinces would have been assured by Pakistan's stake in the plebiscite; the appeal for India's cooperation would have been based on India's commitment to a plebiscite in Kashmir. The Himalaya uplands, Ladakh, Baltistan, Hunza, Nagir, and the Gilgit Agency would probably not have had to be occupied; the disposition of these sparsely-settled areas might have been achieved by arbitration or direct negotiation after the plebiscite. The provinces of Jammu and Kashmir, including the Vale of Kashmir, would have been occupied and the plebiscite would have taken place, in this scheme, after the restoration of law and order and a period in which the decision was explained to the populace.

Access to Kashmir could probably have been achieved most easily through Pakistan, as a railroad passes within thirty miles of the border. Direct air communication could have taken place by use of the airfield at Srinagar. The Force would have needed special equipment for mountainous operations, including transportation usable at altitudes up to 16,000 feet. The special radio communications network of the military observer groups would have been available to supplement Force communications in the field during the withdrawal of the military forces in the phase of demilitarization, and the observer groups could have been used to watch the frontiers after troop withdrawals and during the period of preparing and holding the plebiscite. Small units of the Force could have easily blocked the three main roads into Kashmir from Pakistan and India, as well as the caravan route to Tibet and Sinkiang.

As provided in the resolution of 5 January 1949, the Plebiscite Administrator and UNCIP would have directed the disposition of the armed forces of Pakistan, Azad Kashmir, and India, as well as the militia of the interim government of Kashmir. Political direction would have come from the Administrator, advised by UNCIP; the Force would have been charged with enforcing the withdrawal of the various armed forces, maintaining law and order, and observing the conditions of the plebiscite. Final arrangements might have been made before the plebiscite for the withdrawal of the Force in conjunction with the return of the forces of the country to which the plebiscite indicated the majority of the population wished to accede.

Within the framework of the political agreement reached by UNCIP, a UN Force might have played an active and valuable role in ending the Kashmir dispute through implementing the agreed means to a final settlement. Demilitarization and the plebiscite are the stumbling blocks which have obstructed the settlement of the Kashmir crisis over the past eight years: a decision of the Security Council to send in a UN Force might have made possible a final peaceful settlement.

V. *The Palestine Crisis*

Action by a UN Force in the Palestine fighting in 1948 would have been an enforcement action without the full power to effect a cessation of hostilities, an intervention without agreement on the full purpose of the intervention, and an emergency measure necessitated by the failure to provide adequate means to implement the plan for the partition of Palestine adopted by the General Assembly on 29 November 1947. The conditions normally necessary for use of a UN Force did not exist in the Palestine case. A minimum general agreement to accept the decisions of the UN was completely lacking. A decision to use a United Nations Force in the hostilities in Palestine would have had to be made in the full realization that the Force would have come under attack, would have engaged in large-scale fighting, and would not have been able to effect a military decision with its own power, although it might have been expected to play a significant role in bringing about a cease-fire and a *de facto* acceptance of some of the elements of the partition plan.

The assumption that a Force, if it existed, might have been used in this case is therefore remote from reality. It would be carrying imagination too far to assume that a UN Force would have been allowed to enter Palestine before the termination of the Mandate on 15 May 1948. The firm policy of the British Government, as Mandatory Power, would permit no such international force in Palestine while the Mandate was still in effect. Any movement into Palestine by an international force would have thus been blocked until at least four months after the fighting had begun early in 1948. The Force could not be in Palestine for an orderly take-over of the functions of the British occupation.

The role of a UN Force after the termination of the Mandate would have been dictated by the efforts of the Security Council to bring about a cease-fire. The UN Force, even assuming a strength of 20,000 troops, would not have had sufficient strength to impose a military decision upon the armies of Egypt, Lebanon, Transjordan, Syria, and Iraq; and the Security Council would not have seriously considered such a course until other avenues of agreement concerning a cease-fire had been explored. The British had been unable to keep order in Palestine with an occupation force of approximately 75,000 experienced troops; a UN Force could not have been expected to succeed against the massed armies of the Arab countries, even should the Security Council have found such an action warranted by the Arab behavior.

Fighting in Palestine had begun with the General Assembly's acceptance of the Plan for Partition with Economic Union on 29 November 1947. Attempts by the British to limit the fighting were not successful. After 15 May 1948 fighting became widespread and troops of several of the Arab States formally intervened. Through much of the spring, efforts by the Security Council and the UN Truce Commission set up by the Council to halt the fighting were unsuccessful.

The First Truce, of four weeks duration beginning 11 June, was finally achieved under the Council's resolution of 29 May 1948, which included a declaration that the Council would reconsider the situation in Palestine with a view to action under Chapter VII if the cease-fire was rejected or repudiated after acceptance. Fighting was resumed four weeks later, to be stopped by the strong cease-fire resolution of 15 July 1948, in which the Security Council determined that the situation in Palestine constituted a threat to the peace within the meaning of Article 39. The threat of enforcement action under Chapter VII for non-compliance with the cease-fire order brought about the Second Truce, which lasted with frequent violations and minor incidents to the conclusion of formal armistice agreements in 1949.

Granted a decision to use it, a United Nations Force could have been strategically deployed and well dug-in along the cease-fire line by the expiration of the First Truce, on 9 July. Presence of the Force, coupled with the Council's threat in the resolution of 29 May to invoke Chapter VII, might have prevented the second resort to hostilities.

The Arab determination to continue hostilities, thereafter, despite losses of territory they had suffered in the fighting thus far was an indication of a tenacity of purpose, a political and emotional commitment, a refusal to accept the existence of the new state of Israel, which was to make impossible the conclusion of a permanent settlement for many years. We cannot assume that the use of the UN Force would have had any ultimate effect upon the chances for a political settlement.

However, we may assume that a strong UN Force was introduced into Palestine during the first Truce, and that its presence as a symbol of UN determination to act might have prevented or limited the second outbreak of fighting at the close of the First Truce. An alternate assumption would be the introduction of the Force into Palestine at the time of the Second Truce.

In either case the UN Force might have taken over a number of the duties of the Truce Commission established 23 April 1948 by the Security Council. Belgium, France, and the United States, the only members of the Security Council with consuls in Jerusalem, comprised the Truce Commission. They provided fifty-one officers for the period of the First Truce; these were accompanied by fifty-one guards from Lake Success, plus seventy technicians recruited by the U.S. The same techniques were used to collect the 682 persons who formed the truce supervision organization under the Truce Commission for the Second Truce. This method of recruitment might have yielded to the use of detachments from the UN Force.

The military observers of the truce supervision organization in the Middle East had to keep track of fighting men and war material in Israel, Lebanon, Syria, Jordan, Egypt, Iraq, Saudi Arabia, and Yemen, an area of 1,250,000 square miles with a population of over 40,000,000 persons. Under the terms of the truce resolutions, the introduction of men, war materials, etc., anywhere in the Middle East would constitute a violation of the truce; thus the military observers had to keep supervision over all ports, airfields, lines of communication, roads, railroads, and canals. The manpower and organizational facilities of the UN Force might have been used to expand and improve the personnel involved in the immense job of supervision.

With the conclusion of the Second Truce the UN Force might also have undertaken a number of patrol functions which might have helped to maintain the Truce. Regular patrols of the cease-fire demarcation line, detachment of small units of the UN Force for supervisory assignment with each unit of the armed forces of the several Parties, establishment of demilitarized zones along the demarcation line and in the vicinity of the Holy Places, the demilitarization and international administration of Jerusalem, construction of access roads and fencing where necessary in increasing the efficiency of the patrols—all these would have been suitable extra duties for the UN Force assuming, as always, that the necessary preliminary agreement was obtainable. Fighting in Jerusalem in August and September 1948, continued clashes in the Negev in October and November, might have been handled rapidly by dispatch of mobilized units of the Force.

In the situation in Palestine, occasional outbursts of fighting, border raiding, and attacks on either side of the truce line could not have been *eliminated* by actions of the UN Force. Raiding bands would occasionally slip through the best patrols, and the unanswered problem of the Palestine Arab refugees in Jordan, Syria, and the Gaza area would be continued irritants for years to come. The Force might have been able to reduce such attacks by its patrol functions, by observation of the movements of civilians and soldiers, and by general vigilance as a symbol of continued UN interest.

A force, in summary, might have been useful for patrol duties and to augment the personnel and efficiency of the truce supervision organization after the conclusion of the truce agreements. During the actual fighting the Force could not have been expected to engage all the parties at once, but it might have acted to deter transgression of the lines set up by the General

Assembly partition resolution of 29 November 1947, to protect the Holy Places, and to form an international buffer between Arab and Israeli forces.

THE PROBLEM OF "CONSENT" IN RELATION TO A UN FORCE

by Charles P. Noyes

The purpose of this paper is to examine briefly certain aspects of the problems of obtaining the agreement of the members of the United Nations to make available contingents for a UN Force and of gaining "consent" to its use. The problem of "consent" is taken to cover all relevant questions relating to the willingness of host states, and other states directly involved, to permit such a Force to enter and operate on their territory and otherwise to cooperate with it. This paper, by its very nature, will emphasize the difficulties of establishing and using a UN Force. It does not deal with the many useful purposes that would be served by the existence and use of such a Force or with many of the factors which might lead states to agree to set up and employ such a Force. It deals with only a part of the over-all problem and does not purport to present a balanced view of the whole.

Four types of UN Force will be examined, starting with the present United Nations Emergency Force (UNEF), and adding additional elements intended to give the Force additional usefulness and strength. These are briefly stated here for convenience.

1. The present UNEF.
2. A UNEF type force with a permanent Command, with contingents specifically pledged and held in readiness subject to call by the UN in its own discretion under conditions outlined either in a General Assembly (G.A.) resolution or a treaty.
3. A stronger UN Force, ranging from 20,000 to 50,000 men, with heavier armament capable of and prepared for small-scale military operations.
4. The UN Force outlined in 3 above, combined with meaningful commitments by states to supplement the Force, if necessary.

Clearly, these hypothetical forces are confined within a rather narrow spectrum. We are not considering a military force capable of meeting great power aggression, or overt military action by a communist state against a member of the free world, and have ruled out the use of atomic weapons. Also not considered is a force composed of individual volunteers rather than national contingents. On the other hand we do propose to examine the question whether, and, if so, under what circumstances the Force could be used in a military operation against the military forces of a state.

At this point a brief description of the present UNEF seems necessary. It is an organized military force, comprising national contingents totalling some 6,000 men, with necessary supporting units. UNEF was created by the G.A. and is subject to its directives. It is a subsidiary organ of the UN subject to the orders of its Commander, General Burns, and policy control by the Secretary-General.

The Secretary-General is assisted by an Advisory Committee made up of seven nations—Brazil, Canada, Ceylon, Colombia, India, Norway and Pakistan. The Secretary-General is Chairman of the Committee and consults with it on plans and developments. The Committee itself reports to the General Assembly, and has the right to request a General Assembly session if necessary.

The Force is made up of a UN Command, officers recruited by the Commander individually from nations other than the five permanent members of the Security Council, and national contingents of military personnel accepted by the Secretary-General and placed under the Command by member states. The Command consists of officers of various nationalities. The national contingents come from the following states:

Brazil	India
Canada	Indonesia
Colombia	Norway
Denmark	Sweden
Finland	Yugoslavia

Fifteen other states have offered forces which have to date not been accepted by the Secretary-General. Contingents from the five permanent members of the Security Council are barred by the terms of the General Assembly resolution.

The Force is an organized military force flying the UN Flag and carrying light arms, with necessary supporting units, including medical, engineer, transport, signal, supply, workshop, provost, and post units and other army service elements. Members of the Force wear the uniform of the state to which they belong except for blue UN helmet liners and armbands.

UNEF was established, among other things, "to secure and supervise the cessation of hostilities." The Secretary-General had made clear that the Force was limited in its operations to the extent that consent of the parties concerned was required under generally accepted international law. While the General Assembly was able to establish the Force when members agreed to contribute contingents for the purposes set forth in the G.A. Resolution, it could not station or operate the Force on the territory of a given country without the consent of that country. The Secretary-General also emphasized that the Force was not intended "to influence the military balance in the present conflict and, thereby, the political efforts to settle the conflict." Nor was the Force to be used for "an enforcement action against a member country" or "with a view to influencing a withdrawal of forces." It was "not a Force with military objectives" and, while more than an observers corps, it was "in no way a military force temporarily controlling the territory in which it was stationed."

Egypt, on whose territory the Force would have to be stationed, accepted the idea of the Force. Over a period of time in a series of actions, Egypt consented to the entry and operation of the Force, and ultimately reached written agreement with the UN regulating the status of the Force.

The other parties to the conflict, having agreed to a cease-fire and to withdraw their forces from Egypt, accepted the use of the Force as a buffer between their withdrawing forces and the hostile forces of Egypt. Israel has not yet agreed, however, to the entry of UNEF on its territory, even though the Assembly has approved its placement "on" the Armistice Demarcation line.

The agreement on the status of forces in Egypt is quite far-reaching in its implications. It is based on the principle that the Force is an organ of the UN and shall therefore enjoy in the territory of its members the privileges and immunities necessary to the fulfillment of its purposes, and in particular those set forth in the Convention on the Privileges and Immunities of the United Nations. Officers of the Command have the same rights as members of the Secretariat, but the individual members of the national contingents are treated on a special basis with limited rights exempting them from taxation, customs, and fiscal regulation. The Force itself, as distinguished from its members, is given what amounts to extra-territorial status, with very broad freedom of action within its area of operation, and rights of access, communication and supply. Its bases and military camps are inviolable. The agreement is effective until the Force is withdrawn from Egypt.

The UN is bearing the entire financial cost of the Force other than payment of regular salaries to the members of the national contingents and the provision of their initial equipment. The cost to the UN for the first year will be around $20,000,000. No decision has been reached with regard to the final allocation of these expenses among the member states.

Analysis

UNEF ITSELF

What are the problems of "consent" involved in the establishment and operation of UNEF as presently constituted? As far as the "host" states are concerned, they are not bound by the Charter to accept recommendations of the General Assembly involving the operation of UNEF on their territory. The Secretary-General in his report to the Assembly which it accepted made it clear that this is a basic principle of international law and of the Charter. The application of this principle places any prospective host country in a position to place conditions of various kinds on the operation of UNEF in its territory. In the give and take of the diplomatic bargaining that has taken place between the UN and Egypt, the latter has gained certain important points and has given way on others. Egypt was successful, for example, in rejecting the participation in the Force of contingents from Pakistan, and in restricting the Canadian participation to certain types of personnel. The resulting Force is heavily weighted with national contingents from nations sympathetic to her cause and perhaps even subservient in the final analysis to her will. In a crisis, Egypt by putting pressure on India, Yugoslavia and Finland to withdraw their contingents could probably emasculate the Force. Egypt was also successful in clarifying the purpose and functions of the Force to her advantage. Efforts to give it an occupation task in the Canal Zone failed at an early stage. Similar efforts in the Gaza strip were only partially and temporarily successful and are being frustrated step by step by Egypt's gradual assertion of her legal rights.

From the practical as well as the legal point of view the continuing consent of the host state seems essential to the functioning of UNEF. How could the UN maintain a particular activity or position in the face of insistent demands by the host state that it cease or withdraw? The Force is small, poorly armed, and its line of communications is difficult to protect. Its contingents probably are subject to withdrawal under pressure from Egypt. Any intimation by the Secretary-General that the Force might be ordered to stand its ground against Egyptian armed forces would raise the most difficult practical questions for the nations whose contingents were included in the Force. It seems probable that in the face of a show of force by Egypt to back up a demand, the UN Force would have no alternative to complying under protest. The Secretary-General probably could not, as a practical matter, whatever the legal rights in the situation, take the responsibility for an order which would involve the UNEF in a military action with the host state.

The above considerations apply equally to Israel in the current situation, in her capacity as a prospective host state. Her consent is essential to the operation of UNEF on her side of the armistice line, and she therefore is in a position to bargain regarding conditions. So far Israel has not even accepted in principle the suggestion of the Secretary-General that UNEF be stationed on the Israel side of the frontier. It may be doubted that UNEF as presently constituted will ever be accepted by Israel, in view of the unbalanced makeup of the Force. But assuming this could be overcome, it seems evident that the terms and conditions of such consent would amount to a diplomatic bargain between Israel and the UN, and perhaps Egypt as well.

What about the consent of states directly concerned other than host states? Legally it is clear that the UN may recommend military action against a nation violating the Charter and may with the consent of the nation threatened send forces to its assistance. Israel's consent was in no legal sense a requisite to the establishment or operation on Egyptian territory of UNEF. Nor was the consent of the United Kingdom or France. From the point of view of practical diplomacy, however, the willingness of these three states to accept the basic recommendation of the

Assembly that they withdraw their forces from Egypt and cooperate with UNEF provided the basis for UNEF's establishment in its present form and size, and with its present functions. The "consent" of these states to the broad purpose of the Force as well as their detailed cooperation in the field was obtained—very easily in the case of Britain and France, which had proposed its establishment. UNEF was used successfully to help secure the cessation of hostilities and act as a moving buffer during the withdrawals of the British, French and Israeli forces from Egyptian territory. The Force clearly served a vital diplomatic and even "police" function throughout this operation.

There is a real question whether the UNEF could act effectively in such a situation without such cooperation. If Israel had refused to leave Sharm el Sheikh, for example, or should in the future declare her intention of conducting a reprisal raid in force against the Gaza strip, could the UNEF serve a useful purpose? Again it seems most doubtful as a practical matter that the Secretary-General would deliberately commit UNEF to a military engagement with the armed forces of a state, even though those forces were illegally operating on the territory of another state. The responsibility of the Secretary-General to the states providing contingents and to the men themselves would appear to require a decision to avoid an obviously costly and hopeless military engagement under these circumstances. Any such issue would have to be referred to the diplomatic level for solution.

Acceptance of this conclusion still leaves a wide area within which UNEF can usefully serve the purposes of the UN and strengthen its capability for maintaining an uneasy truce. Its presence is a diplomatic factor of considerable weight. It may serve a particularly useful purpose in controlling and preventing mob action, unofficial para-military or volunteer raiding activity. As long as the state involved does not acknowledge responsibility for such action by its nationals and is prepared to acquiesce in UNEF taking military or police action against them when they are involved in this kind of activity, UNEF may be able to use its limited military force effectively.

A UNEF TYPE FORCE

The first proposal we shall examine for strengthening UNEF involves placing it in its present form and substance on a permanent basis readily available for some future crisis. Specifically we shall assume that all aspects of UNEF remain unchanged except that the General Assembly would establish a permanent UN Command and would arrange for small power contingents to be specifically pledged and held in readiness subject to call by the United Nations in its own discretion under conditions outlined either in an Assembly Resolution or a treaty.

Such an arrangement should enable the UN to mobilize and concentrate UNEF in short order upon a two-thirds vote of the G.A. Participating states would have agreed in advance to provide contingents and presumably they would have expressly or impliedly agreed also not to withdraw their forces without consent of the UN. The General Assembly could therefore act with speed and with knowledge of its power to establish and maintain a UN Force. These are additional elements of strength compared to the present situation.

What are the prospects that the smaller UN members will agree to contribute contingents to a permanent UNEF on this basis? The experience to date, in the Korean and Suez situations and with the Collective Measures Committee's efforts, indicates that the prospects are poor. Some steps forward toward a permanent UNEF may be possible, but it seems unlikely that states will be willing for some time to come to pledge specific forces to UNEF and hold them in readiness subject to call by the UN in its own discretion. This would mean that states would have to agree in advance to permit the call-up and use of their contingents in unknown future circumstances anywhere in the world upon a two-thirds vote of the General Assembly. The contingents could be used against the interests of friendly states and in support of unfriendly states. Even if military action against the forces of states by the "neutral" UNEF here considered were ruled out, it is doubted that the smaller member states would be willing to bind themselves to such an arrangement. Procedurally speaking, the possibility of getting meaningful advance commitments to contribute forces to UNEF by means of a General Assembly resolution seems legally and practically almost insuperable. It could of course be done by treaty, but the problems of working out a fair and workable arrangement and getting member states to adopt and ratify it make this course seem remote.

Assuming such an arrangement were feasible, what would its implications be on the willingness of host states to permit UNEF to operate on their territory? It seems evident that a host state would have greater difficulty in accepting such a Force than the present one. A host state could be expected to screen more carefully the nationality of the contingents called up, since by definition they would not be withdrawn by the contributing country at the host state's request. If a host state were not permitted to veto contingents from states considered hostile or untrustworthy, it might refuse consent entirely. Since the host state's control of the situation in future contingencies would be less, it could be expected to demand greater definition in advance of the specific purposes, functions, and areas of operation, and perhaps formal guarantees against modifications by the General Assembly and particularly the Secretary-General without its consent. The means for control of the Force would become of greater importance to the host state. The question of its confidence in the two-thirds majority group which set the Force in motion in the particular case, in the Secretary-General's objectivity in the situation, in the makeup of an Advisory Committee of the Assembly, would assume added significance.

Similar considerations are relevant with respect to the attitude of states directly involved which are not host states. The added effectiveness of the Force to the UN by the same token increases the difficulties and dangers for them, for almost by definition they will face an unfriendly two-thirds majority in the General Assembly. Questions of definition of function and procedures and sources of control of UNEF in the light of changing circumstances become matters of prime importance for them in determining the extent of their cooperation with UNEF. However, the fact that the host state could not veto contingents or force their withdrawal might eliminate one source of difficulty found in the present situation, and provide, in the eyes of such states, a less unbalanced and more trustworthy instrument to the UN. They would have less cause to fear that the UN could be forced to acquiesce in unreasonable demands by the host state.

On balance the modifications of UNEF here assumed are probably not of sufficient importance to states directly involved to affect in a major way the possibility of their cooperating with it.

In summary this variation of UNEF would be a moderate improvement on the current model, adding significant advantages in the speed with which it could be mobilized. It would be extremely difficult to establish such a Force initially. Once established, the Force might be less acceptable to host states than the present UNEF, but, if accepted, would be a somewhat more trustworthy and effective instrument for the UN within the limits of its agreed mission.

A FORCE CAPABLE OF SMALL SCALE MILITARY OPERATIONS

Let us now add two additional elements of strength to UNEF —more men and heavier weapons, and the intent that in certain circumstances it shall engage in active military operations. Let us assume a maximum Force of 50,000 men drawn by the UN at its discretion from contingents held in readiness by member states just as in the previous hypothesis. What new problems of acceptability does such a fighting force raise among possible host states and other states involved in a dispute? Also what new problems does it involve relating to the acceptability of the Armed Force to contributing states?

If we disregard for the moment the possibility of the use of this Force for active military operations against the organized forces of a state, we can conclude in general that it is simply a more powerful version of the Force discussed above. It would therefore be more effective within the limits of its competence, particularly against para-military or other guerrilla forces. Other than this the problems of consent are basically unchanged.

Once we admit the possibility of organized military action by a substantial UN Armed Force against the forces of a state, several very important questions arise for all concerned. Armed action of this type is coercion. Of whom? To what end? How and with whose help? Coercion is a continuing process and must be controlled, modified, and brought to a conclusion. By what bodies and procedures? To a prospective host state or state directly involved, these are not merely important but crucial questions.

The functions of such a Force can hardly be defined in the same terms as those of the present UNEF. Its purpose would clearly be, under certain circumstances, to "influence the military balance in the conflict and, thereby, the political balance." It would have military objectives and could be given occupation duties, or other tasks involving enforcement action against states. By definition it is no longer purely a neutral organ of the UN, but an element of military power which could be used by the UN for certain purposes to carry out its policies.

This change of character raises many questions indirectly related to questions discussed in this memorandum. Can a Force of this type have the same status as the present UNEF as an organ of the UN? The Convention on Privileges and Immunities seemingly would be stretched well beyond its authors' intentions if it should be held to cover such a military Force. There is a question whether it would be appropriate for the Secretary-General to have control over such a military Force. There are a number of questions as to how far the General Assembly is entitled to go in utilizing such a Force. It can recommend, as in the Korean case, that members join in assisting a state which has been attacked by an aggressor, something which they are already entitled to do under Article 51 of the Charter. It has no authority to invoke sanctions as such under Chapter VII. How far can the General Assembly go in backing up its recommendations for a peaceful solution of disputes between states by a military Force under its control? Is it entitled to occupy territory on its own terms, or to seek to impose particular truce terms or terms of settlement? These are difficult questions, and they are all relevant to the attitude of member states considering participation in such a Force *ad hoc,* and more particularly in committing themselves in advance to provide contingents in the future on UN call. They are also relevant to the attitude of host states and others involved in a particular crisis.

Let us speculate for a moment on the problem this kind of a UN Force presents to a host state, Egypt for example, in the Suez situation. Egypt would have seen immediately that such a Force would have the military capability to occupy the Canal Zone or alternatively Gaza and/or Sharm el Sheikh, and resist efforts to oust it. Once established on Egyptian territory, it could conceivably be used for a number of purposes not originally stated explicitly or agreed upon by Egypt. While legally Egypt might be entitled to demand its withdrawal, the UN could as a practical matter refuse and face Egypt with the necessity of a substantial military action against the UN in an effort to gain its objective. The consequences of such a decision to take military action would of course be extremely grave for Egypt's relations with all members of the UN and particularly those participating in the Force. While the position of host states may remain legally unchanged from previous alternative hypotheses, in practice they will have lost the greater part of their bargaining power once they admit such a Force to their territory. Questions of confidence in the Assembly majority, of definition of the functions of the Force in all conceivable circumstances and of the procedures and sources of control of the Force become crucial issues. One would expect a host state, even if in a desperate situation, to insist on commitments to guard against all foreseeable contingencies before giving its consent to the operation of such a Force on its territory.

Similar considerations apply even more urgently in the case of states directly involved other than host states. They must weigh the possibility that this Force may take military action in unforeseen circumstances against their forces in support of an unacceptable political objective of the UN either alone or in collaboration with the military forces of the host state. They are almost by definition the primary objects of the coercive power of such a Force, and of the coalition of UN states who are ultimately controlling it. They are unlikely to have much confidence that this majority will use its power fairly and may well be led to feel that they must meet strength with strength. The element of coercion that has been injected may involve an unacceptable loss of face, and may make the cooperation of states directly involved less likely and the tasks of diplomacy more difficult.

The problem of establishing this type of Force in advance of a crisis by treaty among member states appears formidable. A non-fighting Force of 6,000 men is very different from a 50,000 man fighting Force. It is difficult to conceive of small states being willing to commit themselves in advance to entrust substantial contingents of their forces to future military decisions of the General Assembly and the Secretary-General. If they undertook such obligations and observed them, their contingents could be forced into military action against a friendly state regardless of whether they approved the Assembly's policies or voted against them. They could be dragged against their better judgment and their will into embarrassing and even impossible situations by an unknown and perhaps shifting coalition of member states. The positions of the great powers, probably always crucial for the success of any military use of a small power UN Force against small powers, could not be foretold. Few countries have strong enough political systems to enable them to undertake and carry out the kind of advance commitment here proposed.

A FORCE CAPABLE OF SMALL SCALE MILITARY OPERATIONS COMBINED WITH MEANINGFUL COMMITMENTS BY STATES TO SUPPLEMENT THE FORCE IF NECESSARY

What new problems arise if we add to the Force considered in the previous section the element that certain member states would be committed to provide reserve contingents in the event that such reinforcements were needed? It seems evident that to the extent that this proposal provides a larger Force at the call of the UN, it would strengthen the hand of the UN, and provide greater assurance of its capability to cope with a crisis. The proposal also involves the so-called "plate-glass" concept. The suggestion is that such reserve commitments provide an important military deterrent, which would give a relatively small UN Force the power of a larger one. This idea may not stand up well under analysis. Clearly, the plate-glass concept relates only to military action against the forces of a state; it has little meaning in relation to military action against guerillas. A plate-glass or trigger Force can be effective if an attack upon it, while immediately successful, will trigger off military consequences which the attacker is not prepared to face. Such military consequences should be certain, quick, and on a scale that is unacceptable to the attacker. Those in control of the plate-glass Force must be sure enough of their deterrent power to be willing to risk the loss of the plate-glass Force.

The UN always has a strong diplomatic deterrent supporting any UN Force in the field, and the implication is strong, if undefined, that it would not permit its forces to be defeated without a major military reaction. There is a legitimate question as to whether the addition of the specific military deterrent provided by the proposed reserve commitments would add greatly to the effectiveness of a UN Force. The reserve forces, while they might be brought to bear more quickly than if no commitments had been made in advance, probably still would take many days, if not weeks, to get into action. The opposing military staff would know in advance the exact status of the UN reserves and could be expected to appreciate fully the relative strength of the UN from a military point of view. There would perhaps be an implication that these reserves constituted an upper limit of forces available to the UN in a particular situation. Unless the reserve commitments were very substantial, it may be that such a system would provide in fact a weaker deterrent than would exist without it. In any event, it does not seem an important element of additional deterrent strength.

MILITARY ASPECTS OF A PERMANENT UN FORCE

by Lt. Col. Charles A. Cannon, Jr.,* U.S.A.
and
Lt. Col. A. A. Jordan,* U.S.A.

I. *Introduction*

The Carnegie Endowment for International Peace has initiated a study of the prospects and possibilities for the creation of a permanent United Nations Force. This particular paper attempts to lay out some of the major considerations and questions of a military nature attendant to the establishment of such a Force, and sets forth some tentative proposals for its organization and employment. Not considered in this paper is the question of whether the United States should support the creation of a permanent UN policing organization; but rather, *if the United States decided to support the creation of a permanent UN Force,* what kind of force should be sought?

On the one hand, it is clear that a large, standing force, capable of sustained combat or of meeting major aggression, should be ruled out since this concept does not represent a feasible goal for the near future. In fact, in view of past and present difficulties between the West and the Soviet bloc, the enforcement provisions and machinery of Chapter VII of the UN Charter cannot and should not be relied upon as bases for the Force. On the other hand, if any type of permanent UN Force is to be established, the successful experience of the United Nations Emergency Force makes feasible a more ambitious approach to the problem than was possible prior to November, 1956. Consequently, the Project Committee for this study has given the authors the task of exploring the military aspects of creating a permanent international force of moderately ambitious, closely defined limits, i.e., not less than 6,000 nor more

---

* The views presented are those of the authors writing as private individuals. They do not represent the views, position, or policies of any government agency.

than 50,000 men, capable of police and limited combat operations, responsive to the General Assembly and prepared for immediate employment.

II. *Assumptions*

A. The UN Force should be designed to execute surveillance, patrol, riot control, and other police type duties, and should be capable of defending itself for a limited time if attacked by small, organized or irregular hostile forces while it is engaged in maintaining or restoring order in an area. The Force will not be utilized in situations in which it would have to make airborne or amphibious assaults in hostile territory or to engage in sustained combat operations against organized national forces.

B. The Force must be capable of operating in any type of terrain or climate, with or without local base facilities, and under conditions ranging from the full cooperation of a local government and populace to the covert or outright hostility of certain elements of the populace. It is not anticipated that the Force will attempt to remain in a country if the host government tries seriously to eject it.

C. If the UN Force is forcibly opposed and cannot handle the situation, it will either be withdrawn or quickly assisted by the national forces of UN member states. It will be unnecessary, therefore, initially to provide plans for major reinforcements or replacements of men and material in the UN Force.

D. It is considered unwise to attempt to move to the optimum force in one leap. Therefore, realistic plans must provide for a carefully phased build-up, designed to achieve the simplest, least controversial gains in the first steps — with the more complex and controversial moves to follow. Furthermore, it seems reasonable to expect that, on achievement of even a relatively small and simple Force in being, the very fact of its existence would facilitate the later objective of developing it into a better equipped, highly mobile Force more capable of policing tense areas or deterring moves against the peace.

III. *General Concept of the Force*

The proposed force will initially be a simple, lightly armed infantry Brigade of approximately 7,000 men. It will be constituted from national contingents contributed by "small" nations (i.e., not permanent members of the Security Council), rather than from individual volunteers. Initially, the force will be essentially a grouping of national contingents (under their own officers and using their own equipment), responsive to the international direction of the General Assembly. The General Assembly will commit and control the forces through an Enforcement Committee, the Secretary-General, his Deputy for Enforcement, and a military staff section (headed by a carefully selected general officer as chief) within the Secretariat. In order to increase its effectiveness and to emphasize its international character, the Force will subsequently be assembled at an international base, trained as a unit, provided with additional and standardized arms, equipment, and tactical transport, and be given the additional personnel required by this augmentation. The cost of the force will be borne by apportionment to all the UN members, except those contributing troops, and with due allowance for any facilities, services, or equipment donated by any members.

IV. *Details of the Proposed Force*

A. The initial organization proposed (see Figure 1) is a Brigade, consisting of two regiments, or six battalions, of 24 line companies with a strength of 200 men each. Six special companies for logistics, maintenance, and administration will be maintained at Force Headquarters. National contributions will be made in packages of company or battalion size for a two-year period. Each contingent should include sufficient personnel and equipment for field duty, e.g. individual arms, clothing, equipment, mess, unit medical personnel, and communications equipment (see note to Figure 1). Since the basic infantry or rifle company is common to most present day armies, such units can most readily be adapted to the structure of the UN Force Brigade. It will be necessary for the more technically developed countries to offer the specialized units shown in Figure 1.

B. Activation of such a Force will entail the following steps (note that although generally in chronological order, several of these can and should be carried out simultaneously):

1. Proposal and adoption of the general concept by the General Assembly.

2. Appointment of an "Enforcement Committee" of the General Assembly composed partially of representatives of countries willing to contribute forces and partially of other members on a rotating basis. The Enforcement Committee, assisted by the Defense Section of the Secretariat discussed below (see Figure 2), would prepare the necessary detailed resolutions for the establishment and maintenance of the UN Force to be presented to the General Assembly.

3. Establishment of a Defense Section within the Secretariat to advise both the Secretary-General and the Enforcement Committee. The Defense Section should consist of internationally recruited, experienced military officers. Divisions of the Defense Section should include the normal personnel, intelligence, plans and operations, supply and civil affairs staff sections, plus other special sections as required, e.g., a special legal section will probably be required to deal with such problems as defining the legal status of members of the Force, developing appropriate regulations for the Force and negotiating required status of forces agreements. The chiefs of sections should, as far as possible, be drawn from or trained by the present UNEF staff. The senior member of the Defense Section, a carefully selected general officer, would be designated Chief of Staff to the Secretary General and/or his Deputy for Enforcement. The Chief of Staff would have no command authority but would serve as the link between the UN Force Commander and the Secretary-General (or his Deputy) for the transmission of orders and reports. The Defense Section should develop plans and procedures for steps 5 through 9, below.

4. Appointment by the Secretary-General of a UN Force Commander, also a carefully selected general officer, for a three- or four-year period. This appointment should be endorsed by the Enforcement Committee, or perhaps the entire General Assembly. He should pick his own staff, including therein nationals from the nations contributing forces.

5. Provision for a garrison location with necessary facilities for the Force. The general area of North Africa would seem most promising for this international base, although an island located in the Mediterranean, Indian Ocean, or Eastern Atlantic might also be considered. If a U.S., British or French base in Libya, Tunisia, Morocco or French West Africa could be made available, with hospital, depots, airfield, barracks, seaport, training areas, and communication facilities, the establishment of the force could be greatly simplified and expedited. It would require up to one thousand international civil servants and local laborers, in addition to the maintenance personnel of the Brigade, to maintain and service a small base with the kinds of facilities mentioned above.

6. Negotiation of commercial air and sea charter arrangements to move the force to its base and, if necessary, to operational areas (see Figure 3). Since commercial charters cannot be relied upon exclusively, the UN Force should have back-up arrangements made with UN members having the air-sea capability to move the Force.

7. On establishment of the base, the UN Force Commander would move there to receive the national contingents which should be phased in by Battalions at intervals of about 30 days. Rotation of these units after two years of service would have to be staggered to avoid a complete turn-over of personnel in a six-month interval.

8. Following the six-month build up, the UN Force Commander would initiate a phased training program to:

a. Develop an effective force with the initial organization and (national) equipment. Emphasis should be on communications, patrol, riot control, and anti-infiltration training.
b. In the last six months of the first two-year cycle, receive replacement units on a phased basis so that new units can begin training for a further modification of the force at the start of the second two-year cycle.

9. Second two-year cycle modifications would include (see Figure 4):

a. Reorganization of one company in each Battalion as a mobile reconnaissance unit on receipt of additional arms, communications equipment, and transport.
b. Addition to appropriate units of sufficient (about 150) armored personnel carriers (preferably tracked amphibious, US type) to give armor protection and mobility to approximately two battalions of the force.
c. Addition of sufficient personnel and light machine guns, recoilless rifles, and heavy mortars to organize one Heavy Weapons Company per Battalion.
d. Beginning of standardization of individual arms, equipment, and field uniforms. This should start as early as possible, perhaps in the first two-year cycle, since it will be vital if the force is called on for strenuous activity. Standardizing on the arms and equipment of a European neutral such as Sweden or Switzerland would simplify the establishment and functioning of the UN supply pipelines which would become a necessity upon standardization.
e. Addition to UN Force Headquarters of an Air Staff Section and a Light Aviation Company (fixed wing). If the national forces can be secured it would also be desirable to attach a helicopter unit to the Light Aviation Company to provide additional personnel and cargo lift capability within the area of operations. If the base has the facilities, it would further be desirable to establish a Naval Staff Section in Force Headquarters and to add a patrol boat or motor launch unit, capable of patrolling a river line or of providing limited tactical water lift for small units.

C. The two-year commitment and staggered, package rotational policy would apply to all personnel in national contingents except individuals evacuated for medical, disciplinary, or other reasons of unsuitability. The General Assembly should seek to have contributing members agree to earmark personnel, who have completed a two-year period of service with the UN Force, as a special reserve available for emergency recall for one or two years following completion of their service. Thus, the equivalent of an additional UN Force Brigade could be made available 30-60 days after call.

D. Pay of personnel should remain a national responsibility, but the UN should undertake the cost of transportation or extra equipment for national contingents. Consideration should be given to raising all personnel to an equitable pay scale by the use of UN funds, paid at the base as a "station allowance."

E. Rough estimates of the overall cost to the UN per man per day under the cheapest conditions (including training at the base, minimal amounts of extra equipment, and the costs of rotation of units) would be between $8.00 and $10.00 per day, or $60,000 to $70,000 per day for a 7,000 man force. This initial cost of approximately $25 million per year does not include funds for the acquisition or building of a UN base. Moreover, if the Force were committed, its expenses would certainly leap upwards — depending on the location and level of activity — and costs might go as high as double the "cheapest" figure.

FIGURE 1

INITIAL ORGANIZATION
(First two-year cycle)*

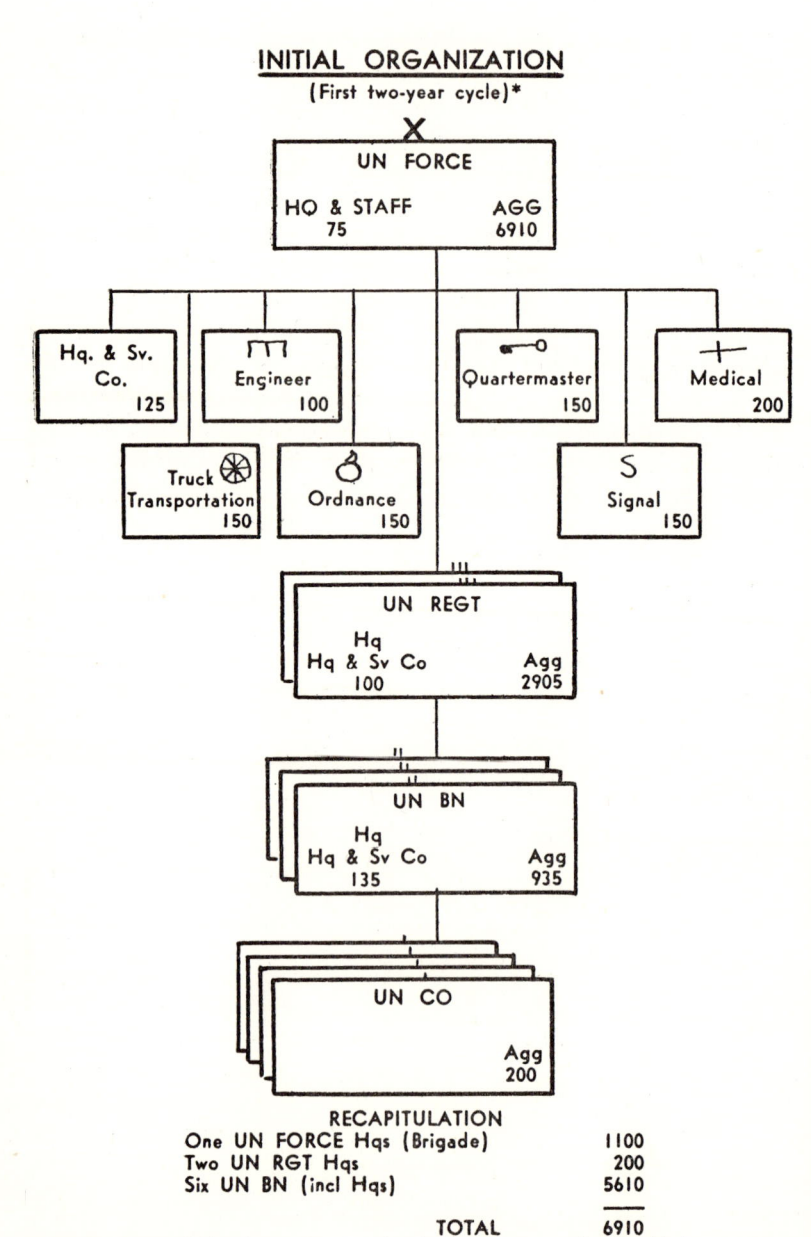

```
                          X
                    ┌───────────┐
                    │ UN FORCE  │
                    │HQ & STAFF │
                    │ 75    AGG │
                    │      6910 │
                    └─────┬─────┘
```

| Hq. & Sv. Co. 125 | Engineer 100 | Quartermaster 150 | Medical 200 |

| Truck Transportation 150 | Ordnance 150 | Signal 150 |

```
                    ┌───────────┐
                    │  UN REGT  │
                    │    Hq     │
                    │Hq & Sv Co │
                    │ 100   Agg │
                    │      2905 │
                    └───────────┘

                    ┌───────────┐
                    │   UN BN   │
                    │    Hq     │
                    │Hq & Sv Co │
                    │ 135   Agg │
                    │       935 │
                    └───────────┘

                    ┌───────────┐
                    │   UN CO   │
                    │       Agg │
                    │       200 │
                    └───────────┘
```

RECAPITULATION

One UN FORCE Hqs (Brigade)	1100
Two UN RGT Hqs	200
Six UN BN (incl Hqs)	5610
TOTAL	6910

*NOTE: One of the first steps in the first two-year cycle should be to standardize communications equipment providing FM voice radio in Co and Bn nets and AM radio in Regt and Brigade nets.

FIGURE 2

COMMAND AND CONTROL ARRANGEMENTS

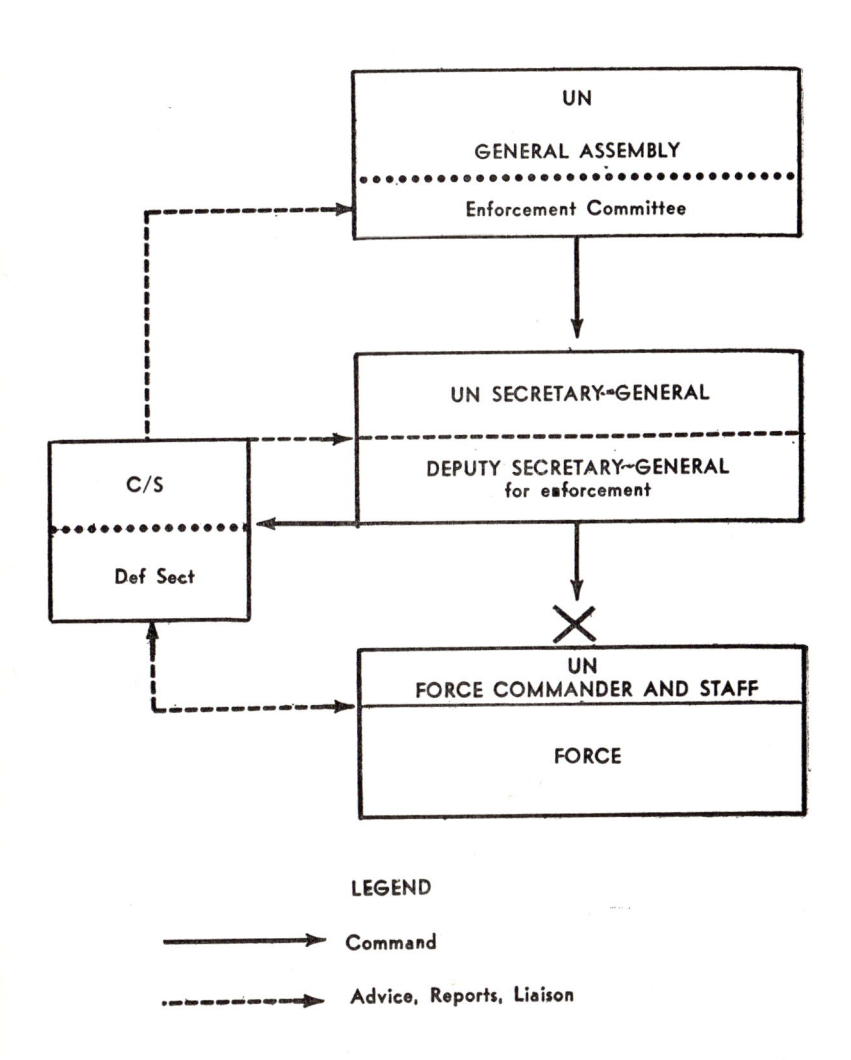

```
                    ┌─────────────────────────────┐
                    │             UN              │
                    │     GENERAL ASSEMBLY        │
                    │·····························│
                    │    Enforcement Committee    │
                    └─────────────────────────────┘
                                  │
                                  ▼
                    ┌─────────────────────────────┐
                    │    UN SECRETARY-GENERAL     │
   ┌────────┐       │                             │
   │  C/S   │       │  DEPUTY SECRETARY-GENERAL   │
   │········│       │       for enforcement       │
   │Def Sect│       └─────────────────────────────┘
   └────────┘                     │
                                  ▼
                                  ✕
                    ┌─────────────────────────────┐
                    │             UN              │
                    │  FORCE COMMANDER AND STAFF  │
                    │                             │
                    │           FORCE             │
                    └─────────────────────────────┘
```

LEGEND

⎯⎯⎯⎯⎯► Command

------► Advice, Reports, Liaison

FIGURE 3

LOGISTICAL ARRANGEMENTS

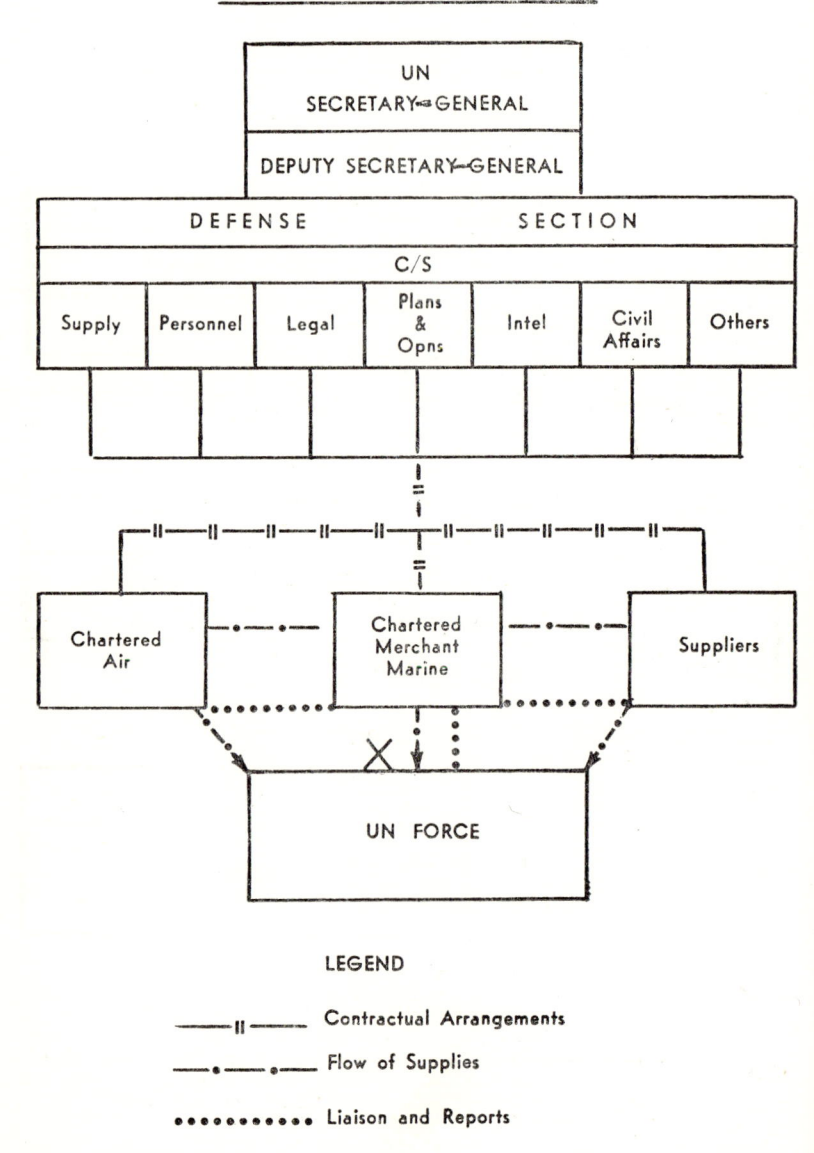

```
┌─────────────────────────────────┐
│        UN SECRETARY-GENERAL      │
├─────────────────────────────────┤
│     DEPUTY SECRETARY-GENERAL     │
└─────────────────────────────────┘
┌───────────────────────────────────────────────────┐
│  DEFENSE              SECTION                      │
├───────────────────────────────────────────────────┤
│                    C/S                             │
├──────┬─────────┬──────┬──────┬──────┬──────┬──────┤
│Supply│Personnel│Legal │Plans │Intel │Civil │Others│
│      │         │      │ &    │      │Affairs│     │
│      │         │      │Opns  │      │      │      │
└──────┴─────────┴──────┴──────┴──────┴──────┴──────┘
```

┌──────────┐   ┌──────────┐   ┌──────────┐
│ Chartered│   │ Chartered│   │   │
│   Air   │   │ Merchant │   │Suppliers │
│   │   │ Marine │   │   │
└──────────┘   └──────────┘   └──────────┘

┌─────────────────────────────────┐
│   UN FORCE   │
└─────────────────────────────────┘

LEGEND

——||——   Contractual Arrangements

——•——•—— Flow of Supplies

•••••••• Liaison and Reports

FIGURE 4

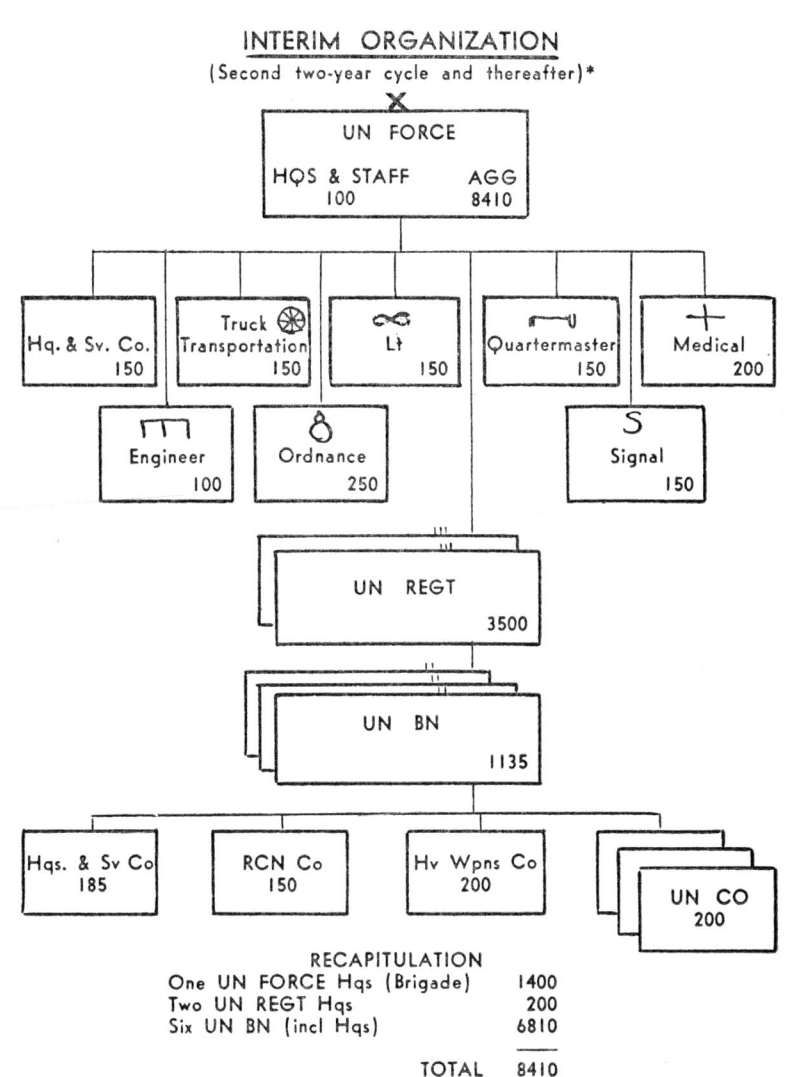

INTERIM ORGANIZATION
(Second two-year cycle and thereafter)*

UN FORCE
HQS & STAFF 100
AGG 8410

- Hq. & Sv. Co. 150
- Truck Transportation 150
- Lt 150
- Quartermaster 150
- Medical 200
- Engineer 100
- Ordnance 250
- Signal 150

UN REGT 3500

UN BN 1135

- Hqs. & Sv Co 185
- RCN Co 150
- Hv Wpns Co 200
- UN CO 200

RECAPITULATION
One UN FORCE Hqs (Brigade) 1400
Two UN REGT Hqs 200
Six UN BN (incl Hqs) 6810

TOTAL 8410

*NOTE: Although not shown in the organization chart, the following additional units would be highly desirable if they could be provided: A cargo and personal helicopter Co; a naval staff section and a patrol boat or motor launch Co; an airborne capability (parachute qualified personnel, equipment, and air transport) in company or battalion size in lieu of one of the regular UN companies or battalions.

EFFORTS TO ESTABLISH INTERNATIONAL POLICE FORCE DOWN TO 1950

by Leland Goodrich

The idea of an international police force, i.e., an armed force organized and used under an international agreement or decision to assist in the maintenance of international peace and security, is much older than the United Nations, both in conception and in application.

An early example of an embryonic international police was the allied force which went to the relief of the foreign legations in Peking at the time of the Boxer Rebellion in 1900. The force consisted of 18,600 men, representing five countries. There was no unified command; it was necessary that the commanders of the cooperating national forces confer each evening, or when necessary, to determine military movements. It was agreed that a majority vote should decide.[1]

League Experience

When the Covenant of the League of Nations was being drafted, neither the British nor the Americans favored the organization of an international force to assist in keeping the peace. President Wilson's idea was that members should use their military forces if necessary to keep the peace but that these forces should remain strictly under national control. A plan proposed by a French Ministerial Commission provided, however, for an international force, composed of national contingents, to be placed at the disposal of the international organ (Council) to assist in executing its decisions and to overcome in case of need any forces opposed to the League in case of conflict.[2]

---

[1] A. S. Daggett, *America in the China Relief Expedition* (Kansas City: Hudson-Kimberly Publishing Co., 1903), pp. 55-57.
[2] David Hunter Miller, *Drafting of the Covenant* (New York: G. P. Putnam's Sons, 1928), Vol. 2, pp. 241-46.

As finally approved, the Covenant did not expressly provide for an international force, though it permitted the organization and use of such force by agreement of the members if circumstances made it appear desirable. For the suppression of aggression, the Covenant relied primarily on sweeping economic and financial sanctions, backed by the broad commitment of Members to guarantee the territorial integrity and political independence of each other against external attack. In only one instance, the plebiscite in the Saar Basin in 1935, was use made of an international force though not on the scale, or for the particular purpose of suppressing the illegal use of force by a state, which the French plan had envisaged. In that case, a force of 3,300 men, comprising national contingents from four countries, was made available to assist in maintaining order in the area.[3] In one other case, the abortive proposal in 1920 to hold a plebiscite in Vilna to determine its future in the dispute between Poland and Lithuania, detailed plans for an international force were made but were not carried out.[4]

The Concept of an International Force in the Drafting of the Charter

In the discussions that took place in the United States Department of State about the establishment of an international organization to take the place of the League, a central problem was that of making adequate armed forces available to the Executive Committee or Council for enforcement action in case of violation of the peace.

Once it was agreed in principle to use the method of national contingents placed at the disposal of the international organization, it became necessary to find answers to other questions relating to the application of this principle. What was to be the size of each national contingent? How was the size to be determined? What was to be its composition? How were necessary facilities, installations, and bases to be provided? Who

---

[3] See F. P. Walters, *A History of the League of Nations* (London: Oxford University Press, 1952), Vol. 2, pp. 586-98; and Sarah Wambaugh, *The Saar Plebiscite* (Cambridge, Mass.: Harvard University Press, 1940).
[4] Walters, *op. cit.*, Vol. 1, pp. 105-09 and 140-43.

would determine when the contingents would be called into service? When called into service, under whose control would they be? Would the effectiveness of the international force require any limitation of national armaments, and how would this be brought about? These and other questions were discussed at great length at various levels of responsibility and final United States proposals were submitted to the Dumbarton Oaks conferees in 1944.[5]

These proposals provided that an "executive council" of eleven members in which the United States, the United Kingdom, the Soviet Union, China, and later France should have permanent membership, should have primary responsibility for the maintenance of international peace and security. By two-thirds vote, including the concurring votes of the permanent members, the Council was to have the power to determine the existence of any threat to the peace, breach of the peace, or act of aggression, and to decide the measures necessary to maintain or restore peace. In case measures not involving the use of force were inadequate, the Council was to be authorized to direct the use of armed force. Member states were to undertake "to furnish forces and facilities when needed for this purpose at the call of the executive council and in accordance with a general agreement governing the number and types of forces and the kind and extent of facilities to be provided." The Council was to assist in the formulating of such an agreement and in doing so was to "take account of the geographical position of the member states, their regional or special obligations, their population, and their relative resources." Member states were to obligate themselves to maintain these forces "in condition of effective readiness." Pending the conclusion of such an agreement, the signatories of the Moscow Declaration of October 30, 1943, and other states in the position to do so were to provide the forces and facilities needed for the maintenance of peace.

Provision was also made for a "security and armaments commission" (the Military Staff Committee of the Charter).

---

[5] U. S. Dept. of State, *Postwar Foreign Policy Preparation, 1939-1945*, Publication 3580 (Washington: U. S. Govt. Printing Office, 1949), pp. 602-03.

Advised and assisted by this body, the executive council was to be responsible for planning and exercising general supervision over any use of military force which the Council might find necessary.

The United States proposals were accepted in substance by the other Dumbarton Oaks conferees with only minor changes. "A special agreement or agreements" was substituted for the one general agreement of the United States plan. Any reference to considerations to be taken into account in determining the size and nature of national contingents was omitted. Although the United States proposals did not make special provision for air units among the national "forces and facilities" to be furnished, it was agreed at Dumbarton Oaks to include a provision that national air force contingents should be held immediately available by members of the Organization to enable urgent military measures to be taken. Furthermore in the text to which the conferees agreed, the "security and armaments commission" of the United States proposals became the "Military Staff Committee." It was made responsible for the strategic direction of the armed forces placed at the disposal of the Council. It was expressly stated, however, that "questions of command of forces should be worked out subsequently."

At San Francisco, the proposals of the Sponsoring Governments, embodying in substance the United States plan, were accepted with little change, in so far as provisions relating to the organization and use of an international force were concerned.

Efforts to Conclude Agreements Under Article 43

Since the Charter provided in Article 43 that forces were to be made available under agreements to be concluded between the Security Council and individual Members or groups of Members, it was clear that the Council would have to decide on the principles governing the size, composition, organization, equipment, supply and use of such forces and facilities as might be placed at its disposal. The Security Council requested the Military Staff Committee, as its first task, "to examine from a military point of view the provisions contained in Article 43 of the Charter and to submit the results of the study and any recommendations to the Council in due course."[6] The report of the Committee, submitted on April 30, 1947, was in the form of forty-one articles.[7] Although the Security Council examined the report in some detail during eleven sessions between June 4 and July 15, 1947, and approved all of the twenty-five articles upon which unanimous agreement had been reached by the Committee, it was unable to resolve the deadlock that had developed in the Committee over key issues, reflected in the sixteen articles on which there had not been agreement. Discussions thus came to a standstill, and it became apparent that agreements under Article 43 could not be concluded in the absence of a definite improvement in the political atmosphere. In 1950 and 1951, the General Assembly urged the Security Council to make renewed efforts to implement Article 43, but the deadlock continued.

The members of the Committee unanimously agreed that the armed forces made available to the Council should be composed of "the best trained and equipped units"[8] of the Member states' land, sea and air forces. They also agreed that the "moral weight and the potential power behind any decision to employ the Armed Forces . . . will be very great, and this fact will directly influence the size of the armed forces required."[9] Nevertheless, the forces should contain sufficient strength to permit the Council to take prompt action in any part of the world.

Disagreement existed with respect to the strength and nature of armed forces to be made available to the Security Council. A wide divergence existed between the views of the United States and the Soviet Union. The United States' position was that since the problem facing the United Nations was that of enforcing peace "in all parts of the world, . . . the United Nations needs, first of all, a mobile force able to strike quickly at long range and to bring to bear, upon any given point in the world where trouble may occur, the maximum armed force in the minimum time."[10]

---

[6] Security Council, Official Records (S.C.O.R.): 1st Yr., No. 1, 23rd Mtg., Feb. 16, 1946, p. 369.
[7] S.C.O.R., 2nd Yr., Special Supple. No. 1, *Report of the Military Staff Committee*, April 30, 1947, pp. 1-32.
[8] *Ibid.*, Art. 4, p. 1.
[9] *Ibid.*, Art. 5.
[10] S.C.O.R., 2nd Yr., No. 43, 138th Mtg., June 4, 1947, p. 956.

The estimates of strength that the United States delegation to the Military Staff Committee presented reflected an emphasis on mobile and striking weapons, such as air force and navy. Furthermore, the quantitative estimates were far in excess of those submitted by other delegations, especially the Soviet Union. The United States estimated that the force might comprise, *inter alia*, 1250 bombers, 2250 fighters, 20 ground divisions, 3 battleships, 6 carriers, 15 cruisers, 84 destroyers and 90 submarines. The U.S.S.R., on the other hand, submitted an estimate of 600 bombers, 300 fighters, 12 ground divisions, 5-6 cruisers, 24 destroyers and 12 submarines.[11]

The Soviet position in regard to the strength and nature of United Nations armed forces was that "in the present situation, it would be sufficient for the Security Council to have at its disposal relatively small armed forces."[12] The Soviet view derived a measure of support from the assumption quite generally made from the beginning that these forces, by virtue of Article 27 (3), would not be used against a permanent member. Furthermore, it appeared to find support in Article 5 of the Report of the Military Staff Committee in which moral weight and potential power behind a Council decision were deemed factors influencing the size of the forces required.

The United Kingdom, France and China also favored small forces, largely, no doubt, because of their inability to make large contributions. Thus, the French delegate maintained that a system of total security would raise practical problems which in present circumstances would be insoluble:

> We should bear in mind, however, that if we could set up a system of security applicable to all conflicts other than those which might arise between permanent members of the Security Council, we should not only achieve something unprecedented in history, but we should also introduce far more security even into relations between the great Powers. The events of the past few years have made it sufficiently clear that minor conflicts have usually preceded major conflicts, and that the former have often been the cause of the latter.[13]

---

[11] See *ibid.*, Supple. No. 13, pp. 133-35; and *Yearbook of the United Nations, 1947-48* (New York: U.N. Dept. of Public Information, 1949), p. 495.
[12] S.C.O.R., 2nd Yr., No. 44, 139th Mtg., June 6, 1947, p. 968.
[13] *Ibid.*, No. 46, 141st Mtg., June 16, 1947, pp. 1007-08.

The Military Staff Committee agreed that the five permanent members of the Council were initially to furnish the major portion of the Forces, while all United Nations members were to have the obligation to place facilities at the disposal of the Security Council if needed for the fulfillment of its tasks. But the Soviet Union and the other permanent members did not agree about the relative size of the contributions of permanent members. The United States contended that in view of the differences in size and composition of the national forces of the permanent Members and "in order to further the ability of the Security Council to constitute balanced and effective combat forces for operations," all the permanent members should contribute *comparable* forces and facilities and, particularly, those elements that they were best able to contribute. The United States, the United Kingdom, France, and China agreed that each nation was to be given the right to offer such forces as it considered reasonable and proper. Each nation would also have the right to contribute armed forces equal to those contributed by other members. Equality was not to mean, however, that "every element of every component . . . would be limited so that it must be equal in strength and composition to the weakest corresponding component or element. . . ."[14]

The Soviet position was that the contributions of the permanent members of the Council should be *equal* both in over-all strength and in composition. "The principle of equality," the Soviet representative argued, ". . . is based on the provisions of the United Nations Charter which place the main responsibility for the maintenance of international peace upon these States," and it "preserves the equal status of the permanent members in respect of the decision on this important question."[15] "The principle of comparable contributions," he said, would lead to a situation in which some members would enjoy "a predominant position as compared to others. . . It might lead to use of the armed forces in the interests of individual powerful States and to the detriment of the legitimate interests of other countries."[16] This danger would stem from the fact that "various types of armed forces do not have identical functions. There is not only

---

[14] *Report of the Military Staff Committee, op. cit.*, p. 12.
[15] S.C.O.R., 2nd Yr., No. 43, 139th Mtg., June 6, 1947, p. 966.
[16] *Ibid.*, p. 968.

the numerical aspect to be considered when deciding the whole problem of placing armed forces at the disposal of the Security Council by agreement, but also the qualitative aspect. If we consider this qualitative aspect of the armed forces, then we shall understand why such a danger exists."[17] However, as a minor concession to reality, the Soviet Union proposed that the Council might excuse a permanent member, at its request, from making an equal contribution.

It was agreed by the five permanent members, however, that irrespective of what principle should govern the contributions of permanent members, the size of contributions of *all* Member nations should be determined by the agreement or agreements concluded by the Security Council with Members concerned. The size of these forces and facilities could not be changed by the will of the Council without the negotiation of a new agreement. Should a state, other than the five permanent members of the Security Council, be unable to contribute armed forces, it might be expected to furnish facilities and other assistance in fulfillment of its obligations under the Charter.

In regard to the provision of Article 45 that members make air forces available to the Council, the positions of the Soviet Union and other permanent members were completely at variance. The Soviet position was that requirements "of national air force contingents . . . immediately available . . . should be based solely on the provisions of Article 43 of the Charter."[18] The other permanent members took the view that the total strength, composition and readiness of national air force contingents to be made available to the Council under Article 43 agreements should be determined in part by the special obligations arising from Article 45.

Still another difference arose among the representatives of the Military Staff Committee when the Chinese and French delegations alone submitted an article envisaging use by a Member state of the armed forces previously made available to the Security Council in the event of self-defense or national emergency.[19] As defined by the French delegate, national emergency would be understood to include "serious national cataclysms such as floods,

---
[17] *Ibid.*, No. 58, 157th Mtg., July 15, 1947, p. 1295.
[18] *Report of the Military Staff Committee, op. cit.*, Art. 16, p. 13.
[19] *Ibid.*, Art. 17, pp. 14-16.

fires, or extraordinary atmospheric occurrences" and "cases when the Government of a Member Nation . . . would be threatened by a faction which would attempt to seize power by illegal means." The United Kingdom, the United States and the Soviet Union delegations maintained that cases of self-defense were adequately safeguarded by Article 51 of the Charter and that the Charter, on the other hand, "makes no specific provision for the release of a Member Nation from its obligations under the Charter in the event of a national emergency." Furthermore, since a precise definition of "national emergency" was difficult to obtain, the inclusion of the term in the Military Staff Committee's report might leave a loophole for states to evade their responsibilities.

In regard to the provision of Article 43 that Members are to make available to the Council, in addition to armed forces, "assistance and facilities, including rights of passage," the Soviet Union insisted on an interpretation that would exclude the provision of bases. Although bases would be provided by agreement between the Member state and the Security Council, foreign troops would nonetheless be continually stationed in territories or waters of other states, thus violating their sovereignty and encouraging the possibility that the bases "would be utilized by some States as a means of exerting political pressure on other nations which provided such bases."[20] Furthermore, the Soviet representative insisted that "the demand for bases contradicts one of the main tasks of the United Nations, the development and strengthening of good-neighbourly relations among States," by constituting a continual source of friction. He also objected to a "general guarantee of rights of passage" on the ground that any state is free to decide whether or not it will grant these rights and, if it does, on what terms.

The other permanent members, however, took the position that provision should be made in the agreements for the use of bases, and, with the exception of France, they felt that there should be "a general guarantee" of the rights of passage and of the use of bases with the proviso that details of this broad guarantee be incorporated in the original or in subsequent agreements. "This is necessary in order that the Security Council may have the freedom of action in planning for the employment of

---

[20] S.C.O.R., 2nd Yr., No. 44, 139th Mtg., June 6, 1947, p. 970.

Armed Forces resulting from the assurance as to the availability of existing bases."[21] The French representative was opposed to general guarantees, but proposed, rather, that specific responsibilities and duties be negotiated and listed in the special agreements.

A similar schism occurred among the major powers regarding the location of the armed forces while not in action. The United States, Great Britain and China held that "Armed Forces . . . when not employed by the Security Council will . . . be based at the discretion of Member Nations in any territories or waters to which they have legal right of access."[22] They considered too restrictive the French position, which called for an enumeration of places where stationing might occur by means of specific agreements under Articles 82 and 83 of the Charter. The Soviet view again reflected concern that the presence of forces of one state within the territory of another, even on the basis of agreement, would constitute a means of political pressure. The U.S.S.R., therefore, proposed that such forces should be stationed within the frontiers of the contributing member, except in cases of action against former enemy states, envisaged in Article 107 of the Charter.

On the questions relating to the manner of employment of armed forces, the members of the Military Staff Committee were in agreement that forces made available to the Council should be employed only by the latter's decision and only for the period necessary to fulfil the task envisaged in Article 42. It was also agreed that use of these forces, whenever possible, should be initiated in time to forestall or to suppress promptly a breach of the peace or act of aggression. Thus, the national contingents had to be held in a special degree of readiness. The Military Staff Committee would be responsible for their strategic direction, while the command of the national contingents would be exercised by Commanders appointed by their national states. On the organization of command, China, the Soviet Union, and the United States favored a provision for an over-all commander, or over-all commanders, without any mention of service commanders, while the United Kingdom and France favored making provision for service commands as well. The five great powers were,

---
[21] *Report of the Military Staff Committee, op. cit.*, pp. 5, 22.
[22] *Ibid.*, pp. 6-7.

however, agreed that the armed forces, when not operating under the Council, "shall be under the exclusive command of the respective contributing Nations."

On the principle governing withdrawal of the force once its mission had been completed, there was again disagreement between the four powers and the Soviet Union. The majority opinion was that the Security Council should not be too rigidly restricted although withdrawal should occur "as soon as possible" in accordance with the provisions of the arrangements governing the location of forces. The application of enforcement measures by the Security Council necessarily varies according to different disputes and, as a result, the conditions of withdrawal cannot be precisely delimited. The U.S.S.R. urged that the forces be withdrawn to their own territories and territorial waters within a time limit of 30 to 90 days after they have fulfilled the measures envisaged in Article 42 of the Charter. A delay in the withdrawal of troops would, according to the Soviet Union, only benefit "certain great Powers contributing armed forces," and would harm the interests of small nations. Nevertheless, under certain circumstances, delay would be justified for a period exceeding the time limit of one to three months. "However, in such a situation the Security Council may take an appropriate decision on postponement."

On the question of logistical support, all the permanent members of the Council were in agreement that Members should provide their respective forces with necessary replacements in personnel and equipment and with all necessary supplies and transport. Specified levels of reserves "to replace initial personnel, transport, equipment, spare parts, ammunition and all other forms of supply" should be maintained by the Member states themselves.

With the exception of Poland, the non-permanent members of the Security Council generally subscribed to the majority positions. The Australian delegate pointed out that the report omitted any adequate definition of the tasks which the United Nations Force would be called upon to perform. Arguing that a definition of these tasks should be one of the first steps in all military planning, he stressed the fact that these tasks would also essentially affect the composition, organization and equipment of forces, in addition to influencing the type of training which component units must be given. He believed that neither the Council, nor the Military Staff Committee, nor the Member governments could proceed without a clearer formulation of them.[23]

Failure of the Security Council to agree on principles governing the conclusion of agreements under Article 43 made it impossible for the Military Staff Committee to make any progress in establishing levels of strength of the national contingents to be made available to the Council. The failure of the Security Council and the Military Staff Committee to reach decisions necessary to the implementation of Article 43 was not due primarily to technical difficulties. It was primarily the result of a political impasse. This was explicitly stated by the Soviet representative in the course of his argument for the principle of equal contributions when he said:

> . . . I should like to draw the Security Council's attention to the fact that the whole question of armed forces being made available to the Security Council by the United Nations under special agreements is not only, and not so much, a technical question as a political one. It is a political problem and should be decided as such. Obviously, in the settlement of this problem there will also arise a number of technical questions which the Security Council will decide in the course of negotiations with the States which make armed forces available to the Security Council. I think, however, that no one will deny that, as I have pointed out, this whole question is political. If we bear this in mind, we cannot take such a light view of the Soviet proposal for equal contributions as certain representatives do.[24]

As a result of this impasse, the Security Council was never provided with armed forces that would enable it to exercise its powers under Article 42 of the Charter.

With the failure of efforts to conclude military agreements under Article 43 of the Charter and thus make available to the Security Council forces and facilities which it could use in the exercise of its powers under Articles 39 and 42 of the Charter, a central part of the Charter system of peace-enforcement failed to become operative. The authors of the Charter had foreseen the likelihood of a transitional period during which this condi-

---

[23] S.C.O.R., 2nd Yr., No. 44, 139th Mtg., June 6, 1947, p. 985.
[24] Ibid., No. 50, 146th Mtg., June 25, 1947, p. 1009.

tion would exist, even under more favorable political circumstances, and had made provision for it in Article 106. Since, however, the condition in fact assumed the character of relative permanency and was due to the failure of the major powers themselves to agree, there was little likelihood that there would be the cooperation among them, looking toward joint action, required to make Article 106 effective.

On one occasion, consideration was given to the possibility of joint action by the permanent members of the Security Council. Following the report of the Palestine Commission that it was unable to implement the plan of partition for Palestine recommended by the General Assembly in November 1947 without the assistance of an effective armed force, the representative of Colombia proposed in the Security Council on February 24, 1948, that the permanent members of the Council be invited to consult, in pursuance of Article 106, with a view to joint action on behalf of the United Nations.[25] However, this proposal was subsequently withdrawn. It was obvious that the growing distrust and hostility that marked relations between the Soviet Union and the Western powers[26] ruled out any possibility of joint military action in Palestine.

The Korean Experience

At the time of the North Korean attack on the Republic of Korea on June 25, 1950, the situation as regards the possibility of United Nations military action was roughly as follows: The Security Council was not in the position to order military measures. While the Security Council might recommend military measures under a liberal interpretation of Article 39, there was no precedent for such a course of action and no serious thought had been given to the procedures that would be followed. Furthermore, there was no very substantial reason for believing that the Security Council would be able to make such a recommendation in a situation where the vital interest of a permanent member would be adversely affected.

Notwithstanding, when informed that the Republic of Korea had been attacked by armed forces from the north, the United

---

[25] S.C.O.R., 3rd Yr., 254th Mtg., Feb. 24, 1948, pp. 292-93.
[26] The Communist *coup* in Czechoslovakia occurred on Feb. 25, 1948.

States Government promptly brought the situation to the attention of the Security Council and took the leadership in proposing measures to be taken. By so doing it brought its own action within the framework of the United Nations and thus obtained broad support for specific measures which it probably would have felt impelled to take in any case. If the Soviet representative had returned to the Council at this time after his absence since January in protest against the seating of the Chinese Nationalist representative, and had used his veto, the United States probably would have sought to bring the matter before the General Assembly. This, however, would have meant a delay which, in view of the fast-moving developments in the military situation in Korea, would have made United States military action in advance of any United Nations decision seem necessary. Since the Soviet representative did not appear at the June 25 meeting of the Council, or subsequently until August, it was possible to get prompt Council action.

1. *Initiation of Collective Measures*

Without advance planning and with continuing uncertainty as to whether and when the Soviet representative would take his seat in the Council, it was necessary to improvise and act on a day-to-day basis in determining the specific steps to be taken. The United States, by virtue of its stake in the future of Korea and the availability and readiness of its armed forces for use, assumed the leadership in the Council in proposing measures to be taken.

From the time of the North Korean attack to August 1 when the Soviet representative resumed his seat, the Security Council adopted resolutions which helped to establish the need of collective measures under the Charter, recommended to members that they take them, and provided the broad framework of organization and direction of the military measures taken. The resolution of June 25 called upon the North Korean forces to withdraw to the 38th parallel and called upon Members to support this action. When informed by the United States and by the United Nations Temporary Commission in Korea that this withdrawal had not been undertaken and that there was no indication that it would be, the Council on June 27 recommended that Members give assistance to the Republic of Korea. The declared purpose of this assistance was to repel the invasion and restore international peace and security "in the area."

The fact that the military attack was overt and deliberate and was initially successful in overcoming the resistance of Republic of Korea armed forces made the rendering of immediate military assistance necessary if the Republic was to be saved. Faced with a rapidly deteriorating military situation in Korea, President Truman on June 26 ordered United States air and naval forces to the support of the Republic. He thus acted in advance of the Security Council's resolution of June 27 and based his action on the terms of the June 25 resolution. Thus United States forces in the Far East under the command of General MacArthur were committed to action well in advance of the arrival of armed forces of other Members. On June 30 United States ground forces were ordered into action.

2. *Response of Members to Council Recommendation*

The Council's recommendation of June 27 was communicated by the Secretary-General to Members on June 29 with the request that they indicate what assistance they were prepared to give. The responses varied greatly.[27] Some members—the Soviet Union and its satellites—denied the validity of the Council resolution on the ground that it had been adopted in the absence of two permanent members. Others—notably the Arab Members—declared they would not give assistance to an aggressor, but took a non-committal attitude towards the Council's recommendation. Still others—especially the Latin American Republics—indicated a general willingness to cooperate but were vague as to the specific assistance they would give. Some Members indicated specific measures they were prepared to take, including the dispatch of units of their armed forces. Generally speaking, these were Members which were associated with the United States in collective self-defense arrangements or had been receiving military aid from the United States and looked to it for support in case of attack. The Secretary-General interpreted fifty-three of the responses as favorable in principle and subsequently addressed more specific requests for assistance to the Members in this category.

---

[27] For summary of replies received, see *Yearbook of the United Nations, 1950* (New York: U.N. Dept. of Public Information, 1951), **pp. 224-29.**

3. Processing of Offers of Armed Forces

The initial offers of military assistance were promptly communicated to and acted on by the United States Government. Once the United States had agreed to organize a unified command, a standing procedure was developed for utilizing armed forces offered by other Members. These offers were made to the Secretary-General who in turn communicated them to the United States representative at headquarters. Preliminary informal discussions often helped to ensure that offers would be of the kind that would be used to advantage. The United States representative transmitted the offer to Washington. Detailed arrangements for the utilization of the assistance were made following bilateral discussions between the United States officials and representatives of the contributing state. Subsequently a formal agreement was concluded defining the conditions under which forces were to be utilized.

Two problems of considerable importance arose in the course of making these arrangements: (1) the minimum strength of individual military contributions to be accepted; and (2) the organization of supplies for the national contingents. The United States government generally insisted that a national contingent should have the minimum strength of a reinforced battalion (about 1200 men) with supporting artillery, that engineer and ordnance units should be able to function as units, and that the contributing state should provide reinforcements adequate to maintain the initial strength. Some offers were declined on the ground of inadequacy, especially offers of volunteers and officers. With respect to supplies, the United States insisted, for practical operational reasons, that there should be only one logistical line of communication, with the one exception of the Commonwealth and those Members using British-type equipment. This made the United States the principal source of supply and created a variety of problems relating to the training of men in the use of the new equipment, the equipping of them, and the making of payment. These difficulties, however, were minimized by what had already been done under Mutual Defense Assistance and other programs, since the Members contributing armed forces had generally been receiving this kind of assistance.

4. *Composition of United Nations Force*

Of those Members which initially or subsequently made specific offers of assistance,[28] twenty-two offered to contribute military forces—ground, naval or air. In a few instances, military units—naval or air—were immediately made available and as soon as they arrived in the area were placed under the command of General MacArthur. In other cases military units were understandably slow in arriving because of time required for processing the offers, training and equipping the forces, and transporting them to the area of operations. The first ground forces of a Member State other than the United States—a United Kingdom unit—did not arrive until the end of August. Others quickly followed. Some offers of military forces were not accepted because they did not meet the standards set by the United States after its acceptance of the responsibility for establishing a unified command, or for political reasons, as in the case of Nationalist China's offer of three divisions of infantry. Generally speaking, the military contributions of Members other than the United States were not of such strength as to be a decisive factor in the military operations in Korea, though their availability was helpful and greatly strengthened the United States' political position by giving the total operation a United Nations rather than an exclusively national character.

In addition to the United States, fifteen Members eventually contributed military forces to the United Nations force in Korea. The contribution of Members to the force at the time of its maximum strength was quite unequal and provided substantial basis for considering the operation as essentially an American one. In comparison with a United States contribution of ground forces of three army corps and one marine division, with supporting elements, the United Kingdom, which next to the United States was the member making the largest contribution, sent two brigades. Numerically, the United States contributed 50.32 percent of the ground forces, 85.89 percent of the naval forces, and 93.38 percent of the air force. The Republic of Korea contributed 40.10 percent, 7.45 percent, and 5.65 percent respectively, and the

---

[28] For summary of offers during 1950, see *ibid.*, pp. 226-28.

fifteen United Nations Members other than the United States the remainder.[29] These figures do not cover important contributions of supporting assistance, such as medical supplies, hospital units and transportation facilities made by other Members, including Denmark, India, Norway and Sweden which did not send armed forces.

5. *Establishment of Command Arrangements*

The establishment of command arrangements presented no great difficulty. The United States had at the time a substantial force in the Far East under the command of General MacArthur, and elements of this force were used initially in Korea. United Kingdom and Dominion air and naval units which were dispatched to Korea immediately following the adoption of the Council's resolution of June 27 were placed under General MacArthur's command. Considering the factual situation, there was no sensible alternative to inviting the United States to establish a unified command of United Nations forces in Korea. This the Security Council did by its resolution of July 7. It also invited Members to place their armed forces sent to the assistance of the Republic of Korea under this command. The United States promptly accepted the invitation, President Truman appointed General MacArthur commanding general of United Nations forces on July 8, and by July 25 the United Nations Command, with headquarters at Tokyo, was fully established. On July 15, President Rhee of the Republic of Korea assigned to General MacArthur command authority over all Korean armed forces during the period of hostilities.

The United Nations Command under General MacArthur was fully integrated into the Far East Command of the United States. General MacArthur's chain of responsibility was through the Chief of Staff of the Army to the Joint Chiefs of Staff, to the Secretary of Defense, to the President of the United States. From the common headquarters of the two Commands, he commanded the U. S. Eighth Army, which included the ground forces of all participating Members and the Republic of Korea, and the Far

---

[29] U. S. Dept. of State, *United States Participation in the United Nations, Report of the President to Congress for the Year 1951*, Publication 4583, (Washington: U. S. Govt. Printing Office, 1952), pp. 273-88.

Eastern Air Force and the Seventh Fleet, which took in all air and naval units contributed by Members for the Korean operation. Consequently the organization of command down to the service level would have been no different if the military force had been wholly American in composition.

It was at the United States Eighth Army Headquarters in Korea that the multinational character of the United Nations Command became most apparent. This became the operating headquarters of the ground forces of all participating Members, in addition to serving that function for the United States Eighth Army. With the exception of the forces of the Republic of Korea, all ground forces contributed by Members were incorporated into United States divisions and brought under the operational command of United States divisional officers. The senior military representative of each Member state contributing forces was accorded the right of direct access to the United Nations Commander "on matters of major policy affecting the operational capabilities of the forces concerned."[30] After July 27, 1951, all Commonwealth units were combined into a Commonwealth division.

The incorporation of military units of Member states in United States divisions and the close integration generally of United States armed forces and those of other members were greatly facilitated by the fact that the countries concerned had previously received United States military equipment and advisers under the various foreign assistance programs. In no case, however, had training and re-equipping reached a point where units were completely combinable or interchangeable with United States units. Experience demonstrated, however, the soundness of the conclusion that "only similar procedures, together with identical equipment and military doctrine, can permit the effective formation of joint forces for joint tasks and the full value of joint command."[31]

Numerous command difficulties arose, none of which proved to be insuperable. While the line of command, for instance, was

---

[30] General Assembly, Official Records, 6th Sess., Supple. No. 13, *Report of the Collective Measures Committee*, 1951, p. 46.

[31] U.S. House of Representatives, 80th Cong., 1st Sess., *Contributing to the Effective Maintenance of International Peace and Security*, House Report 996 (Washington: U. S. Govt. Printing Office, 1947), p. 7.

strictly American, in the issuance of orders a United States corps commander had to recognize the fact that national practices differ. One of the principal devices for obtaining effective cooperation between different national units was the establishment of liaison arrangements. In spite of the difficulties encountered, General Marshall, Secretary of Defense, was able to report in the summer of 1951 that he was much impressed by the complete amalgamation of the various national units into an integrated, co-ordinated, fighting force.[32]

6. *Strategic Direction*

The major difficulties encountered in Korea, and the ones which were least satisfactorily handled, were those relating to the strategic direction of the United Nations force. The Charter provides that "the Military Staff Committee shall be responsible under the Security Council for the strategic direction of any armed forces placed at the disposal of the Security Council." This provision was obviously inapplicable, not only because the Council was not acting under Article 42, but also because of the fact that the Soviet Union, a member of the Committee, was supporting the North Korean authorities against whom the United Nations action was directed.

After the adoption of the June 27 resolution by the Council, Secretary-General Lie and his advisers prepared a draft resolution for limited circulation which would have established a "Committee on Coordination of Assistance for Korea" composed of Australia, France, India, New Zealand, Norway, the United Kingdom, and the United States, with the Secretary-General as rapporteur and with the Republic of Korea invited to send a representative. The proposal was strongly opposed by the United States.[33] Apparently the resolution of July 7 asking the United States to establish a unified command was based on the assumption that the task of coordination, or strategic direction, could be performed by the Security Council, assisted by the periodic reports which the United States Government, in the exercise of

---

[32] U.S. Dept. of State, *Guide to the United Nations in Korea*, Publication 4299, Far Eastern Series 47 (Washington: U.S. Govt. Printing Office, 1951), p. 29.

[33] Trygve Lie, *In the Cause of Peace* (New York: The Macmillan Co., 1954), pp. 333-34.

its responsibility for establishing a unified command, was requested to make.

During the initial period down to September 15, there was no serious problem since there was general agreement that the North Korean attack must be halted and repelled, and that the United States Government, acting through the Joint Chiefs and General MacArthur, was in the best position to decide what was necessary to achieve this result. When, with the Inchon landing of September 15 and the arrival of ground forces of other Members in Korea, the situation changed radically in that a decision had to be taken about crossing the 38th parallel which concerned more than the United States and in which there were possible differences of opinion, the Security Council had ceased to be a possible means of decision. The United States Government asserted the right to make the decision, but preferred to have a resolution of the General Assembly confirming its view. Since the military situation was progressing extremely favorably at the time and there seemed to be good prospects of driving the Communists from Korea and achieving its unification, the great majority of the Members of the General Assembly were prepared to follow the United States' lead. It was clear, however, that the General Assembly was not an adequate instrument for the strategic direction of military operations.

When later the threat and then the actuality of Chinese Communist intervention made it necessary to take important decisions as to how far north the United Nations forces should attempt to go, and what steps should be taken to give assurances to the Peking Government and guard against the expansion of the conflict, two major problems arose of concern to all Members: (1) to what extent was the United States Government free to take decisions after or without consulting other Members; and (2) how firm a control should be exercised over the United Nations Commander, General MacArthur, by the United States Government in Washington as, in a sense, the agent of the United Nations.

These two problems eventually received solutions that under the circumstances were reasonably acceptable to other Members. After the Chinese Communist intervention became a reality, the United States Government adopted the practice of regularly consulting with the representatives in Washington of other Members contributing armed forces. These meetings of the "Committee of

Sixteen" provided the opportunity for information to be given to the Governments of contributing Members concerning the military situation and plans, and thus enabled these governments to present their views on the situation and proposed plans of action. The United States Government, however, always claimed that its responsibility for the conduct of operations was such that it could disregard these views, though in practice it took serious account of them and its decisions were usually influenced by them. This was primarily due to the great importance that Washington attached to maintaining the coalition intact and to having broad United Nations support in Korea.

The second problem proved somewhat more difficult to handle because of General MacArthur's great prestige and the reluctance of officials in Washington to prescribe in detail what the Commander in the field could or could not do. The removal of General MacArthur in April 1951 resulted in a great improvement in the situation and a revival of confidence on the part of other Members in the ability of the United States Government to act with restraint and caution so as to avoid, if possible, the serious expansion of the conflict.

In sum, the procedures of strategic direction were greatly improved in the course of the conflict, and the United States Government, in spite of pressures at home, discharged its responsibilities in such a way as to preserve the "coalition," keep the war limited, and achieve the minimum objectives of the military operation. Nevertheless, the experience did demonstrate the need of giving more serious attention than the United States at least was initially inclined to give to the organization of an effective system of strategic direction of a United Nations military action to repel aggression and restore international peace and security. In the light of this experience, criteria of an effective system might be defined as follows: (1) the political authority that directs the over-all command must be realistically representative of the states supporting the action; (2) the political guidance furnished by the authority must be continuous, direct, strong, certain, and consistent; and (3) the military commander must keep the political authority completely informed of the military situation and his plans.[34]

---

[34] Frederick G. Bohannon, *Some Military Problems of Collective Enforcement Action* (New York: Columbia University Master's Essay, 1953), pp. 35 and 36.

Conclusions

It has not been possible to organize and use military forces for the maintenance or restoration of international peace as was originally planned by the authors of the United Nations Charter. The relations between the Soviet Union and other permanent members have not been such as to permit the conclusion of agreements under Article 43 or other necessary decisions to be taken by the Security Council. For the same reason, joint action under Article 106 has not been possible.

In the case of the North Korean attack on the Republic of Korea, it was possible, owing to a combination of circumstances not likely to be repeated, to initiate collective military measures through the Council's power of recommendation, and to organize and use a United Nations force with success. The lessons of this experience should be of value in case it is found possible to initiate similar action in the future, either through the Security Council or through the General Assembly under the "Uniting for Peace" resolution. It is clear, however, that any use of force following the Korean pattern requires the strong and vigorous leadership of one or more major powers; it must also be recognized that once action of this kind is initiated in a situation where the interests of major powers are in conflict, great restraint is required to prevent that "police action" from developing into a major war. The development of tactical atomic weapons and increasing reliance upon them in national defense establishments make this restraint all the more necessary. In fact, they raise the question whether the Korean pattern of limited military action for limited objectives is likely to be repeated.

A UNITED NATIONS "GUARD" AND A UNITED NATIONS "LEGION"

by Stephen M. Schwebel

I. *A United Nations "Guard": Introduction*

In the Introduction to his Annual Report for 1947-48, the Secretary-General of the United Nations, Mr. Trygve Lie, described a plan he had announced during the Harvard University Commencement exercises a month earlier.[1]

> I have under study proposals for the creation of a small United Nations Guard Force which could be recruited by the Secretary-General and placed at the disposal of the Security Council and the General Assembly. Such a force would not be used as a substitute for the forces contemplated in Articles 42 and 43. It would not be a striking force, but purely a guard force. It could be used for guard duty with United Nations missions, in the conduct of plebiscites under the supervision of the United Nations and in the administration of truce terms. It could be used as a constabulary under the Security Council or the Trusteeship Council in cities like Jerusalem and Trieste during the establishment of international regimes. It might also be called upon by the Security Council under Article 40 of the Charter, which provides for provisional measures to prevent the aggravation of a situation threatening the peace.
> There are many uses for such a force. If it had existed during the past year it would, I believe, have greatly increased the effectiveness of the work of the Security Council, and have saved many lives, particularly in Indonesia and Palestine. It should not be a large force — from one thousand to five thousand men would be sufficient — because it would have behind it all the authority of the United Nations.[2]

II. *The Plan*

On September 28, 1948, eleven days after the assassination of Count Bernadotte, the Secretary-General formally suggested to the General Assembly that "'the formation of a United Nations

---
[1] United Nations Press Release M/446, June 10, 1948, p. 4.
[2] United Nations Doc. A/565, *Annual Report of the Secretary-General on the Work of the Organization, 1 July 1947 - 30 June 1948*, pp. xvii-xviii.

Guard several thousand strong" should be "closely studied and reported upon" by the appropriate committees of the General Assembly.[3] As an immediate measure, the Secretary-General proposed the formation of an 800 man Guard, 500 of whom would be held in reserve in their national homes. He described the "primary positive purpose" of the Guard "to be representative of United Nations authority in support of United Nations Missions in the field and to provide a limited protection to United Nations personnel and property."[4] The Guard would afford security to a field mission's members, secretariat, premises, archives, and other property; furnish such transportation, communications and supply as might be necessary to supplement services available to a mission in the field; maintain order during hearings and investigations of United Nations missions; "patrol points or guard objectives neutralized under truce or cease-fire order of the United Nations;" and "exercise supervisory and observation functions at polling points during the conduct of referendums conducted under United Nations auspices." "Availability of international protective personnel," the Secretary-General wrote, "is a *sine qua non* of a Mission's ability to proceed with the necessary confidence and authority . . . without the suspicion of partiality which the use of local police or national foreign militia engenders. Absence of an independent international body representative of the authority of the United Nations and capable of offering minimum personal protection to United Nations staff has seriously embarrassed the work of United Nations Missions both in the course of hearings and enquiries as well as in the operation of truce arrangements and the rendering of good offices."[5] The experience of United Nations Missions in the field, the Secretary-General submitted, had demonstrated that "there must be available at their disposal adequate representative and protective authority to give effect to their decisions as well as technical service assistance to enable them to function with speed and efficiency."[6]

He was not, Mr. Lie said, suggesting an international army. Both "on practical as well as on legal grounds such a Guard

---

[3] United Nations Doc. A/656, Sept. 28, 1948.
[4] *Ibid.*, p. 7.
[5] *Ibid.*, pp. 1, 8.
[6] *Ibid.*, p. 2.

could not be used for enforcement purposes . . . nor for the purpose of maintaining law and order in an area." But the Guard would "immeasurably strengthen" the hands of United Nations Missions established "for the express purpose of assuring pacific settlements without recourse to the use of force . . ."[7]

The Secretary-General submitted that "adequate constitutional authority"[8] existed under the Charter, notably in Articles 97 and 98, for his establishment of the Guard, provided that the General Assembly gave budgetary approval. For, he contended, he possessed the power to establish units of the Secretariat, if they were required to meet the needs of United Nations organs; and the Guard would be recruited as part of the Secretariat, pursuant to Articles 97, 98, 100 and 101, to fulfill the undoubted needs of United Nations field missions. It would function in a territory "only with the consent, express or implied, of the territorial sovereign."[9]

The Secretary-General described the character, functions, and organization of the proposed Guard in some detail.[10] It would, he emphasized, be "entirely non-military"[11] in character. The Guard would be made available by the Secretary-General at the request of United Nations organs. Its equipment would be limited to "personal emergency defence weapons" (side-arms and light automatic weapons) and transport and communications material (including four armored staff cars); it would "not be organizationally of such a size or character as to be of possible use as an aggressive force." The Guard would "not have the powers, as such, of either a civilian or military police force (such as powers of arrest, quelling of insurrections or, generally, functions implying the use of force for other than personal protective reasons)." But it would be charged with protecting United Nations observers from "undisciplined" attack, and with the guard-

---

[7] *Ibid.*
[8] *Ibid.*, p. 3.
[9] *Ibid.*, p. 5. These words have a ring which is familiar. The phraseology of Mr. Lie's plan does not specify that the Guard would function only with the "continued" consent of the territorial sovereign, but there is nothing in his proposals or the discussions upon them which lends support to a contrary view. Whether a sovereign which once consented to the entry of the Guard would have the right to compel its withdrawal apparently was not discussed.
[10] *Ibid.*, Appendices B and C, pp. 7-11.
[11] *Ibid.*, p. 7.

ing of neutralized objectives. A preliminary estimate of the cost of an 800 man force was four million dollars a year.

III. *The Debate at the Assembly's Third Session*

The *Ad Hoc* Political Committee did not consider the Secretary-General's proposal until the second part of its Third Session, in April, 1949. The late Abraham Feller, who, as general counsel and the Secretary-General's intimate adviser, was prominent in the drafting of the Secretary-General's plan, opened the discussion with an exposition of it. He noted that the amelioration of the Palestine situation placed the creation of the Guard in a less urgent light than it had appeared the previous September. Meanwhile, he stated, "The Secretary-General had been approached . . . by several delegations which had suggested the desirability of further study."[12] The Secretary-General accordingly proposed that the Committee recommend to the Assembly the creation of a small special committee of 10 or 12 members, including the five permanent members of the Security Council, to study all aspects of the problem and report to the Fourth Session. This diplomatic indication that Mr. Lie's plan had met with a mixed reception was more than borne out by the debate which followed.

Speaking first, the delegate of the Philippines noted that the death of Count Bernadotte might have been averted had there been a Guard. He warmly endorsed the Secretary-General's plan, and promptly submitted a resolution embodying his suggestion for the creation of a special committee to study it. The reasons advanced in support of the plan by the Philippine delegate, and by the very few other representatives who unqualifiedly appeared to favor it (namely, Sweden, Haiti, and Peru), did not significantly differ from those of Mr. Lie.[13]

The opposition was more original. Its core was the Soviet bloc; their objections, if not the most influential, were the most fundamental. France, while not contesting the Guard's legality, did challenge its practicality; and a number of States, which gave

---

[12] General Assembly, Official Records (G.A.O.R.): 3rd Sess., Pt. 2, *Ad Hoc Pol. Ctte. Summary Records of Meetings 6 April-10 May, 1949*, p. 24.
[13] *Ibid.*, pp. 35-36. Haiti, however, declaring that "right must be supported by strength," stressed the role of an international force "in maintaining law and restoring international justice."

qualified approval to the principle of the Secretary-General's plan, and unqualified approval to its study, expressed serious doubts on a number of points. The criticism of the plan may be summarized as follows:

In the view of the Soviet bloc, the Secretary-General's proposal was one more step in the progression of Anglo-American perversion of United Nations machinery to imperialist ends. The observer and guard force which had been improvised by the Secretary-General in Palestine, nine-tenths of whom were United States personnel, was a violation of the Charter; the Secretary-General's idea now was to legalize the unlawful.[14] In the last analysis, the Guard was intended to replace the forces envisaged by Article 42 and 43, "to allow the United States and the United Kingdom to continue without restraint their political and military interference in the domestic affairs of other states." The Commissions on Greece and Korea were illegal; a Guard designed to assist such commissions could be no less.

Articles 97 and 98, or other provisions of the Charter bearing upon the Secretary-General's powers, the Soviet bloc argued, hardly authorized him to recruit an (however lightly) armed force, however small. And if the Guard had no connection with the provisions for enforcement laid down in Chapter VII, it was the more contrary to the Charter, since the latter prohibited any resort to force except by application of that Chapter's provisions. The Guard would be distinguished from the forces foreseen by Article 43 only by its size (which could increase), its international (as contrasted with national unit) character, and its illegality.

The Soviet bloc further objected that equipping the force with automatic weapons and with vehicles such as armored cars confirmed their view that the Guard was to be a real armed force.

The less extreme doubts expressed by other delegations emphasized budgetary considerations. "Only when the entire question of the size of a United Nations Guard had been thoroughly examined in the light of what the Organization could afford,"

---

[14] *Ibid.*, pp. 29, 30-33, 40, 43-44. (The observers, who during the second truce period reached 500 strong, were officers drawn from the countries represented on the Security Council's Truce Commission, the United States, Belgium and France. The guards were volunteers from the United Nations Headquarters guard unit, and were of various nationalities.)

the delegate of the Union of South Africa cautioned, "could any decision be taken on the principle of creating such a force."[15] Four millions were proposed for 800 men, the Soviet delegate noted; if the force were expanded as was proposed, the costs could exceed the annual budget of the United Nations.[16] Even the Guard's 800 men, France declared, "would obviously be an expensive and useless luxury."[17]

In all, the French delegation was "unenthusiastic" about the Secretary-General's plan, not on legal grounds — for the legal objections raised did not apply to an 800 man force, and need be considered only were its enlargement to be proposed — but on practical ones. A limited force of 800 men could not effectively protect United Nations missions; past losses of personnel were not due to the absence of such protection; no police force ever had been able to prevent deliberate political assassination. The spirit which should animate the United Nations, the French delegate contended, forbade connecting its prestige with a Guard's eclat.[18]

The South African delegate raised other practical considerations, some of which China, India, and the United Kingdom reiterated. The 300 man active force would have to be recruited with great care to achieve adequate homogeneity "in language, religion and training." Inability to keep the active force constantly occupied would present morale problems. The presence of a reserve cadre of 500 men domiciled in various States presented "the dangers of divided loyalty, differing standards of efficiency and language difficulties." These difficulties, and ones of training, would be heightened with the ultimate expansion of the force to 5,000 men (this was the figure the South African delegate gave). He ventured that the principal source of recruits would be the five great Powers, yet ill-will among their nationals might disrupt the Guard's unity.

Perhaps the most profound objection advanced by South Africa was that of

> the dangers inherent in the exercise of patrol duties in neutralized zones and supervision of elections conducted under United Nations auspices. The exercise of those two functions

---

[15] *Ibid.*, p. 27.
[16] *Ibid.*, p. 31.
[17] *Ibid.*, p. 37.
[18] *Ibid.*, pp. 36-37.

might encourage a tendency to regard the United Nations Guard as a body which bore the responsibility for the execution of the recommendations of the Organization. In practice, the Guard might thus acquire a para-military character which would be utterly incompatible with the avowed purposes for which it had been created.[19]

These para-military functions might draw the Organization into controversy with various States, the South African delegate maintained, and, apart from that, might require a much larger force than had been contemplated or than the United Nations could afford. For example, a whole battalion might be needed to insure free movement of observers in an area as large as Indonesia. The special committe to study the Secretary-General's plan accordingly should consider the feasibility of employing the national police of the countries concerned for guard duties, as an alternative to the creation of the Guard.

The danger of the Guard's clashing with local forces, and the advantages of utilizing national police, struck a responsive note with the Indian and Chinese delegations, as well as the Soviet bloc. Yet the Indian delegate suggested that, if care were taken to construct a non-military United Nations Guard, recruited with full regard to geographical distribution, it should be able to co-operate with local security forces.[20]

The British delegation agreed that "further elucidation" on the status of the Guard in relation to local forces was needed. At the same time, while the Secretary-General had stressed that the Guard would function in a territory only with the express or implied consent of the territorial sovereign, the British delegate pointed out that "the Guard might be most needed precisely where such consent was not available."[21]

The United States joined a number of other delegations in reserving its position on the substance of the Secretary-General's plan, while declaring in favor of the Philippine resolution for the study of it. Particular consideration, the United States delegate said, should be given to the distinction between guard functions and military functions. The United States rejected charges that the plan was contrary to the Charter or improperly

---

[19] *Ibid.*, p. 27.
[20] *Ibid.*, p. 41.
[21] *Ibid.*, pp. 31-32.

motivated or supported. But, it declared, admittedly "some of the proposals of the Secretary-General went too far."[22]

Before the *Ad Hoc* Political Committee voted upon the Philippine resolution, Mr. Feller assured it that the Secretary-General, in proposing his plan, had acted on his own initiative, without pressure or suggestion from any Government. The Committee, by a vote of 41 to 6, with three abstentions, adopted the resolution proposed by the Philippines. "Realizing the need for a thorough study of the matter before concrete action can be taken," the Assembly thus resolved to establish a Special Committee of "specially qualified representatives" of Australia, Brazil, China, Colombia, Czechoslovakia, France, Greece, Haiti, Pakistan, Poland, Sweden, the U.S.S.R., the United Kingdom, and the United States, to study the Secretary-General's proposal "in all its relevant aspects, including the technical, budgetary and legal problems involved," as well as any other proposals by the Secretary-General and Member States for "increasing the effectiveness of the services provided to the United Nations missions by the Secretary-General . . ."[23]

IV. *The Field Service and Panel*

In the face of opposition by two great Powers, the doubts of three others, and the mixed response of lesser States, the Secretary-General retreated. The United States had suggested his plan "went too far"; the Secretary-General not unwisely replaced it with a proposal which was less far-reaching.

"After careful consideration" of the observations made at the Third Session, the Secretary-General submitted "a substantial revision" of his original proposal.[24] Under his revised plan, two new units would be set up, a Field Service and a Field Reserve Panel. The Service, consisting of 300 men, would be part of the Secretariat, but recruited by secondment from national Governments. This uniformed force would provide transport and communications for missions; guard United Nations premises, at Headquarters and abroad; and maintain order during meetings,

---

[22] *Ibid.*, p. 35.
[23] General Assembly Resolution 270 (III) 29 April 1949.
[24] G.A.O.R., 4th Sess., Supple. No. 13, *Report of the Special Committee on a United Nations Guard,* October 10, 1949, p. 6.

hearings, and investigations. The Service would not have any truce or plebiscite functions. It would not regularly be supplied with arms of any kind; in isolated instances, and when permitted by local authority, individual members might be authorized to carry side-arms.

Truce and plebiscite functions would be left to the Field Reserve Panel. The Panel would consist simply of a list of names of men in national service recommended by Governments, which would be compiled, reviewed, and kept current by the Secretariat. The members of the Panel would be called into service only in response to a special decision of the General Assembly or the Security Council, or an organ authorized by them. Membership in the Panel would establish eligibility, not obligation, to serve if called upon. Thus the Panel would need to be large enough to take account of the fact that not all of its members could or would serve at a given moment; and the Secretary-General suggested a list of 2,000. The Panel would, the Secretary-General maintained, enable him to dispense with emergency recruitment of personnel for observation and supervision tasks, and to secure a broader geographical distribution in their selection.

The Field Service, the Secretary-General noted, was designed to render precisely the same services as the Secretariat was already rendering in a less systematic way. The legal basis for its creation would be the same as that of any other Secretariat unit; legal objections made to the former Guard proposal, the Secretary-General ventured, accordingly did not seem relevant. The question of the legality of use of members of the Panel would be the responsibility of the United Nations organ drawing upon it. The cost of the Field Service was estimated at about one million dollars a year.[25]

V. *The Report of the Special Committee*

The majority of the Special Committee approved the Secretary-General's new plan. With respect to the Field Service, the Committee suggested that it be recruited in the normal Secretariat manner, rather than by secondment; and it proposed that

---

[25] *Ibid.*, pp. 6-9.

the Secretary-General consider merging the existing Headquarters Guard Force into the Service. The Service should, the Committee recommended, be employed "only where the use of local services is not practicable."[26] When the cost of maintaining present field personnel were deducted from the cost of the Service, the Committee noted, it was found that the net additional expense was modest: no more than $233,000 a year, and perhaps less. The majority of the Special Committee saw no legal difficulties. The Service could not be considered an armed force; it would stand on the same legal basis as any other unit of the Secretariat. Equally, the Panel would be created for the sole purpose of assisting missions; its members would not constitute an armed force; and the competence of United Nations organs to draw upon the Panel could not be considered by the Special Committee. The Committee accordingly recommended, by a vote of 10 to 2 (2 members being absent), that the Assembly adopt a resolution recognizing the authority of the Secretary-General "to establish the United Nations Field Service, subject to budgetary limitations and the normal administrative controls of the General Assembly."[27] It similarly recommended, by a vote of 9 to 2 with 1 abstention (2 members being absent), the establishment of a "United Nations Panel of Field Observers" to "assist United Nations missions in the functions of observation and supervision. . . ." The delegations of the U.S.S.R., Poland, and Czechoslovakia, equating the Field Force and Panel with the Secretary-General's earlier proposal for a United Nations Guard, attached a vigorous dissent.[28]

VI. *The Debate at the Assembly's Fourth Session*

At the Assembly's Fourth Session, the Secretary-General himself opened the discussion of the *Ad Hoc* Political Committee on the Special Committee's report. In formulating his revised plan, he said, three considerations had been paramount: the necessity for more system and strength in servicing field missions; provision of such servicing efficiently and economically; and "the need

---

[26] *Ibid.*, p. 2.
[27] *Ibid.*, pp. 3-4.
[28] *Ibid.*, pp. 4-5. For an enumeration of the issues raised in the discussions of the Special Committee, see United Nations Doc. A/AC. 29/W.1, July 13, 1949.

to remove any elements of political controversy, a need that was all the more cogent" in view of the Secretary-General's determination that "no proposal of his should serve as a further cause of division among the Members of the United Nations."[29] The recommendations of the Special Committee were wholly acceptable.

The discussion which followed sheds but limited light on problems of an international police force, for most Members were convinced that that was hardly what was under discussion. The Soviet bloc differed, and it renewed and recapitulated all the arguments which had been made against the proposal for the Guard,[30] together with the fresh one that, if the Secretary-General actually had the authority to set up the Field Force, why had he applied to the General Assembly for authorization to do so.

The Secretary-General's new plan met with widespread support. It was considered an improvement over his earlier proposal. The need for economy was still stressed; the importance of securing the guard services of the local State where possible, and of cooperation with local units, was reiterated.[31]

300 mechanics, the delegate of Pakistan noted, did not constitute an armed force.[32] There was some debate over whether members of the Panel should be required to take the United Nations oath, with the result that it was decided that they should.[33] Some delegations expressed doubts about the practicality of the Panel; it would be difficult to keep the list of members

---

[29] *Summary Records of Meetings 6 April - 10 May, 1949, op. cit.,* p. 94.
[30] *Ibid.,* p. 106. Lumping the Field Force and Panel together, the Soviet bloc saw the sum as equal to the Guard. The Polish delegate added this interesting argument: "The United Nations was created as an association of sovereign and equal States and not as a new State . . . still less a super-State. . . . The Member States had agreed to grant certain rights to the Organization, but they had never given it the right to recruit and maintain an armed force of its own. The right to have an army remained the exclusive right of States. Even Article 43 of the Charter made no mention of the United Nations' right to form an army of its own. That article dealt with the undertaking by Member States . . . to make available to the Security Council contingents of their own armed forces. No international army and no international military unit could be founded on the basis of the Charter's provisions."
[31] *Ibid.,* pp. 97, 107, 109-110. Lebanon suggested that the U.N. organ which appointed the mission should decide whether local units or Field Service personnel should be employed, rather than leaving this delicate question to the Secretary-General (at p. 112; and see p. 117.)
[32] *Ibid.,* p. 97.
[33] *Ibid.,* p. 97, 112-113, 117.

up-to-date, and the nomination in advance of persons who would be qualified for any of the diverse tasks which might arise was a problem.[34] The United States, however, appeared to express the general sentiment, apart from that of the Soviet bloc, that the adoption of the Secretary-General's plan for establishing the Service and Panel would be "distinct progress" towards increasing the efficiency of United Nations missions. The revised proposal, in the United States view, had "none of the defects which had led to objections on the part of many delegations, including the United States delegation," to Mr. Lie's original plan. There was no question that the Secretary-General had the legal right to re-organize Secretariat services in the fashion proposed, and to provide observers if requested to do so by United Nations organs; talk of the plan's running counter to Article 43 was obviously unfounded.[35]

In short, the Committee displayed considerable consensus in support of the new proposal. An Israeli amendment which would have authorized the Secretary-General to place Field Service personnel at the disposal of United Nations Missions only in response to a General Assembly or Security Council resolution was withdrawn in the face of substantial opposition,[36] including that of the Secretary-General. Lebanese amendments designed to increase local control over the possible arming of the Service and over the nationality of Panel members were defeated,[37] as was a Polish motion to continue study of the proposal to establish the Field Service and Panel.[38] The resolution on the Field Service proposed by the Special Committee was adopted by a vote of 38 to 5, with eight abstentions; that on the Panel, by a vote of 28 to 7, with 18 abstentions.[39] The General Assembly adopted the resolutions in plenary session on November 22, 1949.[40]

VII. *Conclusions*

(a) " . . . acutely conscious of how different things in Pales-

---

[34] *Ibid.*, p. 100. The United Kingdom took the lead in espousing these views. For other statements critical of the Panel, see pp. 105, 108-110.
[35] *Ibid.*, pp. 98, 103, 105, 109.
[36] *Ibid.*, pp. 104, 110, 116, 118. See also note 48, p. 210 below.
[37] *Ibid.*, p. 118.
[38] *Ibid.*
[39] *Ibid.*
[40] General Assembly Resolution 297 A and B (IV).

tine could have been had the United Nations had an international force at its disposal,"[41] the Secretary-General, initially advanced a plan for the creation of a genuinely international force: a guard, to be internationally recruited by the Secretary-General, apparently to be under his immediate direction, and to be placed at the disposal of the Security Council — and the General Assembly — if not as a "striking force," then nonetheless as a beginning in "the enforcement of peace." The Guard would, among other things, have truce and plebiscite functions; it would be lightly armed for defensive, and equipped for transport and communications, duties. Mr. Lie's proposal, as delineated in his Harvard speech and his Annual Report, was imaginative, radical, and designed to meet an unquestioned need in a cogent (if not legally unassailable) manner. It was unacceptable.

(b) Even after Mr. Lie retreated somewhat to a more modest proposal, the reception remained cool. As has been pointed out, none of the great Powers supported the substance of the Secretary-General's proposal for the establishment of the Guard; and the sparsity of support in other quarters was notable. The reasons of — and perhaps for — the opposition were varied, and some were not without some merit. It is true that the Charter contains no provision for an internationally-recruited force, in contrast with the provision of national contingents; it contains no provision for putting any sort of force at the General Assembly's disposal; yet the truce and plebiscite functions of the Guard — if indeed the Secretary-General's thoughts did not go beyond such — might well have involved the Guard in duties which the Charter contemplated for forces under Article 43. This is not to say that the Secretary-General's plan was lacking in legal basis, but it is to say that legal criticism of it had some foundation. (The same may of course be said of some innovations in United Nations structure which have been carried out.) The financial and practical difficulties were equally real, and possibly more potent. The will to construe the legalities, and to overcome the financial and other practicalities, so as to realize the Secretary-General's plan, was present neither among the great powers nor among the great voting blocs. Internationalism, or the immediate

---

[41] Trygve Lie, *In the Cause of Peace* (New York: The Macmillan Co., 1954), p. 192.

demands of international events, apparently had just not advanced that far.

(c) The Secretary-General accordingly had no choice but to modify his plan, and this he did materially. The Guard was stripped of its truce and plebiscite functions, its arms, its numbers, probably even of its possibility for growth; placing some of these elements in the Panel was more than dividing the sum in two parts. Indeed, in his concessions to the dispositions of nationalism, the Secretary-General went farther than was required when he proposed that the Field Force be recruited by secondment.

(d) The Secretary-General's revised plan met with broad approval on all sides, particularly as the Field Force was concerned, except the Soviet. The modesty of his revised plan made the immodesty of the Soviet opposition appear the more intemperate.

(e) The Field Force and Panel, while certainly "something useful," hardly constitute that international force which Trygve Lie presciently proposed in 1948, and which Dag Hammarskjold could have put to such profound use in 1956.

VIII. *A United Nations "Legion": Introduction*

The proposals for a United Nations Field Service and Field Reserve Panel, adopted in 1949, were not designed to, and in fact did not, provide the United Nations with an international police force capable of coercive policing. The Secretary-General's plan for a Guard, especially as it was transformed into the more limited Service and Panel, contemplated not an implement of collective security, but an instrument of peaceful settlement. Its genesis was essentially in the truce experience of Palestine, not the battle experience of Korea. But, in 1951 and 1952, the Secretary-General suggested plans of a different order.

In 1950, under the stimulus of the Korean hostilities, the General Assembly adopted the "Uniting for peace" resolution. That resolution, among other things, constituted a Collective Measures Committee, which, "in consultation with the Secretary-General" was directed to study and report on "methods . . . which might be used to maintain and strengthen international peace and security...."[42] The Secretary-General, who, throughout the existence of the Collective Measures Committee, played a leading, if not the leading, role in the submission of proposals to it, suggested the establishment of a "United Nations legion."

IX. *The Plan*

As the Secretary-General first proposed his plan for a United Nations Guard in an address at Harvard, so he early spoke of his ideas for a United Nations Legion in a public address before the United Nations Association of Canada:

> Member Governments have been asked to set aside part of their armed forces for United Nations action in case of any future acts of armed aggression. The possibility of creating a separate United Nations Legion composed of volunteers is also being explored.
> I have advocated since 1948 the creation of special United Nations forces. As Secretary-General, I feel it is of the utmost importance that the Member Governments agree to provide these forces and that a United Nations Legion also be established, composed of volunteers drawn especially from those countries unable to set aside special United Nations units of their own. These forces should be at the disposal of the Security Council and the General Assembly.[43]

Subsequently, a principal aide of the Secretary-General, Col. Alfred G. Katzin, clarified the proposal further:

> ...There is no thought on the part of the Secretary-General that a United Nations Legion could be actually organized and operated at the present time as a substitute for national forces acting on behalf of the United Nations..., or that, indeed, a United Nations Legion could operate independently of such national forces to cope with an aggression, or that it could be of such size and composition as to constitute an international army. Primarily, such a Legion would appear to have practical value and utility as an 'organism' within the framework of which additional and supplementary manpower might be organized and through which increased ancillary support and 'some combatant support' might be more

---

[42] G.A.O.R., 7th Sess., Supple. No. 17, *Report of the Collective Measures Committee*, 1952, p. 17.
[43] Alfred G. Katzin, "Collective Security: The Work of the Collective Measures Committee," *Annual Review of United Nations Affairs, 1952* (New York: New York University Press, 1953), p. 212.

easily and more rapidly made available by smaller states than would be the case if the extent and nature of their contributions had to await detailed negotiation at the outbreak of an aggression. . . .[44]

The Secretary-General's proposals were submitted to the Collective Measures Committee as "tentative suggestions . . . not . . . fully developed in their technical aspects."[45] Recognizing that, in resisting aggression, the United Nations could, under existing circumstances, find no substitute for a United Nations force composed of army, navy, and air elements contributed from national forces, the Secretary-General suggested two supplementary techniques of assistance to the UN:[46]

(a) States whose resources would not permit of the contribution of self-contained combat or ancillary units as contemplated in paragraph 8 of the 'Uniting for peace' resolution would be invited to consult as to whether, by resort to a United Nations Volunteer Reserve as contemplated by the Secretary-General, or in any other manner, they could alone or jointly with other States similarly placed, organize in advance combatant or auxiliary units (such as labour or transport units) able to be integrated in a United Nations force to resist aggression; and

(b) Potential strength might be added to forces available to any United Nations Executive Military Authority by enlisting, in the military reserve establishments of States willing to participate, the part-time services of individual volunteers. Such a United Nations Volunteer Reserve "in support of United Nations principles to resist aggression"[47] would, in advance, undertake to be trained and held in reserve to that end. Accordingly, the Secretary-General proposed that principles and procedures be developed between the United Nations and States willing to cooperate, whereby use would be made of individual volunteers for United Nations service.

---

[44] *Ibid.*, p. 213.
[45] *Report of the Collective Measures Committee, op. cit.*, p. 12.
[46] *Ibid.*, pp. 12-13.
[47] *Ibid.*, p. 12.

Under the plan, volunteers would be recruited through the existing national military establishments of the participating states. They would be organized into special United Nations reserve units or groups, and maintained in active training or reserve status within national volunteer reserve establishments, pending their mobilization for service by the United Nations. Co-operating States would be asked to meet the cost of recruiting, equipping, and training the United Nations volunteer reservists as part of their advance contribution to collective security under the United Nations.

Conditions of service by United Nations volunteer reservists would be the subject of agreement between the United Nations and the cooperating States, and should, it was proposed, be sufficiently elastic to meet the special needs and requirements of all concerned. Probably, on account of widely differing conditions and circumstances, detailed arrangements would have to be examined and completed on a State-by-State basis. Thus, for example, these arrangements might prescribe that recruits to a United Nations Volunteer Reserve would be available for national service in the same way as any other national reservists. It might similarly be provided that members of existing national volunteer establishments electing individually to be earmarked for United Nations service as United Nations volunteer reservists would remain subject to mobilization for national service. It could be provided that volunteers would be mobilized for active United Nations service only if an Executive Military Authority were appointed by the United Nations to resist an act of aggression. It could equally be provided that co-operating States would determine individually whether, for internal security or any other reasons, any volunteers held on their reserve establishments could or could not be released for United Nations service. Again, such States and the United Nations Executive Military Authority would decide between them whether United Nations reservists should be mobilized as part of any force contributed to the Executive Military Authority by the State concerned, or as part of an alternative force, or a combination of both. The proposals should be designed to have the utmost flexibility of application to meet the practical needs of a given situation.

As for command arrangements of United Nations Volunteer Reserve units, the Secretary-General urged that they be worked out with the utmost flexibility to suit the practical needs of co-operating States and the Executive Military Authority. He emphasized the paramount importance of recognizing and preserving the international character of the reserve components.

The Secretary-General estimated that "at least fifty or sixty thousand volunteers willing to serve the principles of the United Nations might well become available through a United Nations Volunteer Reserve." The Reserve would provide supplementary strength to other forces seconded to a United Nations Executive Military Authority at the time such an Authority was appointed to resist aggression. /The Secretary-General submitted that his plan for a Volunteer Reserve — a force which would be trained in advance on a part-time voluntary basis — if adopted and implemented, would "solve in large part" the financial, as well as the morale, problems inherent in the existence of a standing force inactive for long periods of time (problems of which the critics of his plan for a United Nations Guard had made much, and with reason)./

X. *The Response*

The record of governmental response to the Secretary-General's plan is relatively sparse. Unlike his plan for the Guard, the Legion was not seriously debated in the General Assembly; no special committee of the Assembly was constituted to consider it (although the Collective Measures Committee was of course competent to do so and did); and no definitive action was taken, apart from its eventual tabling by the Secretary-General himself.

The Secretary-General did not resourcefully struggle for the acceptance of even a modified version of his plan, as he had in the case of the United Nations Guard. His "tentative suggestions" actually were such; they apparently were advanced by the Secretary-General's representative with considerable caution, and with frank admission of the difficulties that stood in the way of the adoption of them or any other plan which would, in varying measure, provide for an international police force. Colonel Katzin's remarks, while directed towards the problems of an international police force in general rather than those of the Legion in particular, embrace the Legion, and are characteristically enlightening:

> ... The absence of unanimity among the Great Powers on collective security arrangements, present world tensions, acts of localized aggression, and guerilla activity in areas of instability make it entirely unrealistic for the United Nations to attempt to pin its hopes on advance pledges of specific forces. Such forces might not bear any relation whatever to the needs of the occasion ... an army of any given size, even though its elements are earmarked in advance for United Nations service, may not be capable of dealing with any aggression which the United Nations is called upon to resist ... while the existence of such armed United Nations forces might, to some extent, allay some public doubts about the effectiveness of the principle of collective security through the United Nations, it would in fact, in all probability, serve very little other purpose.
> ... there would be undoubted advantage to the United Nations to have information in advance, to the greatest extent possible, of the strength of military forces upon which it could rely in the event that it were faced with the responsibility to conduct an armed action. On the other hand, it must be recognized that in the final analysis, and for so long as universal disarmament is not a major part of any over-all United Nations collective-security plan, the United Nations will always have to rely primarily upon the total resources of its Member states to resist an act of aggression. The total resources required may well exceed, in many situations, any small elements of their national armed forces which they might be able safely to earmark specifically in advance for United Nations action.
> ... the mere existence of an armed force of any given strength is not of itself a guarantee that such a force can be effective, no matter how well equipped. Under conditions of modern warfare, resources of a very far-reaching nature, which extend far beyond the mere 'mounting' of a force, are required. Not only must such a force be brought to an area of operations, but it also must be adequately sustained throughout the period of its engagement, whether this extends over weeks, months, or years. Vast ancillary support must be available. Indeed, manufacturing resources of some states in certain circumstances may be required, to a greater or lesser degree, to be directed exclusively or largely to the maintenance of such a force. Commercial shipping and aviation resources may have to be diverted from normal commercial utilization. ... It can well be understood, therefore, without further

amplification, that if the United Nations is to face its responsibilities to counter aggression in a practical manner, then, from the outset, it must look to states for more assistance than the mere provision of a given element of armed strength.

But there are also other elements . . . which must, under present conditions, govern the capabilities of states to be specific on their advance contributions to the United Nations, no matter how clear their good will or how firm their intention to fulfill their pledges to support the United Nations in resisting aggression.

If we look at the commitments of the Great Powers in the first instance, we shall understand that there are vital strategic considerations which limit their freedom of action. An outbreak of aggression in one area must be considered in relation to other troubled areas and areas of potential aggression. Until there is a fully developed and genuine international security system based on controlled forces and limitation of armaments, the Great Powers individually, rather than the United Nations, will have to assess strategic considerations on a world-wide basis. Especially since the Uniting for Peace Resolution is based on the principle of voluntary cooperation of elements from national armed forces, and bearing in mind that such forces would be mobilized by the United Nations only after the outbreak of aggression, it is clearly a matter of great difficulty for the Great Powers to pledge in advance specific forces for service with the United Nations.

The situation of the smaller states can be somewhat different. But because of their lesser resources and because many of them have regional defense commitments which make it difficult for them to earmark additional specific forces for service with the United Nations, their situation, but for different reasons, has put many of them in much the same position as the Great Powers.[48]

The Secretary-General, in outlining his proposals, stated at the outset that, in his opinion, "the creation of any supra-national self-contained standing force, internationally recruited for a fixed period of full-time service and subject, not to the control of any national government, but to a self-contained United Nations command, was administratively, financially, and militarily impractical at the present time."[49] The Collective Measures Committee's unqualified endorsement of this declaration consti-

---

[48] Katzin, *op. cit.,* pp. 207-209.
[49] *Report of the Collective Measures Committee, op. cit.,* p. 12.

tutes one of its few definite reactions to his proposals.[50] The Committee added that, "inasmuch as the Secretary-General's specific proposals do not advocate the organization of a 'legion' in the generally accepted sense of that term, the use of this nomenclature in the context of the present proposals is confusing and misleading and should be abandoned."[51] The Committee observed that it had been unable to give more than "preliminary consideration to the Secretary-General's proposals for a United Nations Volunteer Reserve and was not able to take any decision on the merits, in terms either of their political possibilities or of their military feasibility." It concluded that the proposals deserved further consideration by any continuing body the General Assembly might establish and urged each Member State to consider whether, in its own case, certain features of the Secretary-General's proposals would assist it in carrying out the recommendations of the 'Uniting for peace' resolution."[52]

The General Assembly's consideration of the report of the Committee was not extended, and references to the Secretary-General's plan were few. Australia, the United States, New Zealand, the Netherlands, and France, in varying degree, supported the plan for a Volunteer Reserve.[53] However, no mention was made of a United Nations Legion or Volunteer Reserve in the resolution adopted by the General Assembly in response to the Collective Measures Committee's report.[54]

The third and, to date, the last report of the Collective Measures Committee, under the caption, "Question of a United Nations Volunteer Reserve," declares:

> The second report of the Collective Measures Committee, in dealing with the question of the formation of a United Nations Volunteer Reserve, indicated that the Committee had been able to give only preliminary consideration to the proposals made by the first Secretary-General of the United Nations in this regard. The Committee was subsequently advised that the Secretary-General did not wish, for the time being, to proceed with the proposals. The Committee is of the

---

[50] *Ibid.* Both the Secretary-General and the Committee took care to limit their statements to the time at which they spoke.
[51] *Ibid.*, p. 12.
[52] *Ibid.*
[53] G.A.O.R., 7th Sess., 1st Ctte., 573rd Mtg., March 12, 1953, pp. 440, 442, 448, 453, 461.
[54] General Assembly Resolution 703 (VII), 17 March 1953.

opinion that no further action or study by it is required on this question."[55]

The Committee in this fashion recorded the Secretary-General's decision, at least "for the time being," to yield to the dual pressures of the depreciation or disinterest of Members, and the doubts of his Secretariat colleagues most closely concerned. For reasons that governments perhaps did not choose to reveal fully, and for reasons (not necessarily the same) that Colonel Katzin alludes to in the passages quoted from his paper, the verdict, in 1952 and 1953, was that the Secretary-General's plan for a United Nations Legion was not "practical."

---

[55] United Nations Document A/2713.

Index

Advance planning: See **Setting up UN police force.**

Afghanistan, UN police in, 40

Aggression, UN role, 31, 71, 113
  Anglo-French-Israeli action, 2
  cease-fire support, 115
  equal blame, where, 89
  great powers' attitude, 114, 115
  nuclear weapons' use, 73
  size as UN factor, 72
  threatened, UN action, 114

Air lift to Italy, 24-27

Algeria, UN police role, 41

Anglo-French-Israeli action in Egypt,
  aggression, as 2, 13
  bargaining position aim, 2
  ostensible purpose, 1, 2
  troop withdrawal price, 2

Armistice agreements and UN, 14

Atomic weapons: See **Nuclear weapons.**

Bacteriological weapons, 42

Bargaining power,
  host country's: See **Host state's rights**
  UNEF as aiding, 11

Bases of UN police force,
  Art. 43 discussion, 180
  Chapter VII reliance, 161
  costs, 77-79
  location, 79
  7,000-man force, 165

Belligerents' separation aim, 2

Bernhoft, C.G.A.H. 25

Bolivia and Gran Chaco, 50

Border control, 14, 44, 74, 128, 146

Boxer Rebellion analogy, 47

British action in Egypt: See **Anglo-French-Israeli action in Egypt.**

Buchanan, W., opinion poll, 66

Buffer, UNEF as, 12, 150

Bunche, Ralph, 21, 25

Burma, UN police in, 40

Burns, E.L.M., 7, 28, 31

Canada
  UNEF genesis, role in, 4-6
  UNEF in Egypt, troops for, 27-31

Capodichino air lift, 24-27

Carnahan, A.S.J., 68

Carrizosa, Eduardo, 25

Cease-fire,
  demand for in UN,
    Britain's conditions, 8, 9
    India's demands, 6
    police force as condition, 5
  Hammarskjold report, 11
  Indonesia, 132
  UN patrol of, 6-9, 14, 74, 115

Charter of UN,
  peacemaking duty, 43
  police force in, 51-55, 173
    See also **Permanent UN police force; Prototype forces to 1950.**

Chemical warfare control, 42

China,
  Red China as host state, 88
  Red China in Korea, 192

Chinese civil war, 38, 39

Coercion in peacemaking, 42

Cold war and UN force, 60

Collective Measures Comm., 62
  UN Legion report, 214-216

Colombia,
  Leticia dispute, 51
  UNEF, in planning of, 7

Command and staff, UN force, 71
  advance planning for, 86
  choosing, 76
  Gen. Assemb. role, 79, 80
  headquarters committee, 80
  immunities, UNEF, 150
  Korean crisis, 189-191

Command and Staff, UN force (*cont.*)
  rotation of officers, 76
  Secretary-General role, 80
  six-thousand-man force, 76
  UN organization, in, 7, 8

Committing troops for UN police force: See Permanent UN police force.

Communist expansionism, UN police force in, 40, 41, 55

Composition: See Troops of UN police force; UN Emergency Force.

Consent of parties,
  Generally, 148-160
  advance commitments, 154, 159
  atomic war as factor, 89
  Egypt, 16, 18, 22, 33, 150
    See also Egypt.
  equal blame, where, 89
  force size as factor, 156
  forces dependent on, 148
  future conditions, predicting, 89
  host state's rights: See Host state's rights.
  non-host states, 152-155
  Palestine crisis, 143
    See also Egypt.
  Pearson-Dulles concept, 88
  permanent UN force. 153-156
  plebiscite patrol, 36-38
  scope of problem, 148
  setting up UN force, 88, 89
  Soviet satellites, 89
  status of forces pact, 17, 150
  treaty, by, 158
  troop selection, 16, 88, 151, 155
  UNEF problems, 43-45, 151-153
  world community interest, 89

Contributing state's obligations, 87

Control of UN police force,
  among states, 87
  contribution factor, 73
  day-to-day control, 99
  host state rights, 151, 155
  logistics factor, 73
  UN control, 64, 181
  UNEF, of, 9, 12

Cooling-off period aim, 2

Cordier, A. W., 4, 5, 25

Criminal prosecution, 17

Crisis function of UN force,
  ad hoc action, 81
  aggression barrier, as, 33
  balancing of dangers, 119
  basic assumptions, 123, 124
  basic questions, 122
  better settlement terms, 33
  Communist expansionism, 40
  evaluating, 122
  Greece, in, 124
  Indonesian crisis, in, 130-136
  invasion, to repel, 114
  Kashmir dispute, 137-143
  mass-destruction weapons' supervision, 42
  national police, aid to, 41
  Palestine, 43-45, 143-147
  peace force function, 92, 93
  power as factor, 124
  probable procedure, 33
  Southeast Asia, in, 40
  speedy action. 33
  troops' effectiveness, 45
  typical situations, 32-45
  UN voting as factor, 120

Cyprus, UN police force in, 41
Czechoslovakia troops, UNEF, 24

Deterrent effect, 34, 35, 91, 136, 159
  Egypt, in, 2
  5-10,000-man force, 74
Diplomatic problems, 22-24, 153
Disarmament, 71, 72, 103
Domestic affairs of a nation, UN police force in, 41, 116
Dulles, J. F., 3, 64, 88
Duration of service, 17, 18

Earmarking troops: See Permanent UN police force, Committing troops for.
Eden, Anthony, 8
Egypt,
  Anglo-French-Israeli action in: See Anglo-French-Israeli action in.
  balancing rights of, 15
  consent as UNEF factor, 16
  permanent UN force, 32-34
  status of forces pact, 17, 150
  Suez and, 2, 14, 151
  UNEF, permission of to enter, acceptance, 8, 150
    Canadian troops, 27-31
    composition veto, 16
    diplomatic, 22-24
    good faith factor, 18
    Hammarskjold plan, 9, 23
    nationality bars, 27-31

INDEX

political pressure danger, 88
Soviet support, 10
status quo restoration, 9
troop acceptance, 25-31
troop withdrawal, 3, 9, 17, 18
veto of troops, 16, 18, 22, 33
Eisenhower, D.D., 3
Emergency Force, UN: See UN Emergency Force.
Enforcement of peace by UN: See Peace enforcement by UN.
Engen, Hans, 7, 21
England: See Great Britain.
Equipping UN force, 27
See also Financing: Logistics.
advance planning, 82, 85
atomic weapon control, 72
base unit cost, 78
costs: See Financing
political effects, 55
seven-thousand-man force, 163
UNEF, 27
Extraterritoriality, 151

Face-saving under UNEF, 11
Fedayeen raids, 14, 44, 74
Feller, Abraham, 198
Field Reserve Panel, 202-208
Field Service: See UN Field Service.
Fighting force,
earmarked contingents, 91
UNEF as not, 12
UN Legion, 63
Financing UN police force,
apportionment, 105, 151, 167
costs,
air lift to Italy, 24-27
apportionment, 84, 151
bases, 77-79
control dictated by, 73
fifty-thousand force, 72
five hundred thousand men, 72
Hammarskjold formula, 19
high cost, 19
major force, of, 71
man-day, 72, 167
nuclear weapons factor, 72
pledge basis, as, 84
richer countries, 85
setting up UN force, 84
seven-thousand-man, 75
UN budget compared, 72
UNEF, 18-20, 151
UN Legion, 211
Flanders, R. E. 68
Formosa, UN police in, 38, 39
France,
Egypt action: See Anglo-French-Israeli action in Egypt
UNEF acceptance, 9, 12
Freedom of action retention, 61
Frelinghuysen, P., Jr., 68

Gaza strip, 43-45, 151
General Assembly of UN,
cease-fire res. by, 3, 4
command role, 79, 80
lack of confidence in, 61
permanent UN police force, sentiment for, 68-71
setting up UN police, 81, 90
UNEF legal basis under, 15
UN Guard debate, 198-202
Geneva Protocol terms, 49
Germany, UN police in, 45
Gormley, John, 25
Gran Chaco dispute, 50
"Grand Design" analogy, 47
Great Britain,
See also Anglo-French-Israeli action in Egypt.
UNEF acceptance, 9, 12
Great powers and police force,
exclusion, 11, 12, 94, 105
Hammarskjold plan, 11
threatened aggression, 113
UN force opposing, 116-119
world opinion effect, 116
Greece, UN action in, 124-130
Greek city states analogy, 46
Guard, UN: See UN Guard.

Hammarskjold, Dag,
Palestine border patrol, 44
status of forces pact, 17
UNEF, part in, 4, 7,
assembling, in, 9
financing formula, 19
rounding up troops, 21
UNEF plan by: See UN Emergency Force.
Hammarskjold reports,
precedents under, 11-20

Hammarskjold reports (*cont.*)
    awareness of setting, 11
    consent of parties, 16
    Egypt's sovereign rights, 15
    financing of UNEF, 18-20
    great powers, as to, 11
    neutrality, 13
    police duties of UNEF, 12
    political control, 12
    world community rights, 15
  Secretary-General under, 12
    Advisory Committee, 12

Headquarters of UN force, 77, 86

Host state's rights, 87
  See also Egypt.
  advance planning for, 88
  bargaining for, 151, 158
  consent, 18, 88, 152
  Egypt situation, 16, 88
  occupation, as to, 151
  permanent UN force, 153-158
  political pressure danger, 88
  Soviet satellite, 89
  troop selection, 88, 155
  troop withdrawal, 152, 157
  UNEF problems, 151, 152
    See also Egypt.
  UN force control, in, 155
  unrecognized state, 88
  veto power, 55, 155
  waiver of, 88
  world community interest, 88

Hungary, UN role in, 34, 116

India,
  cease-fire resolution and, 6
  Kashmir plebiscite: See Kashmir plebiscite.
  UNEF, in genesis of, 6, 7
  UN police role in, 40

Indonesian crisis, 130-136

International police force, attempts to 1950: See Prototype forces to 1950.

Intervention, 41, 46

Invasion and UN police, 114

Israel,
  See also Anglo-French-Israeli action in Egypt; Palestine crisis.
  host of UNEF, as, 43-45, 152
  imposed peace fear, 44
  troop withdrawal by, 2

Kashmir dispute, 137-143
Kashmir plebiscite,
  attitudes of parties, 36-38
  imposing settlement, 36
  UN police role in, 36-38, 144
Katzin, A.G., 209, 213
Korean crisis, UN force in,
  Generally, 184-193
  Chinese intervention, 192
  collective measures, 185, 194
  command, 189-191
  composition of forces, 188
  earmarking of troops, 57-61
  offers of troops, 187
  organization defects, 56
  UN action in,
    "police action," 56, 57
    recruitment, 38
    strategic direction, 191-193
    U.S. participation, 39, 56
    veto absence, 55-57
Krishna Menon, V. K., 6, 7, 29
Krugman, J. E., 66

Lall, A. S., 6, 7, 21
Lane, Abbe, and morale, 86
Laos, UN police force in, 40
League of Nations attempts, 48-50, 171
  treaty efforts, 49
Leech, G. C., 25
Legal problems, UN force, 75
Legion, UN: See UN Legion.
Length of stay of troops,
  UNEF: See UN Emergency Force.
Leticia dispute, 51
Lie, Trygve, 62, 195, 207
Lodge, Henry Cabot, 9
Lofgren, S. A., 25
Logistics,
  advance planning in, 85
  Korean police action, 187
  seven-thousand-man force, 163
  UN debate on, 182
  UNEF, 24-27, 150

MacArthur, D., 189, 193
Manpower situation, 112
Mass-destructions weapons, 42
  See also Nuclear weapons.

INDEX

inspection by UN, 72, 73
use of by UN, 73
Menon: See Krishna Menon, V. K.
Military balance and UNEF, 11
Military operations of UN,
  acts outside host pact, 157
  bases, 77-79, 161, 165, 180
    See also Bases; Permanent UN police force.
  concept of UN force, 163
  conflict, influencing, 156
  consent factor, 156-169
    See also Consent of parties; Host state's rights.
  great-power exclusion: See Great powers and police force.
  immunities, effect on, 157
  influencing conflict, 156
  military objectives of, 157
  non-host interests, 158
  occupation duties, 157
  range and scope of, 162
  reserves for, 159, 162
  restraint needed, 194
  seven-thousand men, 163-167
  size of force: See Size of police force needed.
  small-nation attitude, 158
  small scale force, 159
  strategy, 191-194
  treaties concerning, 158
  troop withdrawal demand, 157
  UN Charter concept, 194
  U.S. support factor, 161
Military Staff Committee, 53, 170
Missiles, UN control of, 42
Morale problems, 86
Mutual Assistance Draft, 49

Nasser, Gamal Abdel,
  UNEF, view of, 1
  veto, 16, 18, 22, 23, 33
Nationality difficulties, 75
  Egypt, in, 16, 22, 27-33
Navigation, freedom of, 14
Nehru, J.: See Kashmir plebiscite.
Nepal, UN police force in, 40
Neutralism and UN force, 35
Neutrality of UNEF, 13
New Zealand UNEF troops, 23
North Korea as host state, 88
Norway and UNEF, 7
Nuclear weapons,
  aggression, to repel, 73
  attack on UN force by, 73
  consent concept change by, 89
  control, 42
  cost of UN force, factor, 73
  policing, 72, 73
  stalemate resulting, 104
  strategic framework, 111
  UNEF as factor, 3
  use of by UN, 73, 105

Occupation duties, 151, 157
Opinion polls on UN force, 66
Owsley, C. J., 25

Pakistan,
  Kashmir plebiscite, 36-38
  UNEF, troops in, 23
Palestine crisis,
  See also Egypt; Israel.
  UN possible role in, 143-147
Palestine problem, 43-45
  compromise in, 43
  Gaza border patrol, 43-45
  Soviet opportunism, 43
  UN troops in, 43
    consent factor, 44
    Israel's attitude, 43-45
Paraguay, Gran Chaco and, 50
Patrol, UN, 14, 44, 74, 128, 146
Peace and fighting forces distinguished, 91
Peace enforcement by UN,
  cost: See Financing.
  defining objectives, 71, 72
  disarmament as factor, 71
  nations' attitudes, 69, 70
  public opinion polls, 66-69
  size of force needed, 71-77
    See Size of police force needed.
  UNEF as start, 66
Peace force, suggested.
  Big Five exclusion from, 94
  cease-fire, following, 93
  consent of states, 100
  control over, 92, 99
  earmarking troops for, 100
  feasibility of now, 100
  fighting force, as not, 91
  functions, 91-93
  procedure of, 92
  recruitment, 100, 101
  size of force, 100
  UNEF experience, 96

INDEX

Peace Observation Comm., 62
  peace force functions, 97-100
  working out details by, 92
Peaceful settlement, police force functions, 13, 92
Peacemaking, imposed, 42-45
Pearson, L. B.,
  Canadian troops and, 29-31
  "consent" concept, 88
  Suez action, in, 2
  UNEF genesis, part in,
    assembling, in, 9, 21
    author of, as, 1, 2
    cease-fire resolution, 3-6
    conferences, 3-5

Permanent UN police force,
  ad hoc setting up, 81
  aggression function: See Aggression, UN role.
  Algerian role, possible, 41
  alternatives to, 120
  attempts to 1950: See Prototype forces to 1950.
  bases: See Bases.
  Boxer Rebellion analogy, 47
  central authority and, 46
  Charter provisions, 51-55
    Art. 43 debate, 52-55
    Charter concept, 173-175
    Military Staff Comm., 53
  coercion factor, 42
  Collective Measures Comm., 62
  command: See Command of UN force.
  committing troops for, 57-60
    advance pledges, 81, 84, 154, 159
    cold war effect, 60
    failure rationale, 60
    freedom of action and, 61
    Gen. Assembly factor, 61
    Korean action, 57-59
    reinforcements, 162
    small scale operations, 159
    smaller nations, by, 154
    suggested resolution, 91
    U.S. policy, 60
  Communist expansion and, 40
  composition, consent to, 37
  Congressional resolution on, 68
  consent factor in, 153-166
    See Consent of parties.
  contributions to, 53
    "equality principle," 53
    states' obligations, 87
  control: See Control of UN police force.
  cooperation failure, 53
  cost of: See Financing.
  defining, difficulty of, 71
  deterrent effect: See Deterrent effect.
  disarmament as factor, 71
  duration of service, 76, 181
  early attempts: See Prototype forces to 1950.
  effectiveness of, 37, 45
  enforcement of peace by: See Peace enforcement by UN.
  Egypt crisis, 32-34
  equipment: See Equipping UN force.
  feasibility of, 161
  fighting force, question of, 12, 61, 63, 91
  financing: See Financing.
  first step, as, 106
  forces outside UN, 55
  freedom of action and, 61
  functions and value of,
    aggression, to stay, 33, 35
    bacteriological weapons, 42
    better settlements, 33
    border control, 44, 74, 75, 128, 146
    cease-fire patrol, 74
    chemical warfare, 42
    crises, in: See Crisis function of UN force.
    deterrent effect, 34, 35, 74, 117, 159
    domestic order keeping, 41
    future usefulness summarized, 106, 111-121
    insulating states, 74
    invasions, 32, 114
    military: See Military operations of UN.
    moral barrier, as, 33, 34
    national police aid, 41
    nuclear weapon control, 42
    other than stated, 157
    peace interposition, 42
    plebiscites, in, 35-38
    political window, as, 34
    size factor: See Size of police force needed.
    summarized, 106, 162
    wars that never happen, 106
  fundamental difficulty, 46
  future usefulness,
    aggression, to combat, 113
    cease-fire, in, 115
    internal conflict, in, 116
    manpower factor, 112

INDEX

specific situations, 113
strategic framework, 111
summarized, 106, 111-121
Gen. Assembly action, 68, 90
general concept of, 163
"Grand Design" analogy, 47
great powers and: See Great powers and police force.
headquarters, 77, 80, 86
host state's rights: See Host state's rights.
ideal solution, 81
intervention, 41, 116
invasion, repelling, 114
Korean situation, in, 38, 39
manpower situation, 112
military aspects of: See Military operations of UN.
missile control, 42
moral authority of, 91
morale problems, 86
new look at problem, 105
non-host states' rights, 155, 157, 158
opinion polls on, 66-69
ordering into action, 55
outside home territory, 54
Palestine problem, in: See Palestine problem.
panacea, as not, 45
peace enforcement by: See Peace enforcement by UN.
peace force, suggested: See Peace force, suggested.
Peace Observation Commission function, 92
peacemaking, effect on, 104
personnel legal problems, 75
policy considerations, 35
political control, 87
political pressure by, 36
pre-UNEF: See Prototype forces to 1950.
privileges and immunities, 150, 157
rationale and logic of, 46
recruitment: See Recruitment.
regional alliances, 60
reinforcements for, 162
religion of personnel, 75
Roman Empire analogy, 47
self-determination role, 41
setting up: See Setting up.
size of force: See Size.
Southeast Asia, in, 40, 41
Soviet Union, 95
speed of settlement by, 33
stationing, 54, 64, 181

outside home territory, 54
where most needed, 54
strategic direction, 191-194
suggested appeal for, 90-92
training program, 165
transportation, 165
treaties concerning, 158
troops: See Financing; Size; Troops.
typical situations: See Crisis function of UN force.
uniformed forces, effect, 34
UNEF as not permanent, 96
Uniting for Peace Res., 59, 61
veto of troops: See Veto.
volunteers: See Volunteers.
world opinion backing, 119

Peru, Leticia dispute, 51

Plebiscites,
See also Kashmir plebiscite.
Saar basin voting, 51, 173
UN force role in, 35-38

Police force, international: See Permanent UN police force; Prototype forces to 1950; UN Emergency Force.

Political balance and UNEF, 11, 13

Political control, 12, 87

Political pressure by UN,
Anglo-French-Israeli view, 9
danger to host state, 88

Political pressure body, UNEF,
Hammarskjold report, 10, 11
Kashmir plebiscite, 36
United States view, 10, 11
world opinion, mobilizing, 119

Precedents of UNEF: See Hammarskjold reports.

Privileges and immunities of UN force, 150, 157

Prototype forces to 1950,
Boxer Rebellion forces, 47
Congress' 1910 res., 48
Geneva Protocol, 49
Gran Chaco dispute, 50
"Grand Design," 47
Greek city states, 46
Korean experience, 184
League of Nations, 48-50, 172
Leticia dispute, 51
Mutual Asst. Draft, 49
Roman Empire precedent, 47
Saar basin plebiscite, 51
UN Charter concept, 173-175
air forces, 179

INDEX

Prototype forces to 1950, UN Charter concepts (*cont.*)
  Art. 43, under, 175-184
  bases, matter of, 180
  composition of force, 176
  contribution formulae, 178
  control and use, 170
  logistics, 182
  Military Staff Comm., 170
  national contingents, 173
  period of use, 181
  scope contemplated, 179
  stationing of force, 181
  strength of force, 176
  withdrawal of troops, 182
Vilna 1920-21 dispute, 50
Public opinion polls, 66-69

Raids: See Border control.
Recruitment of UN force,
  career officers, 76
  directly-recruited, 75
  host country consent, 37
  Korea, for service in, 38
  Lie's comment, 63
  peace force, suggested, 100-102
  personnel problems, 75
  seven-thousand-men force, 75
  UN Legion, 63, 64, 211
  volunteers: See Volunteers.
Regional alliances, 55, 60
Religion as troop factor, 75
Roman Empire precedent, 47
Roper, Elmo, poll, 66
Russia: See Soviet Union.

St. Laurent, Louis, 5
Saar basin plebiscite, 51, 173
Sanction by UN force, 157
Satellite, consent of, 89
Saukkonen, Aimo I., 25
Secretary-General of UN,
  See also Hammarskjold; Lie.
  command role, 12, 80
  peace powers of, 52, 55
  veto power effect, 55
Self-defense, UNEF and, 15
Self-determination of peoples, UN force role in, 41
Setting up UN police force,
  ad hoc, 81
  advance preparation, 81-88
    advance promises, 82
    command, as to, 86
    costs, spelling out, 84
    facilities available, 82
    headquarters plan, 86
    logistics, 85
    moot points, 88
    morale problems, 86
    speed advantages, 160
    UNEF experience, 82
  consent element, 88, 89
  control problems, 87
  costs, spelling out, 84, 85
  first step, as, 106
  Gen. Assemb. res., 90
  Gen. Assemb. role, 81
  host state's rights, 88
  paper permanent force, 81
  pledged force, 81, 84
  political control, 87
  seven-thousand-man force, 164
  states' obligations, 87
  training program, 185
  UNEF experience, 81, 86, 89
Sieger, E. W. R., 25
Size of police force needed,
  See also Financing.
  5-10,000 men, 74
  6,000-man force, 76, 161
  7,000-man force, 163-167
  50,000-man force, 72, 156-159, 162
  500,000-man force, 72
  aggression size factor, 71
    except by great power, 72
  cost factor, 71-74, 77-80
  formulae, 53
  gradual accretion, 162
  guaranteeing world peace, 71
  large standing force, 161
  military operations factor: See Military operations of UN.
  nuclear weapons factor, 73
  objectives factor, 71
  peace force, suggested, 100
  quota force, 71
Skliarov, I. A., 56
Southeast Asia and UN force, 40
Sovereign rights of states, 15, 16
Soviet Union,
  exclusion from UNEF, 12
  manpower of, 112
  Middle East aim, 45
  Palestine problem and, 43, 45
  peace force interest, 95, 104, 199
  UNEF attitude, 3, 7, 10
Sparkman, J. J., 68
Stationing UN force, 54, 64, 181
Status of forces pacts,
  criminal prosecution, 17

INDEX

Egypt, with, 17, 150
Stavropoulos, C. A., 17
Suez Canal,
  Anglo-French action, 2
  Canadian view, 2
  UNEF function, 14, 151

Tibet appeal, 40
Transportation of UN force,
  air lift to Italy, 24-27
  seven-thousand-man force, 165
Treaties,
  League of Nations, 49
  UN military operations, 158
Troops of UN police force,
  See also Financing; Logistics.
  acceptance by host, 88, 151
    Israel refusal, 43-45
    permanent UN force, 155
  advance commitments, 154, 159
  bargaining power of, 2
  Egypt, in: See Egypt.
  length of service, 181
  nationality problems, 16, 18, 22, 33, 75
  presence, effect of, 2
  reserves, 159
  selection, veto, 16, 55, 88, 151
  withdrawal,
    See also UN Emergency Force: Length of stay.
    Egypt attitude, 17, 18
    host state's rights, 157
    Israel, from Egypt, 2
    request for, 152, 157

Uniforms, UNEF, 27, 150
  effect of, 34
UN Charter: See Charter of UN.
UN Command, 7, 8
UN Emergency Force,
  accident of history, as, 1
  Advisory Committee for, 12
  assembling, 21-31
    air lift, 24-27
    Canadian troops, 27-31
    country cooperation, 21, 22
    diplomacy, 22
    Egypt: See Egypt.
    Italy, in, 24-27
    lessons learned, 27, 28
    nationality bars, 27-31
    uniforms, 27
  assistance function of, 13

atomic war factor, 3
bargaining position aid, 11
Britain as UN policeman, 12
buffer, as, 150
cease-fire function, 4, 9
composition of,
  Egypt's veto power, 16
  great-powers' exclusion, 11
  Korean crisis, 188
  nationality questions, 25-31
Congressional resolution, 66
consent of parties to: See Consent of parties.
contributing states, 149
  obligations of, 87
control of, 9, 12
cooling-off function, 2
costs: see financing, *infra*.
criminal prosecution in, 17
described, 149
diplomatic problems, 153
draft resolution for, 6, 7
duration, 9
Egypt's attitude: See Egypt.
enforcement organ, as, 13
equipment for Egypt, 27
extraterritoriality, 151
face-saving under, 11
financing, 18-20, 151
  See also Financing UN police force.
  ability-to-pay formula, 19
  apportioning, 19
  "basic rule," 18
  equipment, salaries, 18
  Hammarskjold formula, 19
  reluctance of states, 19
  UN, payments by, 18
  U. S. offer, 19
France as UN policeman, 12
functions,
  armistice agreements, 14
  assistance, 13
  battle zone, in, 14
  belligerents' separation, 2
  border patrol, 4, 14
  buffer force, as, 12
  cease-fire, 9, 14
  conflicting views, 9
  cooling-off period, 2
  Egypt's consent factor, 16
  enforcement as not, 13
  facilitation, 13
  fighting force, as not, 12, 106
  Gaza strip, in, 151
  Hammarskjold view, 14
  inferences of, 14
  insulating, 15
  limitations on, 150

INDEX

UN Emergency Force, functions (*cont.*)
  navigation freedom, 14
  observation, 13
  peaceful settlement, 13
  police force, as, 12
  political, 9, 13
  preliminary question of, 9
  presence, effect of, 153
  securing compliance, 14
  status quo, *re*, 9
  stop fighting in Egypt, 8
  Suez area, in, 14, 151
  summarized, 149, 150
 genesis of,
  Anglo-French-Israeli action in Egypt, 1-5
  Canada's view of, 4
  cease-fire debate, 3-5
  Dulles' view, 3
  Hammarskjold's part, 4, 5
  lack of time, 4
  Pearson's part in, 2-6
   See also Pearson, L. B.
  Scandinavia's part, 7
  Soviet view of, 3
  UN Command: See UN Command.
  U. S. view, 3
 great-powers' exclusion, 11, 12
 Hammarskjold plan
  cease-fire basis, 11
  conferences leading to, 7
  Egypt's acceptance, 8
  face-saving under, 11
  pressures involved, 9, 10
  reports: See Hammarskjold reports.
  UN approval of, 8, 20
  UN Command proposal, 7
 Hammarskjold reports: See Hammarskjold reports.
 host state's rights, 151
  See also Egypt.
 legal basis of, 15
 length of stay, 17, 18
 military balance effect, 11
 military force, as, 106, 149
 morale problems, 86
 nationality difficulties, 16, 22, 27-33, 79
 nations' sentiments on, 69
 neutrality of, 13
 non-fighting force, 106
 observers' corps, 13
 organization, 149
 original concept of, 1, 2
 parties accepting, 150
 peace enforcement start, 66
 permanence, question of, 96
 placing of forces,
  consent: See Consent.
  status of forces pacts, 17
 police duties, 12
 political balance and, 11, 13
 political pressure by, 9-11
 Port Said activities, 74
 precedents established: See Hammarskjold reports.
 presence of, effect of, 153
 principles governing,
  Hammarskjold report, 10-20
  military balance, 11
 privileges, immunities, 150
  extraterritoriality, 151
 resolution setting up, 21
 self-defense by, 15
 setting up, 21
 stationing, question of, 9
 status of forces pact, 17
 success of, 1
 temporary measure, as, 96
 transportation of, 24-27
 uniforms, 27, 34, 150
 withdrawal, question of, 9
  See also Troops of UN.
 world community rights, 15

UN Field Reserve Panel, 202, 208

UN Field Service, 202-204

UN General Assembly: See General Assembly of UN.

UN Guard, 62, 63, 195-208
 army, as not, 196
 committee to study, 202
 functions, 195-198
 Gen. Assemb. resolution, 206
 Headquarters Guard and, 204
 legality of, 207
 Lie plan for, 195
 peaceful settlement by, 208
 plan described, 195-198
 police force, as not, 205
 power to establish, 64, 197
 revised proposal, 202
 size and organization, 196
 summary account, 206-208

UN Headquarters Guard, 204

UN Legion, 208-216
 aims, 209
 appropriateness of term, 215
 command, 211
 composition, recruitment, 63
 control, 214
 costs, 211
 fighting force, as, 63

INDEX

Gen. Assembly action, 198-206, 215
Lie plan for, 209-212
rationale of failure, 64
service conditions, 211
UN reserve, as 210, 211
volunteer recruitment, 211
UN police force: See Permanent UN police force; UN Emergency Force.
UN Security Council: See Security Council of UN.
UN Volunteer Reserve, 63, 210-212
United States,
Formosa, in, 38, 39
Korean action, 39, 56, 188
strategic direction, 198
peace force interest, 104
regional alliances, 60
Resolution of 1910, 48
UNEF attitude, 3, 10
Uniting for Peace Res., 59, 61
appeal, terms of, 92
UN Legion proposal, 208
Urrutia, F., 21

Vance, R. F. C., 25
Van Wagenen poll, 67
Vaughan, D. B., 25
Veto,
Korean crisis, 55-57
UN troops, of, 16, 55, 88, 151, 155
See also Consent; Host state's rights.
Egypt, in: See Egypt.
Viet Nam, UN police role, 40
Vilna dispute, 50, 173
Vitetti, Leonardo, 24
Volunteers,
recruitment difficulties, 75
seven-thousand-man force, 75
suggestions for, 62
UN Legion, for, 64, 211, 212

Weapons of mass destruction, 42
See also Nuclear weapons.
World government, UN as not, 16

DATE DUE

MAR 8 1970

APR 2 8 1970

DARTMOUTH COLLEGE
3 3311 00964 6474